Sex, Violence and Crime

Foucault and the 'Man' Quest.

What happens when you *sex* violent crimes? More specifically, what happens when you make men's violence against women the subject of a conversation or the focus of scholarly attention? The short answer is: all hell breaks loose. Adrian Howe explores some of the ways in which this persistent and pervasive form of violence has been named and unnamed as a significant social problem in Western countries over the past four decades. Addressing what she calls the 'Man' question – so named because it pays attention to the discursive place occupied, or more usually vacated, by men in accounts of their violence against women – she explores what happens when that violence is placed on the criminological and political agenda.

Written in a theoretically-informed yet accessible style, *Sex, Violence and Crime – Foucault and the 'Man' Question* provides a novel and highly original approach to questions of sex and violence in contemporary Western society. Directed at criminologists, students and, more widely, at anyone interested in these issues, it challenges readers to come to grips with postmodern feminist reconceptualisations of the fraught relationship between sex, violence and crime in order to better combat men's violence against women and children.

Adrian Howe teaches social policy at RMIT University, Melbourne, Australia.

Sex, Violence and Crime

Foucault and the 'Man' Question

Adrian Howe

Routledge·Cavendish
Taylor & Francis Group

First published 2008 by Routledge-Cavendish
2 Park Square, Milton Park, Abingdon, Oxon OX14 4RN

Simultaneously published in the USA and Canada
by Routledge-Cavendish
270 Madison Ave, New York, NY 10016

A GlassHouse book

*Routledge-Cavendish is an imprint of the Taylor & Francis Group,
an informa business*

Transferred to Digital Printing 2010

Typeset in Times by RefineCatch Limited, Bungay, Suffolk

British Library Cataloguing in Publication Data
A catalogue record for this book is available from the British Library

Library of Congress Cataloging-in-Publication Data
Howe, Adrian.
   Sex, violence, and crime : Foucault and the 'man' question /
Adrian Howe.
      p. cm.
   1. Women – Violence against.   2. Postmodernism – Social
aspects.   3. Feminist theory.   4. Foucault, Michel, 1926–1984 –
Influence.   I. Title.
   HV6250.4.W65H69 2008
   362.83 – dc22   2008010510

ISBN13: 978–1–904385–92–9 (hbk)
ISBN10: 1–904385–92–3 (hbk)

ISBN13: 978–1–904385–10–3 (pbk)
ISBN10: 1–904385–10–9 (pbk)

ISBN13: 978–0–203–89127–8 (ebk)
ISBN10: 0–203–89127–9 (ebk)

Contents

Acknowledgements

This book is based on a 20-year engagement with persistently challenging questions about sex and violence. It is founded more specifically on a subject I have taught in Australia and the UK that I call Sex, Violence and Crime (SVC). The subject was first taught at La Trobe University from 1990–2000, a period I look back on as a high point, within and outside the academy, of feminist confrontation with the massive social problem of men's violence against women and children. So my first thanks goes to all those back then, too many to name, who taught me new ways of understanding and conceptualising sexed violence – my SVC students at La Trobe who were so passionate about the issues and so constructively critical of how they should be taught; workers in the sexual assault field who shared their experientially-based knowledges with us, and the many feminist scholars who enriched this field of inquiry with such highly diverse and theoretically rigorous analyses. I also thank all those students and colleagues who supported the teaching of SVC in the UK, and all who encouraged me to write this book. I owe a special thanks to the three readers who provided insightful and compelling critical commentaries on the manuscript that spurred me on to complete it. I was very fortunate indeed that two former SVC students, Katie Curchin and Danielle Tyson, were available to work as research assistants on this project. Making contributions well beyond the usual research assistant duties, they brought to this project invaluable 'insider' knowledge of the complexities and pitfalls that face anyone who tries to theorise sexed violence. I cannot thank them enough for their diligence in keeping my arguments on track and reassuring me about SVC's continuing relevance today. I am also extremely grateful to my friend Sarah Ferber who took time out from her own research in order to provide a greatly-appreciated outsider perspective on the penultimate draft of the manuscript. The final draft benefited immensely from that brilliant insight and devastating wit that we who are privileged to be her friends know only too well. Thanks to all those whose opinions I canvassed about the publisher's request that I change the title, with apologies to those who opted for the original *Sex, Violence and Crime in a Postmodern Frame*. Beverley Brown, thank you for commissioning the book, for offering your usual incisive comments on early drafts and for suggesting ways to appropriate the subject of men's violence from radical feminism. Alexia Peniguel, thank you for granting me permission to reproduce 'Ode to Foucault' (and for writing it!), and finally thanks to RMIT University for research funds to assist with the completion of this book.

Introduction
Ode to Foucault and other paradoxes

What happens when you *sex* violent crimes – that is, when you insist that violence is located within sexed, or as some prefer to call them, gendered relationships? What happens, more specifically, when you take men's violence against women as an analytical object, perhaps the focus of scholarly attention or of an undergraduate criminology course? The short answer is: all hell breaks loose. The longer answer requires a book. *Sex, Violence and Crime – Foucault and the 'Man' Question* jumps into the fray, exploring some of the ways in which men's violence against women has been named and un-named as a significant social problem in Western countries over the past 40 years. During that time, some governments, most recently in Britain, have made so-called 'domestic violence' a policy priority. Yet questions remain about how men's violence should be framed and most effectively resisted. Remarkably, it is also still unclear whether, after decades of exposure, it is now culturally permissible in Western societies to hold men (and not their mothers, wives or girlfriends) responsible for their own violence. This book addresses what I call the 'Man' question, so named because it pays attention to the discursive place occupied, or more usually vacated, by men in accounts of their violence against women. Querying whether explanations can be provided for men's violence that do not discursively erase it or, worse, deteriorate into excuses for it, I take non-feminist criminologists to task for faltering on the 'Man' question. But while criminology is my primary target, the critique developed here applies to any bid in any field to deny, explain away or obfuscate the unpalatable evidence of men's pervasive violence against women. In short, this book explores the possibilities for and the prohibitions against speaking out about that violence today.

That might seem like enough for one book, but this one attempts something more. It strives to confront the social problem of men's violence without sounding like the kind of feminist who put that issue so firmly on political and law reform agendas in Western jurisdictions over the last third of the twentieth century – the so-called, and usually self-defining, 'radical feminist'. Acknowledging the ground-breaking work of radical feminists is one thing; being mistaken for one is quite another. That is not a situation any self-respecting poststructuralist feminist wants to find herself in, especially if she has set herself the task of developing a distinctively postmodern feminist analytical framework. Leaving aside, for the moment, what it might mean to be *for* the postmodern, my chosen postmodern framework is Foucauldian, after Foucault, a philosopher who would have rejected both the feminist and the postmodern label, and who was a past master of strategies of denial on the question of men's violence. But we are getting ahead of the story. Suffice it to say from the start that sexing violence is a complex business. For all that, this is a modest book. At least, it has a relatively modest goal. It explores what happens when sex, violence and crime, and more particularly, men's violence against women, are placed on the criminological and political agenda – when they are 'put into discourse', as Foucault might have inquired, if he had ever turned his mind to the place of men in criminological inquiry.

This is bound to be a controversial book. Even calling men's violence 'men's violence' incites outrage, whether the setting is a university tutorial, a dinner party, a family gathering or a casual pub conversation. One is met immediately with qualifying 'buts': *but* not all men are violent; *but* women are violent too; but, but, *but* she had it coming, 'she asked for it' retaining its privileged place as the most deeply culturally ingrained excuse for men's violence in Western societies. As for the responses of non-feminist criminologists to feminist investigative research on the asymmetry of violence 'between the sexes', they are no more sophisticated. Camouflaged as etiological research, so-called 'expert' explanations for men's violent acts invariably deteriorate into apologies that run the gauntlet from the abjectly sycophantic to the self-consciously defensive. While such apologies can be strident, it is more common to find an unselfconscious agent-deleting manoeuvre that presents the violence as a weird kind of disembodied abstraction, yet at the same time manages somehow to trace a causal chain back to a woman, usually the violent man's hapless mother. Indeed, in some sections of the academy in the United States, and now in Britain, it is argued that, contrary to feminist claims, women are equally if not more violent than men. Moreover, if mainstream criminology's erasure of men from violent narratives is astonishing, the speedy scramble to unsay men's violence can be electrifying, even in the array of so-called 'critical criminologies'. If there is one thing that has remained constant over the two decades during which I have taught criminology, it is that even the simple act of naming men as the main perpetrators of most forms of violence creates havoc in non-feminist forums. Saying without qualification, as this book does, that men are responsible for most forms of serious violence courts danger; it is tantamount to declaring war on the civilised discourses of erasure in which criminology and related disciplines couch the question of men's violence.

Making excuses for men's violence is as endemic in Western culture as blaming women for it. It took one leading English newspaper just a month to find boyhood photographs of a man alleged to have flown one of the planes into the World Trade Center. The headline evinces the standard criminological agenda of searching for underlying causal factors: 'Do these snapshots of a teenage boy in Cairo contain clues to what turned him into a killer?'. Beneath it is a photo of a boy being hugged by his mother. The adjoining text quotes his father describing him as a pampered mummy's boy: 'I used to tell her that she is raising him as a girl'.[1] The inference is obvious: mums have much to answer for when pampered sons grow up to be enraged killers. As we shall see, criminologists frequently resort to this mother-blaming ploy to explain men's lethal violence. By challenging these exculpatory discourses, whatever form they take – media crime reports, 'expert' criminological explanations, casual conversational asides – I hope to provoke debate within and beyond criminology.

Laughing derisively at excuses for men's violence against women is not all that this book does. Western feminism has a long history of causing trouble by asking uncomfortable questions. What, exactly, makes violence sexual? At what point do sexual practices become 'deviant' and 'dangerous'? When does the eroticisation of dominance cross over into violence? Just what is the sex of so-called 'sex crime'? Asking sex crime to declare not only its sex but also the sexed identities of its perpetrators raises hackles inasmuch as these queries return us, inevitably, to the question of men. One of the central challenges of this book is to raise these issues without being dismissed as an un-nuanced 'man-hating' radical feminist locked into an unpalatable man-versus-woman binarism.

Honing the target

Since the late 1960s, feminist researchers have amassed a great deal of evidence relating to men's pervasive violence against women and children. One of the main purposes of this book is to ask how their work has impacted on criminology. Given the discipline's ostensible interest in addressing crime in all its manifestations, one might reasonably have expected it to pay close attention to the now widely-documented social problem of men's violence and its criminalisation in Western jurisdictions. While feminist criminologists have responded impressively to this challenge, non-feminist criminologists have struggled with the question of the relationship between men and men's violence. Before proceeding, two points must be made clear. First, men do not have a monopoly on non-feminist or masculinist perspectives, defined here as viewpoints on gendered relationships that privilege, sometimes explicitly, more usually implicitly, men's interests over women's. Such perspectives can be and sadly, too frequently, are, held by women. Second,

1 *The Independent*, 12 October 2001.

as we shall see, masculinist perspectives range from defensive and near-hysterical anti-feminist stances to more moderate non-feminist viewpoints, some of which may even make token references to feminist work, but which nonetheless remain androcentric or male-centered. The response of masculinist criminologists, be they the unreconstructed variety or the ostensibly reconstructed feminist-touting types, to voluminous research reports testifying to men's routine violence has been, on the whole, tortuous at best. Indeed, the lengths to which they will go in order to un-name the pervasive problem of men's violence frequently strain credibility. At least, they would defy the belief of anyone who had not actually familiarised themselves with criminology texts, as Foucault had when he asked, in feigned or genuine puzzlement:

> Have you read any criminology texts? They are staggering. And I say this out of astonishment, not aggressiveness, because I fail to comprehend how the discourse of criminology has been able to go on at this level.[2]

That was in 1975, but little has changed to make non-feminist criminology less astonishing when it comes to accounting for men's violence against women and children.

Not that this would have bothered Foucault. He had little interest in any form of men's violence. This is somewhat puzzling. One might have thought that violence, and sexual assault in particular, would have posed central issues for Foucault when he came to analyse the relationship between sexuality and power. Yet surprisingly, rape and child sexual assault did not warrant close attention in the eyes of a philosopher who waxed eloquent about sexuality; about subjugated knowledges of struggle and conflict, and about the impact of power at the 'local' level, say in the family; and who, in his final work, focused on the care of the self, a masculinist self to the last. Consider, for example, the position Foucault took in his famous debate with feminists about whether rape should be framed as a crime of sex and whether the rapist should be punished as a criminal.[3] It was, he thought, a relatively simple matter to 'produce the theoretical discourse' demonstrating that sexuality should never be 'the object of punishment'. For him, there was 'no difference, in principle, between sticking one's fist into someone's face or one's penis into their sex'. It followed that rape had nothing to do with sexuality. Yet he never did provide the theory to support these assertions. Nor did he ever explain why he thought his view that 'rape didn't have to be punished as rape' because it was 'quite simply an act of violence' was a 'very

2 Foucault, 1980a, p 47.
3 Foucault, 1988a, pp 200–2.

radical position'. As for child sexual assault, Foucault's analysis, such as it was, did not extend beyond musing that 'there are children who throw themselves at an adult at the age of ten – so? There are children who consent, who would be delighted, aren't there?'. In such cases, there was 'no reason to punish any act'.[4] The injury to the child was not something that detained him. Somehow this massive abuse of power at the local level, frequently within the family, escaped his notice. The sexual assault of a young girl in rural nineteenth-century France was simply a 'bit of theatre', 'an everyday occurrence in the life of village sexuality', just one of many 'inconsequential bucolic pleasures'.[5] The unequal distribution of harms in such encounters – the injury to the individual child and the social harm to children as a group versus the harm of punishing an individual sex offender – simply passed him by.[6]

For Foucault, the key question was how sex, and not sexed violence, is 'put into discourse' in 'our part of the world'.[7] No wonder he was merely 'astonished' by criminology. Only those outraged by men's violent criminal acts need to go further, by condemning the discipline's staggeringly inadequate and defensive response to report after report about intolerable levels of men's sexual and homicidal violence. One thing is already clear, however. Before proceeding to this book's main agenda – unpacking the alibis and apologies set on foot whenever men's violence is foregrounded as a social problem – a disclaimer is in order. Given that being called 'anti-male' is a common fate for any woman who refers to men's violence as 'men's violence', it is well to begin with assurances that there is no anti-male agenda here. On the contrary, the critique developed here applies to any apologist for men's violence, whatever their sexed identity. After all, the worried self-identified feminist woman who is troubled by the possibility of upsetting a 'sensitive' male colleague might resort to an apologist strategy just as quickly as the defensive old-school male criminologist confronted by one of those irascible feminist sisters hell-bent on calling men's violence men's violence. For example, I have witnessed a senior woman academic, one well-published in feminist criminology, rushing to defend a junior male colleague and close off discussion when a feminist critique was on foot in a seminar on 'gender issues' in criminology. I have also heard a feminist academic claim that courses focusing on men's violence against women and children are too fraught, too 'emotional'. Clearly, some feminist women have a problem with feminist women who talk too openly about men's violence. In view

4 Foucault, 1988a, pp 204–5.
5 Foucault, 1979, p 31. Teresa de Lauretis was the first to note the 'paradoxical conservatism' of an historian of social history attuned to questions of power and resistance who dismisses child sexual assault as a 'bit of theatre': de Lauretis, 1984, p 94.
6 For a feminist gloss on the concept of 'social harm', see Howe, 1987.
7 Foucault, 1979, p 11.

of these sensitivities, it might pay to feign an apologetic tone when raising the question of men's violence. So readers, be assured, this book is not, heaven forbid, 'anti-men'. It is concerned rather with the array of apologies for men's violence, whoever speaks them, in the criminological arena, in criminal courts, in the media and in everyday conversation.

Teaching sex, violence and crime

> But I lost a lot of friendships – if anyone said something stupid about violence or rape, I used to say, just fuck you.[8]

This is the book students have been asking me to write for nearly two decades. It is based on lectures written for my undergraduate criminology course, 'Sex, Violence and Crime', or simply 'SVC'. The course began as a lecture series called 'Women Who Kill'. This lecture series, my first, was devised as an addition to a mainstream undergraduate criminology course in an Australian university at a time – the 1980s – when its criminology programmes were bereft of feminist teachers and courses. Within a year, the 'Women Who Kill' lecture series had spawned a drama, performed by students, about the Lindy Chamberlain case, Australia's most infamous miscarriage of justice. Chamberlain's trial by media was the perfect vehicle for exploring the profoundly sexed, misogynist nature of media constructions of 'the criminal woman' and, more broadly, of the production of knowledge about violent crime.[9] Shortly thereafter, the lecture series, drama and all, moved out from the mainstream course and transmogrified into SVC. Violent, murderous women and the whole complex question of women's involvement in and responsibility for interpersonal violence remained on the syllabus. But the focus now shifted to men, the social group responsible for almost all the violent acts conventionally known as sex crime and also for the vast majority of assaults and murders that I eventually came to name as 'sexed violence'.

This book extends the project I commenced in *Sexed Crime in the News*. That project aimed to disturb the complacency and self-evidence of so-called 'sex crime', recognising that even if sex crime is narrowed down to crimes involving sexual violence, definitional problems persist. Sexual assaults followed by murder are treated as sex crimes in criminology texts and in the media, but what does murder have to do with sex? Is family violence sex crime? Paedophilia would appear on most conventional lists of sex crime, but would father-daughter rape? What about marital rape? Why is it not reported as sex crime? What makes violence sexual, and to whom? How can

8 Alice Sebold quoted in K Viner, 'Above and Beyond', *Guardian*, 24 August 2002.
9 See Howe, 2005.

'sex crime' be destabilised, so that crimes involving sexual violence are no longer readily classified quite so simply as 'sex crime', while others, notably the domestic or private variety, are left out of the equation. As I suggested in *Sexed Crime in the News*, calling sex crime 'sexed crime' not only problematises the 'sex' of crimes of violence; it also acknowledges that women are not the only sex. The common sense understanding of sex crime might conjure up the image of a molested or mutilated female body, but men also have sexed bodies. Speaking about 'sexed crime' helps to sex violence by raising questions about the fundamental though usually ignored sexed and sexual aspects of that violence. It also assists in the seemingly never-ending project of breaking down the arbitrary division separating public from privatised forms of men's violence against women.[10]

I defined sexed crime very broadly in *Sexed Crime in the News* as covering all forms of violence in which the gender – or should that be the sex? – of the perpetrator or victim is relevant to the violent act. It includes so-called 'domestic violence' as well as sexual assaults committed on men, women and sexual minorities in the private and public spheres. Sexed violence, I suggested, was violence that can only be fully understood in the context of human relationships that are profoundly sexed, but not often recognised as such, precisely because they are dismissed as having something to do with a vaguely defined, amorphous 'gender'. That is why 'sexed violence' is the preferred term in this book, 'gender' having received quite a trashing from poststructuralist, feminist and queer theorists for subordinating sex and sexuality to gender, or neglecting them altogether.[11] More broadly, the questioning of the sex of sexual violence has unravelled the taken-for-granted ways in which sexed and gendered relations are represented in accounts of sexed violence.

Since its inception in 1990, SVC has interrogated every concept that is conceivably relevant to the question of men's violence against women and children. Besides such obvious candidates as 'sexual violence' and 'sex crime', we have questioned 'interpersonal violence', 'intersexual violence', 'men', 'women', 'violence', 'crime', 'abuse', 'sex', 'gender' and 'experience'. And what would be the point of addressing the 'Man' question without taking on board Third World, postcolonial, black, Asian and other minority feminist challenges to white Western feminism's essentialising and universalising tendencies? What would be the value of an interrogation of non-feminist representations of men's violence that does not simultaneously expose the racialised and frequently racist underpinnings of all sexed discursive practices? What self-respecting white Western postmodernist feminist, thoroughly sensitised to the always already contingent nature of broad-based

10 Howe, 1998, p 6.
11 See Howe, 1998, pp 3–6; Smart, 1994.

claims, could resist critiques that problematise dominant speaking positions and dismantle authoritative voices? Who in the postmodern camp, and most especially the Foucauldian camp, would not jump at the chance of honouring the subjugated voices of ethnic and racial minorities, of white working-class women and sexual minorities, by interrogating her own speaking position and owning her sites of privilege? And who amongst us, even if we claim to speak only about the effects of men's violence on their victims, and not *for* the survivors, could not be stopped in her tracks by Linda Alcoff's superlative Foucauldian-inflected analysis of all the political and conceptual problems that beset anyone attempting to speaking for others?[12]

Teaching in the field of sex, violence and crime has been an immensely rewarding experience. There have been moments of great poignancy and indomitable courage as students revisit violent episodes in their childhoods or in their adult lives in order to reframe them in ways that ensure responsibility falls on the violators, and not themselves as victims. According to students' testimony, given year after year in seminars, essays and private correspondence, writing about previously undisclosed or unspoken violations of their own bodies and psyches can be part of a healing process. Most crucially, it can assist the transformation process from victim to survivor, then to states of identity that are no longer states of injury. There has also been much anguish and despair as students come to grips with the pervasiveness of men's violence and of the vast array of excuses for it in Western culture. Many have arguments with their families, partners and housemates, ignoring my advice not to take SVC home. Many lose friends, as rape victim and novelist Alice Sebold did, when anyone said something stupid about rape or any other form of men's violence. There have been other moments of great hilarity induced by reading criminological accounts of violent crime or, just as ludicrous, women's magazines passing as manuals on how to please men sexually. Most rewarding of all has been the constant scrutiny of our own discursive practices when it comes to naming and explaining sexed violence. The personal and conceptual input of a generation of students has been profound, forcing me to rethink every aspect of my teaching, including my subject matter, my assumptions and omissions, my theoretical and political orientation, methods of assessment, choice of video and film clips, even my style and lecture delivery. Pedagogically, SVC has been pushed and pummelled every which way, and is all the better for it.

Teaching SVC has also been fraught and crisis-ridden in ways that have not been conducive to a productive learning experience. Throughout its first decade it fought off interference from a hostile, overtly anti-feminist managerial fraternity for whom the linking of 'sex and 'violence' with 'crime'

12 Alcoff, 1990–1.

had spelt trouble from the start. It signalled feminism. It oozed dissent. It was read, accurately, as code for an avowedly counter-hegemonic reading of criminological accounts of criminal violence. After a great deal of opposition from all levels of management, including attempts to re-name it 'Crime and Society' – so much safer, 'Crime and Society', blanched of sex and violence – as a prelude to abolishing it altogether from the curriculum, SVC survived.[13] It was taught for several years in the UK where it continued to create havoc by exposing the pervasiveness of men's violence as well as the absurdities that pass as knowledge about sex, violence and crime in the media, in criminology texts and in so-called 'common sense' understanding of social relationships. And now it has returned to Australia where it is about to become a core course in a social science programme at a metropolitan university.

For a postmodern frame

Over the past 30 years, many fields of inquiry in the humanities and social sciences have been transformed by theories that emerged under the sign of the 'postmodern'. There is even a branch of critical criminology calling itself 'postmodern criminology'. This dubious exception aside, postmodernism has had a limited impact on criminology, a discipline that remains, even in some of its so-called 'critical' manifestations, obstinately modernist and positivistic. Moreover, as we shall see, even avowedly postmodernist criminologists parade androcentric white Western perspectives as universal views, without a passing thought for reflexivity, the hallmark of a postmodern analysis. For the most part, criminology, including its self-defined 'critical' wing, has baulked at taking on board postmodern feminist perspectives developed in a host of other disciplines. It thus remains untouched by poststructuralist feminist scholarship that has produced devastating critiques of precisely the kinds of celebratory masculinist representations of male heroism and male violence that are, interestingly, often more pronounced in 'critical' accounts of interpersonal violence. The failure of so-called postmodern criminology to come to grips with analyses of the representation of violence such as that of Teresa de Lauretis and Elisabeth Bronfen or even my own critique of masculinist celebrations of violent 'transcendent' men is a startling example of this oblivion.[14]

Why this work has failed to register with non-feminist criminologists is a matter of speculation, although one of them has at least recognised that there is a problem. In his introduction to *The Futures of Criminology*, an

---

13 See Howe, 2000a, and Thornton, 2006 for commentaries on the conservative attacks on feminist pedagogy in the context of the retreat from a social contextual approach to law and legal studies in an Australian university.

14 de Lauretis, 1987; Bronfen, 1992; Howe, 2000b.

edited collection that engages with postmodern theories in order to assess their potential to transform criminology, David Nelken asks:

> ... why, with the major exception of feminist writing, is there such unwillingness to engage with current intellectual debates over the way social developments have affected the possibility of representing reality and telling the truth?[15]

His answer reiterates one of the standard anti-postmodern chants: such debates, he warns, can lead to 'theoretical incoherence and practical impotence' (modernist theories, evidently, offering the consoling coherence and potency he craves). Displaying the typical timidity of the anti-postmodernist, Nelken is nervous about the prospect of going 'too far' in the direction of reflexivity and deconstruction and he worries about the impact of some forms of postmodern writing on 'the normal proprieties of intellectual debate'.[16] But who, exactly, determines what these normal proprieties are? Refusing such limits and taking Nelken's inquiry further, we might ask why postmodern feminists are so willing, and non-feminist criminologists of any stripe so reluctant, to engage with contemporary social theories. Could it be that non-feminists of any theoretical ilk are threatened by challenges to dominant modes of representation? Whatever the reason, postmodern feminists need to find an audience for the critiques of criminological paradigms that criminologists refuse to hear.[17]

It would not do, however, to suggest that all feminist criminological work falls on deaf ears in non-feminist criminological circles. Indeed, some of us working under the sign of feminist criminology have been lauded as exemplary 'border-crossing' criminologists.[18] Even here, however, non-feminist criminologists have not signalled any recognition of the significant differences of opinion that have lead some feminists to want to cross disciplinary borders and others to renounce criminology altogether. Maureen

---

15 Nelken, 1994, p 7.
16 Nelken, 1994, p 18.
17 Identifying a similar problem of masculinist oblivion to the work of 'oppositional critical theorists' within science studies, Donna Haraway puts the matter succinctly:

> Either critical scholars in antiracist, feminist cultural studies of science and technology have not been clear enough about racial formation, gender-in-the-making, the forging of class, and the discursive production of sexuality through the constitutive practices of technoscience production themselves, or the science studies scholars aren't reading or listening – or both.

> Haraway, 1997, p 35.

   She suspects that the problem is the failure of mainstream science studies scholars to engage with critical work.
18 Lippens, 1998, p 333 citing Cain, 1990; Smart, 1990a, Naffine, 1997 and Howe, 1994.

Cain, for example, has argued for a 'transgressive' feminist criminology, one that aims to 'break out' by starting the analysis outside the discursive boundaries of mainstream criminology.[19] In contrast, Alison Young insists that feminist conversations with criminology start from within its borders. In her view, 'there is no need to demand the abolition or abandonment of criminology'. Young thus distances herself from Carol Smart's position, at least insofar as Smart has been 'taken as suggesting that criminology should be abandoned by feminists'.[20] That puts a rather gentle gloss on what Smart actually said about the discipline. What she said was that 'the core enterprise of criminology is problematic', that feminist efforts to transform criminology 'have only succeeded in revitalising a problematic enterprise', and that, 'as feminist theory is increasingly engaging with and generating postmodern ideas, the relevance of criminology to feminist thought diminishes'.[21]

For Smart, criminology is problematically positivistic in its basic presumption that a verifiable knowledge or truth about crime can be established such that once we have worked out the causes and have the right universalising theory, we will 'know what to do' and a solution to crime can be discovered. Connected to this, criminology subscribes to the modernist faith that science can reveal the truth about human behaviour and will eventually bring about progress. However, as Smart observes, modernity is now seen by postmodernists as 'synonymous with racism, sexism, Euro-centredness and the attempt to reduce cultural and sexual differences to one dominant set of values and knowledge'. It is also 'male or phallogocentric' and white. Accordingly, clinging to modernist thought is 'not only antediluvian; it is also politically suspect'. In short, it was very difficult to see what modernist modes of thought like criminology had to offer feminism.[22]

While I agree with Smart's indictment of criminology, not all feminists do. Some have opted to remain within the discipline, claiming that the development of feminist perspectives in criminology is still 'a project under construction'.[23] And while some took the anti-essentialist crusade against the category of 'woman' to the point of declaring that 'the criminal woman does not exist',[24] at the other end of the spectrum, light years away from post-structuralist interrogations of essentialising categories, many continue to undertake empiricist studies in the name of 'feminist criminology'. Yet for all the diversity of feminist responses to criminological questions over the last decade, few have come to terms with the implications of Smart's critique. As

19 Cain, 1990, p 10.
20 Young, 1996, p 26.
21 Smart, 1990a, p 70.
22 Smart, 1990a, pp 72–5, 84.
23 Gelsthorpe and Morris, 1990, p 4.
24 Carlen, 1985, p 10.

she explains, criminology might claim to be a *savoir*, an objective or technicist scientific body of knowledge that eschews value judgments and leaves the allocation of responsibility and blame to the juridical and ethical realms, but its discourses are replete with the white, Western, Eurocentric and phallogocentric biases that Smart and other postmodernists attribute to modernist modes of thought. This is especially apparent in non-feminist criminological analyses of men's violence. Indeed, on the evidence of their repeated failures to face up to the asymmetry of sexed violence and, worse, their alibi-providing complicity with violent men, non-feminist criminologists are utterly unredeemable and constitutionally incapable of providing insights into the explosive encounter of sex and violence that I call sexed violence.

If holding non-feminists to account for making a myriad of excuses for men's violence spells trouble, so too does opting to present sex, violence and crime in a postmodern frame; for this writer, a Foucauldian feminist frame. There are other postmodern feminist interpretive paradigms, notably Derridean deconstructivist and also psychoanalytical ones. These have made valuable contributions to the project of sexing the postmodern, and by no means do I wish to argue for the superiority of 'my' postmodern frame over others. It is just that, for me, Foucault, despite – or perhaps perversely, because of – his many foibles on sex/gender questions, remains the main man. The great French philosopher who paved the way out from the confines of conventional penology by redefining punishment as penality has much to offer anyone bent on breaking out of criminological and other modernist paradigms. Most crucially, he provides the methodologies for doing so. First, he gifted us Foucauldian discourse analysis (although he did not call it that). Second, and related, he taught us how to problematise thought. 'Problematisation', the relentless practice of problematisating or breaching the self-evidence of what is, is a practice that this book follows, albeit with a feminist spin that sometimes leaves the Master himself looking analytically thin when it comes to exploring sexed violence.[25] But that is no reason to sideline him, much less to refuse to deploy his ideas about the relationship between power and truth and, especially, about the power of dominant discourses to 'fiction' truths, as he put it.[26] Who amongst those who are subjugated or who feel disempowered in any way could refuse his invitation to perceive discourse as the power to be seized?

> . . . as history constantly teaches us, discourse is not simply that which translates struggles or systems of domination, but is the thing for and which there is struggle, discourse is the power which is to be seized.[27]

25 See Foucault, 1984a, pp 381–90; Howe 1994, pp 120–1 and pp 209–10.
26 Foucault, 1980b, p 193.
27 Foucault, 1984b, p 110.

Thus does Foucault enjoin us to engage critically and passionately with dominant discourses, criminology included, subjecting them to a critical interrogation he called 'problematisation', defined as an attempt to 'make problematic and to throw into question the practices, the rules, the institutions, the habits and the self-evidences that have piled up for decades and decades'.[28]

As if all that were not enough to turn young heads, Foucault's notion of an *'insurrection of subjugated knowledges'*[29] is just the tonic for those seeking a way to find their own critical voices and to speak out against ostensibly objective, but in fact, hopelessly sex-biased criminological explanations of interpersonal violence. Such is the pulling power of the theorist who encourages the subjugated to resist domination at their own 'local' level, that one student was inspired to write a song, 'Ode to Foucault', recording her excitement at her first encounter with him in the mid-1990s:

According to *Cleo*, as the modern girl I was it
I had a work life, a social life, I knew where to find my clit
I could change a car tire without getting dirt on my power suit
I did safe sex, I did pap tests, I was working on the perfect root

According to *Cosmo*, I had a long way to go
There were so many things about men I didn't know
Like what they really like in bed and what really makes them come
And how they'd like me to be strong but soft and not too bright
But not too dumb

And I thought, hey what about what I want, I mean isn't this the
     nineties?
Aren't we allowed to have demands and aren't we the ones who should
     define these?
And why are all these men and women speaking for me?
I've got a voice, I've got thoughts, listen to my reality

I'd almost given up hope, I thought I could see no end
I was hurting and angry and the search for the perfect orgasm was
     driving me round the bend
And on a whim, or maybe because I couldn't think straight, I joined
     this class
Hoping against hope for some hope that might last

It was there I first met him, it was there our eyes met
Well, his image on a projector was as close as I could get

---

28 Foucault in Gandal, 1986, p 127.
29 Foucault, 1980c, p 81, original emphasis.

And I knew I'd found a man who would be strong and stand by
  for me
Who wouldn't care what I did in bed, who wouldn't bitch or talk
  over me

Now I was in a state of bliss, I was in a state of constant discovery
He taught me new ways of thinking about my own and others' history
But my friends became quite jealous at how I was so in the know
They said 'we're not going to ask you out again if all you do is talk
  about fucking Foucault'

So some of them went their way and some of them came my way
And I just twisted and turned and made my own highway
I worked out he wasn't a saint, he wasn't that good with women
In fact when it came to feminism he was in the deep end barely
  swimming

But I'll always hold him dear as my first poststructuralist crush
The intensities of our study sessions to this day make me blush
I'll never replace him, he made my world shine
I guess you could say he was my very first time.[30]

This book is a lengthier homage to Foucault. It is a journey exploring what a Foucauldian feminist methodology can bring to an understanding of how men's violence against women and children is represented – 'put into discourse' – in Western societies. There are some who feel that the time of discourse analysis is past. They clearly have not cast a critical eye over criminology texts and media representations of men's violent assaults on women and children. The abundance of agent-deleting texts transforming official statistics on wife murder and child sexual assault into non-gendered and non-sexed 'interpersonal' violence screams out for a demystifying discourse analysis.

Getting by with some help from our friends

SVC might be a love affair with Foucault, but for those not fully satiated, our bit on the side is the influential Italian Marxist Antonio Gramsci. One can go a long way with Gramsci's remarkably adaptive concept of 'hegemony', his key to understanding that class domination works by means of consent as much as brute force. Even more inviting is his notion of counter-hegemony, one that foregrounds the question of agency – the power to act on your own behalf. Today, hegemony and counter-hegemony are no longer

---

30 Alexia Peniguel, 1998, cited with permission.

tied to class politics and class antagonisms as Gramsci understood them. We now have recourse to notions of white hegemony, masculinist hegemony (or, more usually, hegemonic masculinity) and hegemonic heterosexuality or simply, heterosexism, to deepen our understanding of domination and sub-ordination. We also have an expanded conception of counter-hegemony, one that includes the notion of an avowedly counter-hegemonic under-graduate course like SVC that encourages students to adopt critical perspec-tives, not just on criminological questions, but on every conceivable social issue. In the process, they gain an understanding that members of subordin-ated groups who appear to have adopted masculinist viewpoints, values and behaviours antithetical to their interests, might be described as 'hegemon-ised'. For example, women who subscribe to the idea, common in women's magazines, that they should compromise their own sexual desires in order to attract or keep a man might be said to have formed their world view under conditions of hegemonic masculinity. Such a feminist re-deployment of Gramsci's theorisation of the way class oppression works is frowned upon in some criminological circles today.[31] But that only makes the exercise all the more enjoyable. Foucauldians, amongst others, have no time for conceptual pieties. The more purists demand verisimilitude, the more post-modernists indulge our critical faculties, paying homage to our Master's directive that 'the only valid tribute' to innovative thought is 'to use it, to deform it, to make it groan and protest'.[32]

There are many things that this book is not. First, it is far from being the first feminist encounter with either Foucault or Gramsci, or even the first *ménage à trois* with them. Many feminists have pressed themselves happily against Foucault and some have even married him to Gramsci with conceptually stimulating results.[33] Nor does this book offer to make a theoretical breakthrough that will explain at last why men are so violent, much less 'solve' the problem. It has absolutely no interest whatsoever in engaging with criminological inquiries into the link between criminality and masculinity. Indeed, the very idea of postulating some Archimedean point of leverage to explain sexed violence is repellent to anyone who believes that any such etiological impulse is fundamentally flawed and ethic-ally suspect. Nor does this book bother to defend feminist scholars who have deployed postmodern theories against criminology from allegations that they have succumbed to a fear of being tainted by criminology's 'empirical

---

31 Hall, 2002. See Connell's (2002) response in defence of the concept of 'hegemonic masculinity'.
32 Foucault, 1980a, pp 53–4.
33 For a very relevant example of a Foucauldian feminist interrogation of incest, see Bell, 1993. For an interesting argument championing Gramsci as 'a prime candidate for a feminist agenda, possibly challenging the eminent place Foucault enjoys in feminist discourse', see Holub, 1992, p 200.

referent', namely crime.[34] They are more than capable of defending themselves; and besides, this book has no such fear of empirical referents. Taking as its focus the discursive construction of men's violence against women, a form of violence about which there is a great deal of empirical research, it provides a Gramscian and Foucauldian-inflected critique of how men's violence is spoken about in Western culture today. In short, this book tests the limits of the sayable and unsayable in this massively-documented yet still highly fraught area.

Alternatively, it might be read as a sharing of the joy experienced by those introduced to a language that describes their experiences of violence and subjugation without re-subjugating them, and a methodology that works as a toolkit for exploring sites of pain and privilege, collusion and potential sites of resistance to violence in their own lives. In other words, *Sex, Violence and Crime – Foucault and the 'Man' Question* is a guide for anyone interested in thinking critically in the field of sexed violence. It aims to show, first – courtesy of Gramsci – just how prevalent, or hegemonic, apologist discourses are in that field. Second, it aims to ensure – courtesy of a take on Foucault's summation of his own project – that 'certain phrases' (excuses and alibis for violent men) are no longer 'spoken so lightly' and 'certain acts' (men's assaults on women and children) are 'no longer, or at least no longer so unhesitantly' performed. In sum, my hope is that this book makes another contribution to that seemingly never-ending Foucauldian project of breaching the self-evidence of the way things are, of trying to change 'people's ways of perceiving and doing things', and of participating actively in the 'difficult displacement of forms of sensibility and thresholds of tolerance'.[35] As Foucault himself might have said, I could scarcely hope to achieve more than that.

A final introductory point: it should be acknowledged from the start that postmodernism has had a very bad press. It has frequently been held responsible for a host of perceived evils, notably the debunking of Western culture and even the decline of civilisation. Defenders of the literary canon and other unreconstructed pillars of various modernist faiths rail against postmodernism's supposed excesses, often without bothering to read postmodern theory and almost always without understanding it. Amongst its many alleged faults, postmodernism is said to be incomprehensible to all but a few arcane theorists who have no sense of the 'real world'. This antipathy is alive and well across a range of disciplines, including criminology, where postmodern methodologies such as discourse analysis and deconstruction have been denounced in favour of a more pronounced focus on 'the real'. This

---

34 Carlen 1990, p 111, citing, e.g. Carol Smart and Beverley Brown. See further Howe, 1994, pp 213–5.
35 Foucault, 1981, pp 11–12.

anti-postmodern *animus* still permeates many criminological texts today, although not in any profound or arresting way. It suffices for the unreconstructed modernist to make sweeping unfounded pronouncements that postmodernism is responsible for the demise of 'objective knowledge' or, perhaps, the women's movement and women's studies departments, or for halting any kind of progress in the modern world. Moreover, if the condemnation is sufficiently anguished, it can even cause erstwhile proud critical criminologists to renounce their former allegiance to contingency, uncertainty, reflexivity and all that their anti-positivism once entailed.

Eminent critical criminologist Stan Cohen is a case in point. His entertaining account of the politics of denial in *States of Denial: Knowing about Atrocities and Suffering* might have served as a helpful precursor to this book, but for two insurmountable conceptual obstacles. First, by reassembling the private/public distinction carefully dismantled by feminist scholars during the last third of the twentieth century, Cohen relegates violence against women to the private, domestic sphere. Safely airbrushed of male agents, the discursive field he refers to as 'domestic violence against women' appears ever so fleetingly as an example of 'private' or 'everyday' human suffering and a precursor to the main event: 'the worlds of mass suffering and public atrocities' that preoccupy Cohen.[36] Second, his account of denial strategies deployed in the face of human suffering, the outright and less outright denials, discrediting of whistleblowers, re-naming and justifications – the very same strategies that this book exposes, albeit in the context of men's violence – is unremittingly anti-postmodern. Throughout *States of Denial*, postmodernism is paraded as a sign of disintegration, fragmentation, ethical turpitude and 'mindless relativism'. Moreover, it is condemned as pathologically indifferent to all truths about atrocities and suffering, while postmodernists find ourselves lumped together with psychopaths, moral idiots and late capitalist Thatcherite individualists.[37] Past masters of forgetting and denial, we are said to be insane enough to 'seriously "interrogate" truth claims about, say, infant mortality in Bangladesh', and good for nothing except repeating 'the stupid idea that there must always be another point of view'.[38] For Cohen, the idea 'that there can be no access to current or historical reality from outside a vantage-point of power' is the most 'pernicious element' of the postmodern critique of positivism or Enlightenment rationality. Incensed by such an anti-foundational critical practice, Cohen feels compelled to speak for the critical criminologists of the 1960s and to take responsibility for what he sees as the unintended effects of their anti-positivistic stance. Speaking for all – standard operating procedure

36 Cohen, 2001, pp 15 and 51.
37 Cohen, 2001, p 8.
38 Cohen, 2001, pp 187 and 244.

for unreconstructed modernists – he declares: 'All of us who carried the anti-positivistic banners of the sixties are responsible for these philosophical high jinks'. It follows that he believes that critical criminologists should all have the good grace to stand up and say that the infinite relativism that he attributes to the postmodern-infected 'cultural left' is definitely 'not what we meant'.[39]

Cohen does not produce any evidentiary basis for his parody of postmodern theories. This comes as no surprise: unsubstantiated assertion is elevated to an art form in the anti-postmodern camp. This is not the place to get caught up in the long drawn-out debate over the merits and demerits of a postmodern sensibility, save for a brief comment about Cohen's misreading of the postmodernist take on the relationship between power and truth. I turn once again to Judith Butler's superb response to postmodernism's detractors who, she argues, are so busily engaged in a 'self-congratulatory ruse of power' that lumps together a diverse range of critical perspectives under 'the sign of the postmodern' that they miss its main point. That point, she argues, is precisely to question what it is that authorises such an 'act of conceptual mastery'. Taking a position that 'places itself beyond the play of power', that 'lays claim to its legitimacy through recourse to a prior and implicitly universal agreement' is, Butler argues, 'perhaps the most insidious ruse of power'. What form of 'insidious cultural imperialism', she asks, 'legislates itself under the sign of the universal'? So, postmodernism – or poststructuralism, her preferred term – insists that power pervades all conceptual frameworks, including that of postmodernism's critics. Crucially, however, the imbrication of all speaking positions in a 'field of power is *not* the advent of a nihilistic relativism incapable of furnishing norms, but, rather, the very precondition of a politically engaged critique'. That is, recognising and fully owning one's privileged speaking position is our first ethical duty. Postmodernists, then, do not abolish foundational categories, much less indulge in mindless relativism. Our goal is rather to interrogate (a word Cohen despises) just what it is that established foundations and putatively universal truths authorise and legitimate and what, or who, is excluded by them. For example, any text that resorts to a universalising 'we' must, as Butler insists, be 'exposed for its highly ethnocentric biases' or, for that matter, any bias that might inform a privileged speaking position.[40] Cohen's biases are transparent. He tells us he belongs to a 'tiny subculture' that is privileged middle-class, intellectual, English-speaking, 'culturally Anglo-American', yet 'cosmopolitan, deracinated'.[41] Overlooking his highly privileged speaking position as a white man, he leaves tantalisingly open the

---

39 Cohen, 2001, p 281.
40 Butler, 1992, pp 5–7, original emphasis. Butler argues that strategies of resistance to modes of domination can be formed without recourse to foundations, such as Cohen's universal and objective truths. She claims that 'contingent foundations' will suffice.
41 Cohen, 2001, p 299.

question of whether a postmodern-inflected sensitivity to acts of conceptual mastery might have helped him write a less masculinist book, one that did not relegate violence against women to the private sphere.

As for the postmodernism-versus-poststructuralism terminological conundrum, it need not detain us. At times I have written under the mantle of postmodern feminism; at others, I have shared Butler's preference for speaking of positions and strategies that are influenced by poststructuralist theories.[42] For example, in *Punish and Critique*, my study of critical approaches to punishment and penality that move beyond the confines of penology, criminology's twin discipline, I located myself under the sign of the postmodern. I have stuck with postmodernism here, but I do so in the belief that the choice of nomenclature is, ultimately, inconsequential. What matters is the methodology, in our case, the Foucauldian methodology of paying attention to the discursive constructions of truth and the intersections of power and knowledge that are exposed when sex, violence and crime are placed in a postmodern frame.

A taste of what's to come

While this book follows the trajectory of SVC, it is not a history, much less a litany of the course's successes and failures. Nevertheless, the first four chapters do follow Part One of the lecture programme which, for all the modifications and revisions made since SVC's inception, retains much of its original format. We begin with what turns out to be the far from self-evident question of sex. Chapter 1 introduces my Foucauldian feminist method of examining how sex and violence are 'put into discourse' in women's magazine articles on heterosexual sex. By reproducing a mode of a very familiar form of sex talk, these magazine articles provide a vehicle for breaching the self-evidence of heteronormativity, thus putting into question 'sex', as in having sex, and also sex as in having a sex, or a sexed identity – something Foucault paid much less attention to.

In the second half of the twentieth century, feminist scholars in a range of fields of social inquiry problematised the taken-for-granted meaning of 'sex' and 'gender'. They also amassed a great deal of evidence relating to men's pervasive violence against women and children in all Western jurisdictions. It might have been expected that this new knowledge would have impacted significantly on criminology, given the discipline's ostensible interest in addressing crime in all its manifestations. Alas, no. Chapter 2 provides a critique of mainstream criminological accounts of violent interpersonal crime, focusing on the discursive strategies deployed by apologists for violent men in order to counter insistent feminist naming practices.

---

42 Butler, 1992. Carol Smart comments on the overlaps between postmodernism and poststructuralism and her preference for the latter term in Smart, 1995.

Chapter 3 is billed as a 'postmodern case study', one that might confound readers, at least initially, inasmuch as it is both for and against Foucault. The focus is the Pierre Rivière case, made famous by Foucault and his followers waxing eloquent about the nineteenth-century French peasant who killed his mother, sister and brother and then wrote an account of his deeds. Most commentators, feminists included, have subscribed to Foucault's narrow reading of the case as a perfect illustration of the power of the controlling discourses of law and medicine. By contrast, Chapter 3 provides a critical reading of the case and its reception in order to expose the limits of a masculinist analysis, including putatively 'postmodern' ones that fail to even notice that the case is a case of 'family' violence. This sets the scene for Chapter 4's engagement with so-called 'critical criminologies' that celebrate men's violent acts, including violence against women. Here we see how self-defining 'critical' criminologists get caught up in the excitement of sexed violence, abandoning critical insight for emotional attachment to violent men. As we shall see, they might purport to make an epistemological and political break with positivist paradigms. But when faced with the evidence of pervasive men's violence, non-feminist critical criminologists soon retreat into victim-blaming etiologies and antediluvian conceptualisations of 'gender' reminiscent of the old-order criminology they claim to have supplanted.

Chapter 5 addresses two of the key 'internal' questions faced by the feminist movement, questions which arose within the movement when it placed men on the political agenda. First, no sooner had the largely white Western women's movement put men and men's violence on the political agenda in the late 1960s than black and other minority ethnic women challenged white feminism's formulation of and answers to the 'Woman' question – the question, that is, of how diversely situated women should be represented. Second, in the 1980s, feminists informed by poststructuralist theories began challenging radical feminism's essentialising and totalising constructions of gendered relationships. While Chapter 5 explores how these interventions explode the notion of a monolithic feminist project, Chapter 6 provides some genealogies of the practice of naming and un-naming men's violence focusing on the formulation of domestic violence policies in Britain at the turn of the new millennium. With men still un-named as agents in the government's 'Violence Against Women' initiatives, the stage has been set for more discursive battles between, on the one hand, feminist activists and scholars who have endeavoured to make men's violence against women a policy priority and, on the other, all those non-feminists who have fought so voraciously to recuperate for men all the ground lost to criticism. That these battles are being fought under the rapidly changing conditions of globalisation makes feminist framings of the 'Man' question all the more fraught.

My first plan for the Epilogue was to pen a confession to having evaded the tricky questions. What about women's agency and responsibility for acts of sexed violence? What are we to make of women who collude with men's violence or who participate in violent acts themselves? And what is to be done about all this sexed violence? Do postmodern feminist theories do more than liberal or radical feminisms to assist survivors to find a voice? Do they help create more resistant subject positions for women to occupy? But in the end, I decided to limit the Epilogue's task to that of responding to the suggestion that the time of discourse analysis has passed. I then leave off where we began – with a will to continue challenging the tactics of denial, equivocation and erasure relied on by violent men and their apologists in the face of compelling evidence of widespread violence against women in Western societies.

Chapter 1

Let's talk about sex, baby

> At the bottom of the page she had written . . . BEWARE OF FOUCAULT, as if the philosopher was a particularly savage dog.[1]

'The best orgasm of your life!', 'How to reach orgasm every single time!', 'When it's ok to fake it'. For more than three decades now, articles in women's magazines have urged young women to discover (or, more precisely, perform) heterosexual sexual bliss. But sex advice columns do much more than that. By reproducing a mode of very familiar sex talk, they enable us to listen – courtesy of a feminist adaptation of Gramsci's theory of hegemony – to the sounds of hegemonic heterosexism clanking into gear. The never-ending stream of advice to young women on how to be properly sexed, sexual and prepped to please their man also supplies a rich body of material for breaching – courtesy of Foucault – the self-evidence of 'sex'. Indeed, magazines like *Cosmopolitan, Cleo* or *She* cry out for Foucauldian discourse analysis; that is, for testing Foucault's famous assertion in volume 1 of his *History of Sexuality* that what matters, when it comes to sex, is not 'whether one says yes or no to sex', or 'whether one formulates prohibitions or permissions, whether one asserts its importance or denies its effects, or whether one refines the words one uses to designate it'. What matters is to account for the fact that sex is spoken about and to discover:

> . . . who does the speaking, the positions and viewpoints from which they speak, the institutions which prompt people to speak about it and which store and distribute the things that are said. What is at issue, briefly, is the over-all 'discursive fact', the way in which sex is *'put into discourse'*.[2]

What matters, in short, is how sex is talked about. For Foucault and

1 Duncker, 1997, p 13.
2 Foucault, 1979, p 11, emphasis added.

Foucauldians, sex – and by extension, violence and crime – are first and foremost discursive practices. It follows that checking how sex, violence and crime are 'put into discourse' is this book's method of choice for planting them firmly in a postmodern frame.

Some caveats before we begin. This book does not have space to explore the development of what has been called, after Foucault, the 'postmodernisation' or denaturalisation of sex.[3] Engaging with the massive body of 'prosex thought' inspired by Foucault's three-volume history of sexuality is simply beyond its reach.[4] Nor can we spare the time to get immersed in the equally voluminous feminist debates for and against the deployment of his ideas for feminist ends.[5] My more minimalist goal is to create a *usable* Foucault, a Foucault amenable to anyone interested in forging a critical understanding of sex and sexed violence. Naturally, the first question that springs to mind is: how much sex do we need for that? Some may say they cannot get enough, but we need enough to grasp Foucault's reconceptualisation of sexuality as a discursively constituted event involving a technology or technique of the self.[6] And we need enough to comprehend what Rosalind Coward meant when she declared that every manifestation of sexual activity, including male aggression, far from being 'natural', is a 'ritualistic enactment of cultural meanings about sex'. Sex, she said, is 'never instinctual' – sex is 'always an activity wrapped in cultural meanings, cultural prescriptions and cultural constraints'.[7] Drawing on these insights, Chapter 1 takes the first small steps needed to inculcate a postmodern feminist sensibility around questions of sex in order to lay the groundwork for the challenges made to non-feminist perspectives on men's violence against women in the next three chapters. It also aims to disabuse readers of the notion that 'Radical feminism *is* feminism' as non-feminists appear to assume is still the case today.[8]

The coming of soul-less sex

Let us begin with an illuminating early twenty-first century magazine discussion of 'modern' sex. The October 2003 British edition of *Cosmopolitan* sets itself apart from the madding crowd of glossy women's magazines that have urged young women, in issue after issue, onto better and better heterosexual sex. Remembering the (undisclosed) time of her 'first proper boyfriend', a time when she and her girlfriends 'relished our newfound sexual power', the editor – a self-declared 'modern-day feminist' – reflects on the 'new worrying

---

3 Simon, 1996.
4 Berlant and Warner, 1998, p 547.
5 See, e.g. Haug *et al*, 1987; Bell, 1993; Butler, 1993.
6 Foucault, 1985, p 11.
7 Coward, 1987, pp 239–40.
8 MacKinnon, 1983, p 639, emphasis added.

trend' she calls 'Soul-less Sex'. While 'soul-less sex' is not defined in the editorial, it soon becomes apparent that it is code for the recent much-publicised spectacle of young English women drinking themselves into comas, acquiring sexual transmitted diseases at alarmingly high rates in the process, and topping the European teenage pregnancy scales at a rate of two, three and six times more than their Italian, French and German counterparts respectively.[9] The editor blames these worrying new trends on 'soul-less sex', which is 'the opposite' of the 'open approach to female sexuality' that the editor had enjoyed when she was younger, which if one can guess from her photograph was some 10 years earlier. Back then, she says:

> We didn't feel ashamed about one-night stands, we didn't judge each other and we weren't embarrassed by our enjoyment of sex. This, we thought, is what feminism is all about.

Moreover, it was magazines like *Cosmo* that had 'helped make this proud sexuality possible':

> Along with millions of other women, we felt able to expect satisfying sex. We didn't always get it, but we knew we deserved it (unlike our mothers and grandmothers).

Now something had gone awry. Feminism was supposed to mean 'more choices in all areas of our lives'. The arrival of soul-less sex, however, was a headache for the editor of 'the only magazine that gives women open and entertaining sexual advice'. Certainly, the behaviour of young women obsessed with sex with men they did not know which had caught the British media's attention was worrying, but *not* – she assures us – because she had an issue with 'the number of men a woman chooses to bed'. The problem was rather that young women 'feel they *must* be part of this new trend'; that they 'feel pressured because suddenly sex is the cool, fashionable thing to do'.[10]

Our worried *Cosmo* editor taps into a question that has been posed by feminist analysts for some time now – just how sexually liberating for women is all this magazine sex talk? Have all the hints on how to have seamless orgasmic sex 'every single time' failed to live up to their promise? One view is that magazines aimed at young women should not be admonished for trying to turn their readers into 'passive clones of male desire', because 'if you actually take the trouble to read magazines like *Cleo, Cosmo*

---

9 Chlamydia infections have increased dramatically in the UK over the past decade. In 2000, syphilis had increased in women by 53%, leading to new campaigns to reach the 'reckless' young: *Independent*, 4 August 2002.
10 Editor, *Cosmo*, 2003, original emphasis.

or *Dolly*, you get a very different picture'.[11] Well, do you? In this chapter, I do take the trouble to read the magazines. I also take up the challenge of taming the savage dog – the challenge of rendering Foucault's frequently difficult, sometimes convoluted, and occasionally circular theories about the power of discourses less scary to the uninitiated. We will pick up more methodological clues from Foucault for studying the power of discourse in Chapter 3. Here we are concerned with developing a Foucauldian reading of discourses about sex – predominantly sex as in having sex. Finally, a brief reference to sex as in having a sex will serve as a reminder of just how complex 'sex' is.

Sex and method – taming the beast

Some readers might prefer to bypass questions of method in order to get straight down to business – the business of sex. It may be a matter of indifference to them that Foucault wrote a great deal about methodology, as well as about sexuality. No doubt they will be relieved to learn that as this book is not a methodological tract, it will not be delving into the detail of Foucault's notes on method. Nor will it get side-tracked by the extensive literature assessing his history of sexuality. As already mentioned, the heated debates between his feminist admirers and detractors, between those who have followed and those who have adamantly declined to follow any of the Foucauldian paths are not our concern here either.[12] Instead, this chapter explores reading strategies for those interested in taking what is sometimes called 'the postmodern turn'.

Expanding on the question of terminological confusion between postmodernism and poststructuralism that was raised in the introduction, let us begin with a discussion of these terms that takes place within a criminology text. According to Maggie Wykes, criminology has experienced a 'critical turn' that 'blended feminism with post-modernism, particularly with the post-structural philosophical aspects of post-modernism'. She sees this distinction between postmodernism and poststructuralist theories as crucial inasmuch as 'post-modern critique', in her view, 'merely celebrates a frivolous kind of dismissal of all attempts to account for change in the world'. Poststructuralism, on the other hand, challenges objective truth because it recognises that power is imbricated in the production of truth; that regimes of truth are forged from a 'will to power'. Such an understanding, she says, is 'epitomised' by Foucault's work.[13] That Foucault himself not only refused

11 Lumby, 1999, p 8.
12 See, e.g. Ramazanoglu, 1993. For an overview of feminist deployments of Foucault's ideas about the policing and disciplining of sexed and sexualised bodies, see Howe, 1994, Chapter 5.
13 Wykes, 2001, p 18.

this label, but insisted that he did not know what the terms 'postmodern-ism', 'structuralism' or 'poststructuralism' meant, is of no consequence.[14] What is pertinent however, is that a clear exposition of poststructuralism and of how Foucault's work fits the description, can be found in Chris Weedon's ground-breaking book advocating the usefulness of poststructur-alist theory for feminist practice.

Poststructuralism, Weedon explains, is the name given to theoretical posi-tions developed from the work of Derrida, Lacan, Kristeva, Althusser and Foucault. Its 'founding insight' is that 'language, far from reflecting an already given social reality, constitutes social reality for us'. This 'insight', as she calls it, is the very heart of the matter, the key to unlocking the post-modern door. Discourses give the world meaning; they do not simply trans-late a given or 'fixed reality'. For example, what it means to be a woman, or a man, is not constant, fixed, essential or eternal. Rather, 'the meanings of femininity and masculinity' vary across time and between cultures. But while all poststructuralist theories agree on this point – that 'meaning is constituted within language' rather than being a given – different forms of poststructuralism theorise the production of meaning in different ways. Derridean deconstruction, for example, looks at the relationships between different texts. In Weedon's view, however, it is Foucauldian theory, with its analytical focus on historically specific discursive relations and social practices, that is 'of most interest to feminists'.[15]

Discourse, it should be made clear from the start, is not interchangeable with 'language'. A 'critical concept' that refuses the 'supposed given unity of particular domains of knowledge', 'discourse' has been defined as 'a sys-tem of language, objects and practices', one that 'implies a practice both of speech *and* action; who, it asks, speaks on a particular object or event and when, where and how?'.[16] Discursive practices can be economic, social and political. As Weedon explains, Foucault used the concept of 'discursive field' to explore the relationship between language, social institutions, subjectivity and power. Discursive fields consist of 'competing ways of giving meaning to the world and of organising social institutions and pro-cesses'. Law, the political system, the church, the family, the education system and the media are all located in a particular discursive field. Within each field, some discourses support the status quo, while others contest it, and are consequently 'dismissed by the hegemonic system of meanings and practices as irrelevant or bad'. This is the fate, for example, of dissenting

---

14 Foucault, 2000. For his opposition to labels, see *The Order of Things*, where he dismisses as 'half-witted', commentators who persisted in labelling him a 'structuralist': 1973, p xiv. See further Foucault, 1989a and 2000. One scholar claims that Foucault was a 'consistent postmodern in that he would never have called himself a postmodern': Hoy, 1988, p 38.

15 Weedon, 1987, p 22.

16 Haug *et al*, 1987, p 191, emphasis added.

discourses such as feminism that seek to challenge dominant or 'hegemonic' discourses.[17]

What is distinctive about Foucault's approach is his linking of discourse and power and his emphasis on the social and institutional effects of discourse, especially its role in 'the constitution and government of individual subjects' – that is, of who we are. Power, he argued, was exercised on individuals not only through institutions such as psychiatry and the penal system, but also via 'the discursive production and control of sexuality'. It followed that the analytical focus should be on the discursive fields which constitute madness, or punishment of sexuality. The aim in each case is to 'uncover the particular regimes of power and knowledge at work in a society and their part in the overall production and maintenance of existing power relations'. Discourses are crucial to Foucault in the establishment of regimes of truth because, as Weedon explains, they are 'ways of constituting knowledge, together with the social practices, forms of subjectivity and power relations which inhere in such knowledges and the relations between them'. But discourses are 'more than ways of thinking and producing meaning'. They also constitute:

> ... the 'nature' of the body, unconscious and conscious mind and emotional life of the subjects they seek to govern. Neither the body nor thought and feelings have meaning outside their discursive articulation, but the ways in which discourse constitutes the minds and bodies of individuals is always part of a wider network of power relations, often with institutional bases.[18]

In short, discourses are powerful, some much more than others, as we shall see. For now, Foucault gets the last word on the power of discourse – discourse, he said, is 'the power to be seized'.[19]

Sex, discourse and the power of truth

As it happens, sex is a very good place to start discussing the method that Foucault himself referred to, at least on one occasion, as 'discourse analysis', a method that treats discourse not as 'a set of linguistic facts', but as 'games, strategic games of action and reaction, question and answer, domination and evasion, as well as struggle ... a strategic and polemical game'.[20] Not only does the first volume of Foucault's *History of Sexuality* offer, as Weedon

17 Weedon, 1987, pp 35–7.
18 Weedon, 1987, pp 107–8.
19 Foucault, 1984a, p 110.
20 Foucault, 2002, pp 2–3.

points out, a clear and accessible account of his theoretical method; a whole chapter of that book is devoted to method. Starting with Foucault's definition of his objective as 'an analysis of the discourses of sex and their implications for the constitution and government of the sexual subject', Weedon turns to the famous passage on page 11 which we commenced quoting at the beginning of this chapter. Here we learn that exploring how sex is 'put into discourse' is no simple matter. It involves examining the 'polymorphous techniques of power', no less, and locating:

> . . . the forms of power, the channels it takes, and the discourses it permeates in order to reach the most tenuous and individual modes of behaviour, the paths that give it access to the rare or scarcely perceivable forms of desire, how it penetrates and controls everyday pleasure . . .

And there is still more to be gleaned from page 11, notably Foucault's aim in writing his history of sexuality. Far from wanting to ascertain whether discursive productions and their effects of power lead to formulations of 'the truth about sex', his goal was rather 'to define the regime of power-knowledge-pleasure that sustains the discourse on human sexuality in our part of the world'.[21] In other words, his focal concern is the relationship between language, power, subjectivity and social institutions, including sexuality. He wants to discover how social relations are produced and sustained 'in the discursive production of historically specific sexuality, the subjects which it constitutes and governs, and the emergence of resistance to this power'.[22]

From the eighteenth century, so Foucault's argument goes, sex became a pivotal focal point for the exercise of power in Western societies. Sex, he said, 'must not be described as a stubborn drive' in need of subduing, but rather 'as an especially dense transfer point for relations of power' – including, interestingly, relations of power 'between men and women', as well as between 'young people and old people, parents and offspring, teachers and students, priests and laity, an administration and a population'.[23] Furthermore, sex and sexed bodies are not historically constant, but are instead discursively constituted in historically and culturally specific ways. As such, they are sites of continuing struggle. Sex then, does not exist 'outside of its realisation in discourses of sexuality'; it has 'no essential nature or meaning'.[24] However, as a crucial site of power, sexuality has become central to subjective identity – to who we are.

---

21 Foucault, 1979, p 11. Clearly, one cannot overemphasise the importance of p 11, except perhaps to university students prepared to tear it out of a library copy (with belated apologies to La Trobe University library).
22 Weedon, 1987, p 118.
23 Foucault, 1979, p 103.
24 Weedon, 1987, pp 118–19.

Fond though he was of exploring how sex, bodies and subjectivities have been policed, Foucault famously rejected the 'repressive hypothesis', the notion that prohibition is the key to the history of sexuality. Not that he denied that sexuality has been repressed and prohibited in Western societies. He was adamant that it had been. His argument was rather that since the eighteenth century there has been a veritable deluge of discourses about sex, 'a discursive ferment', even an 'institutional incitement to speak about it'. The 'great process of transforming sex into discourse' was led by the development of a science of sexuality which led in turn to a 'policing of sex' – not, crucially, via 'the rigour of a taboo' – but 'through useful and public discourses'.[25] Of all the incitements to speak about sex, confessional speech was for Foucault the dominant form through which individuals are subjected to the power of discourses in Western societies – those of the science of sexuality, medicine, psychiatry, psychoanalysis, ethics, pedagogy, demography, biology and political science. As Weedon explains this point, to speak or confess is to assume 'a subject position within discourse and to become *subjected* to the power and regulation of the discourse'.[26] The subject is at once constituted by discourse, and subjected to it, and he – always already he in Foucault's texts, or she, in Weedon's – has his or her position as subject 'guaranteed by the "expert" enquiring voice'.[27] Resistance is possible, however, for where there is power, there is resistance. Indeed, 'points of resistance are present everywhere in the power network'.[28] By rejecting the idea of an essential sexuality, Foucault opens sexuality up to 'history and change', making resistance possible through the clash of contradictory discourses that provide the opportunity for 'contradictory subject positions and practices'.[29]

We shall return to the question of power and resistance in Chapter 3, but it will assist our discussion of sex to linger longer with the methodological pointers that Foucault drew from his understanding of the inextricable connections between discourse, power and knowledge, or truth. Power, he argues, produces truth, or rather 'effects of truth' and it does so, crucially, through discourse. In every society, he says, there are 'manifold relations of power' which permeate 'the social body' and which crucially, cannot be established, consolidated or implemented without the production, accumulation, circulation and functioning of a discourse'. Indeed:

> There can be no possible exercise of power without a certain economy of discourses of truth . . . We are subjected to the production of truth

25 Foucault, 1979, pp 18–25.
26 Weedon, 1987, p 119, original emphasis.
27 Weedon, 1979, p 120.
28 Foucault, 1979, pp 26 and 95.
29 Weedon, 1979, pp 123 and 125.

through power and we cannot exercise power except through the
production of truth . . . we are forced to produce the truth of power that
our society demands, of which it has need, in order to function: we *must*
speak the truth; we are constrained or condemned to confess or to discover the truth.[30]

Each society has 'its regime of truth, its "general politics" of truth' – or discourses which it accepts and 'makes function as true'. Each has mechanisms
for distinguishing true from false statements, procedures for acquiring the
truth and determining who can be 'charged with saying what counts as true'.
There is then, a 'political economy' of truth, involving discursive battles 'for
truth', in which truth and power are intimately connected. Indeed, as 'truth
is already power', analysts should not attempt to separate truth from power,
but rather to detach 'the power of truth from the forms of hegemony, social,
economic and cultural, within which it operates at the present time'.[31]

Detaching the power of truth from hegemonic discourses is almost the last
piece of methodological advice we shall take from Foucault for now. It
might be helpful, however, to say a bit more about the key concepts of
hegemony and counter-hegemony, and also to acknowledge something that
Foucault did not – his debt to the Marxist theorist, Antonio Gramsci.[32] To
mark this book's debt to Gramsci, it is not necessary to discuss his 'proto-
structuralist understanding' of the materiality of language that anticipated
late twentieth-century poststructuralist theories, as Renate Holub does. Nor
do we need to contrast his micro history of sexuality with Foucault's.[33] It
suffices to register Gramsci's signature concept of 'hegemony', pivotal for
understanding that consent is vital for the successful imposition of domination. For Gramsci, the hegemony or domination of the ruling class is
secured, on the one hand, by the state's repressive institutions, the police,
army and prisons which coerce a population into consenting to the rule of
the dominant economic group. But on the other hand, and more importantly, hegemony is forged in 'civil society', through institutions ranging
from education, religion and the family to 'the microstructures of the practices of everyday life', all of which contribute to 'the production of meaning
and values which in turn produce, direct and maintain the 'spontaneous'
consent of the governed to the political and social status quo.[34] Hegemony,
as Raymond Williams defines it, is 'a lived system of meanings and values,
not simply an ideology, a sense of reality beyond which it is, for most people,
difficult to move, a lived dominance and subordination, internalised'.[35]

30 Foucault, 1980c, p 93, original emphasis.
31 Foucault, 1980d, pp 131–3.
32 Holub, 1992, p 13.
33 Holub, 1992, pp 20, 28 and 195–7.
34 Holub, 1992, p 6.
35 Quoted in Holub, 1992, p 104.

Gramsci's concept of hegemony is highly versatile, capable of 'probing relations of power on a microstructural as well as on a macrostructural level'. By grasping 'power relations in the interstices of everyday life', it has the potential to probe 'relations of domination in the most intimate practices of everyday life', including sexual practices.[36] No wonder Foucault, fascinated as he was with the microphysics of power and with dominant and subordinated knowledges, became interested in the idea of detaching the power of truth from the hegemonic discourses in which it was enmeshed. As Holub explains, what both share – 'or perhaps this is something Foucault adopted from Gramsci' – is the idea that consent to domination is produced from within social relations, within 'microstructures that inform the practices of everyday life'. Where they differ is their approach to the question of the ubiquity of power. They agreed power was everywhere, but Gramsci, much more than Foucault, emphasised unequal power relationships and *why* power exists, whereas Foucault concentrated on understanding *how* power operates.[37] Foucault is quite explicit on this point – he was not interested in 'why certain people want to dominate', but rather in how power operated 'at the level of ongoing subjugation, at the level of those continuous and uninterrupted processes which subject our bodies, govern our gestures, dictate our behaviours'. He wanted to grasp how subjects come into being – how, as 'an effect of power', their bodies, gestures, discourses and desires come to be 'constituted as individuals'.[38]

Freed from the Marxist preoccupation with ideology, Foucault was able to pursue an inquiry into the relations of truth and power that are constitutive of hegemony.[39] More broadly, his method might be described as he himself came to describe it: as a series of 'problematisations'. Simply put, question the self-evidence of that which is, throw everything into question, dissipate 'what is familiar and accepted'.[40] The goal of a 'history of thought', as Foucault came to define his life's work, was to 'define the conditions in which human beings "problematise" what they are, what they do, and the world in which they live', even their sexual world. How do we come to recognise ourselves as sexual subjects? What are the 'games of truth by which human beings came to see themselves as 'desiring individuals'? These were some of his central concerns.[41] In short, his goal was to question who we think we are right down to our most intimate moments.

That, in brief, was Foucault's counter-hegemonic strategy, and that

---

36 Holub, 1992, p 197.
37 Holub, 1992, pp 199–200, emphasis added.
38 Foucault, 1980c, pp 97–8.
39 See Smart, 1986, pp 159–64.
40 Foucault, 1988c, p 265.
41 Foucault, 1985, pp 5–10.

should be quite enough methodological advice for now, quite enough to understand his central point that discourses on sexuality, and not only those claiming to tell the truth about sex, are operations of power. It is time now to see how sex is put into discourse today, but with this final clarification: while Foucault explored how a strangely ungendered sexuality – sexuality *per se* – entangled neutered individuals in power/knowledge relations, feminist work concentrates on how sexuality, and female sexuality especially, has been organised around the institution of heterosexuality.[42]

Disclaimer – but I'm *not* a radical feminist

Getting down at last to sex (or rather, discourses about sex), we might begin with 'foreplay', if only to see how tricky talking about sex can be. In commonsense understanding, 'foreplay' is what happens immediately prior to heterosexual sex, before the 'real thing', from the man's point of view, or what might happen, if you are lucky, from the woman's point of view. In an age where mutually-satisfying heterosexual sex is a widely-acclaimed aspiration, we might have expected 'foreplay' to have disappeared from sex talk. Yet it has managed to retain its place in popular culture. Decades-old 'jokes' about the Anglo-Australian male's idea of foreplay – 'G'day love, I'm home' or 'Brace yourself, Sheila' – have twenty-first century counterparts. In one recent English version, a cartoon depicts a man shouting 'Fore' as he swings a golf club while standing on a bed next to his irate wife who complains: 'you know that's not what I mean by foreplay'. The continuing salience of 'foreplay' in popular discourses about sex gives rise to a conundrum: if foreplay is what you do *before* you have sex – 'real' sex – as penile penetration of a vagina (or any orifice, for that matter) is still coded today, then it follows that other sexual activity (lesbian sex comes to mind) is not sex. But if that is so, how have representations of sexual relations between women come to have such a prominent place in popular culture and in pornography? Why are they registered as 'sex' when, if there is no penis in sight, one might expect them to be dismissed as merely 'foreplay'?

Already we appear to steer off course, diverting into a philosophical dialogue about the real, or worse, into a confrontation with heterosexuality, and we have not even got past foreplay. This is one of the enduring troubles with sex: it can lead one astray. Here however, it is leading straight to an insistent marking of a distinction between radical feminist and poststructuralist feminist perspectives on sex. Catherine MacKinnon can stand in as our token radical feminist. In the 1980s, before her infamous apostasy – marriage, to a man – Mackinnon placed probing questions about sexual intimacy and violence onto the feminist agenda. Consider, for example, her

42 Bell, 1993, pp 24–5.

stunning query: 'What is the etiology of heterosexuality in women?'[43] – what causes women to opt for heterosexuality? Such a question might have qualified as one of those Deleuzian shocks to thought that rock us out of established ways of thinking.[44] But beyond querying whether heterosexuality's pleasure is 'women's stake in subordination', MacKinnon was not interested in exploring the etiology of heterosexuality in women. Nor, of course, am I, causal questions being something any self-respecting postmodernist spurns. Nevertheless, MacKinnon's question is illuminating because it hones in on the construction of heterosexual rather than 'deviant' sexual desires, thereby problematising normalcy, which is always thrilling for Foucauldians.

If asking questions about the etiology of heterosexuality in women is interesting, querying what causes heterosexuality in men is not. The answer to *that* question is surely self-evident. Heterosexual men get access to women and what more could anyone want? But again we digress. Still, it is worth noting that the evidence unearthed first by feminist investigative research and later by government crime surveys of widespread sexual and physical assaults on women by men they know is precisely the evidence which gives MacKinnon's etiological question a purchase today. Sidestepping this question, which would take us into psychoanalytical theory and outside the ambit of this book, I want to reformulate her positivistic 'why' question into a 'how' question – how is heterosexuality promoted as women's 'natural' sexual identity? Or, giving it a Foucauldian feminist gloss, how is heterosexuality put into discourse today?

Now this Foucauldian query, I am at pains to point out, is fundamentally different from a radical feminist one. Briefly, MacKinnon is focally concerned with demonstrating that violence and intimacy are linked; that heterosexual sex is forced sex; that violence and abuse are central to sexuality as women live it. Modern sexuality, she insists, is 'based on male force'. The appearance of women's consent to sex concealed the reality of force on which sexuality is based. Inviting us to compare victims' reports of rape with women's reports of sex, she suggests they 'look a lot alike'. She also thinks victims' reports of rape are very similar to 'what pornography says sex is'. Indeed, 'the major distinction between intercourse (normal) and rape (abnormal) is that the normal happens so often that one cannot get anyone to see anything wrong with it'.[45]

Feminist scholars have not needed MacKinnon's assistance to see that something is very wrong with hegemonic constructions of 'normal' heterosexual sex. They have also found much that is problematic about MacKinnon's radical feminist framing of the issues, not least her dismissal of the

---

43 MacKinnon, 1989, p 324.
44 Bottomley, 2004, pp 49–50.
45 MacKinnon, 1989, pp 336–7.

possibility of women's sexual agency – of a woman's capacity to consent to sex, of women's heterosexual desire. Still, radical feminist analysts like MacKinnon should be thanked for putting the question of the link between sex and violence so sharply onto the feminist agenda. Helpfully too, radical feminist preoccupations with the violence of heterosexual sex provide a nice contrast to the Foucauldian feminist focus on the violence of representational practices. How, Foucauldian feminists might ask, are sexed bodies discursively constituted and policed, say, in women's magazines? A never-ending stream of feature articles claim to provide the truth, even the 'real truth about men and sex', but what is this truth, and has it changed over the last decade or so?

Reading *Cosmo*

The February 1991 issue of *Cosmo*, one of my all-time favourites, contains no less than three feature articles on sex in its 16-page *Sex Report*. 'Sex is Back', screams the report's first headline. The author, not so sure, is 'determined to seek out the truth'. The truth, she discovers, is that women were not asking men to use condoms, mainly because the men were so resistant to that request. The problem is that in the 'age of AIDS', heterosexual women are at greater risk from HIV-AIDS than heterosexual men. It follows that women had 'some serious sorting out to do'.[46] The next article in the sex report is titled: 'Why he wants you to do that!'. What, exactly? The columnist explains that she received hundreds of letters from men frustrated that their wives and girlfriends would not 'shave off their pubic hair; talk dirty in bed; make love in a garter belt, black stockings, and high, high heels; or masturbate for them'. Nor were they willing to 'make love in public places or go out for the evening without underwear beneath their skimpy clothing'. The columnist explains why:

> Many women find these requests threatening. They bring us face-to-face with a darker side of male sexuality than we want to see. And they make us feel unappealing.[47]

The trick, she says, is to overcome women's resistance by altering their attitudes to the sex practices men wanted from them. For instance, shaving off your pubic hair is not such a big deal – it need only occur occasionally, say twice a year. Moreover, help is at hand from a male psychologist who assures women that this particular request is not camouflage for a man's lust for prepubescent girls, but simply a desire for a woman to appear vulnerable.

46 Zorn, 1991, pp 86–7.
47 Bakos, 1991a, p 88.

As for the other unsatisfied male sexual demands, such as talking dirty in bed or masturbating for him, women readers are advised to regard these demands as 'arousal variations'. After all:

> They are neither painful nor illegal. So would it really hurt to try them out at least once? Besides, if you really do not want to try them, you can always say no without feeling like a prude.[48]

Next, the *Sex Report* considers the results of a survey indicating that men felt they were not getting enough of 'the two sex acts they wanted more of', namely, anal and oral sex. Indeed, 'there were indications that some women were 'openly hostile to both practices'. Sympathetic to men who were sure they could 'overcome our objections if we'll let them try', the writer explains how she advises 'men who want anal sex (or any other sexual practice) badly to let their women know how intensely they desire it'.[49] The key to a successful negotiation is for the man to go at her pace and arrange a 'signal word that, when spoken by her, means unequivocally, go no further'. The code word cannot be 'no' because 'some people', apparently, call out 'no' or 'oh no' in the heat of passion, when actually they mean 'yes'. Once this issue is settled, the man has to offer her something in return, perhaps 'the fulfilment of her number-one sexual wish'. Trying anal sex at least occasionally may not 'meet his frequency needs', but a committed sexual relationship involves 'compromises on both parts'. While readers may be left in some doubt about what compromises were being asked of men, the advice to women who are loath to perform oral sex on men is crystal clear. They should place the penis on one side of their mouth in order to prevent it going deep enough to 'trigger the gag mechanism'. So, notwithstanding *Cosmo's* own surveys indicating that women were tired of men's sexual demands that left them feeling used and pressured, women readers are told to negotiate 'a minimum numerical requirement – for example, anal sex twice a month or a long fellatio session once a week in exchange for whatever you want sexually'.[50]

According to *Cosmo's* 1991 *Sex Report* then, the truth about sex is that sex is what men want, that it involved compromise on the woman's part and imaginative reinterpretations of men's demands as 'arousal variations'. The underlying message about 'modern sex' is that women are not doing enough of what men wanted sexually; that they are frustrating men; that men and women want different sexual practices, and that women's sexual desire is, or should be, subordinate to what men want sexually. Moving on, the March 1992 edition of *Cosmo*, which boasted the biggest sales worldwide in the

---

48 Bakos, 1991a, p 131.
49 Bakos, 1991b, p 94.
50 Bakos, 1991b, p 97.

magazine's history, contained a 76-page booklet, *Men, Love and Sex – What Every Woman Should Know About Men*. Claiming to seek out and tell the truth about sex, or even the 'real truth about men and sex', the booklet sets about exposing the 'real truth' by unravelling 'the amazing sexual secrets that give insight into the male mystique'. Turning randomly to the chapter on oral sex, we find Secret Number 5: 'men always love receiving oral sex from a woman'. Ignoring the fact that this must be one of the late-twentieth century's worst kept sexual secrets, the author proceeds to advise women about what men dislike about the way women perform oral sex. Women who 'suck on a penis as if they are milking a cow' is ranked as pet hate number one. While a specific remedy is not supplied for pet hate number 4 in the oral-sex-for-men department – 'women who give oral sex in total silence' – it is clear that the 'the real truth about men and sex' is that some kind of noise is required on the part of a woman performing fellatio.

The March 1992 issue of *Cosmo* contained another illuminating feature article about sex. 'The Great Swallowing Controversy and Other Dilemmas of Modern Sex' was written by a woman who says she is fed up with men's demand for oral sex and that most of her friends felt the same. The 'sub-doona' question that had plagued her since puberty is a familiar one: 'Am I normal?' – a question prompted by the fact that she had always found performing oral sex with men to be tedious at best, 'vomit worthy' at worst. A 'lightning survey' of her friends had highlighted a 'general consensus' on this issue. In fact, only one had enjoyed the practice in question. For the rest, mention of 'the great swallowing controversy' had 'inspired choruses of "yuks" '. That was not their only complaint. Evidently, 'good old-fashioned sexual intercourse' also left a lot to be desired, at least for this woman, who had always found it 'infernally frustrating'. She found some solace in a friend's complaint that her husband believed that 'foreplay' was 'something you are forced into if there isn't time for the "real thing" '[51] – a sign that the traditional distinction between 'foreplay' and 'the real thing' was still alive and well in 1992. But dissenting voices, if that is what they were, were soon eclipsed in *Cosmo*. The July 1992 edition was memorable for a new development, a feature article on faking orgasm, 'If You Can't Make It, Fake It', written by the author of the 'great swallowing controversy' who had apparently had a change of heart about the importance of pleasing her man sexually. Worried about the propriety of a sexual lie? Worry no more: it is all a question of 'plain, old-fashioned politeness':

> Give the guy a break. His buttocks have been pumping like pistons . . . If your partner has been giving you his sexual all, isn't it pretty picky to lie there . . . silently sending out the message, 'Failure'? Wouldn't it be

51 Feltz, 1992a, pp 96–7.

altogether kinder . . . to take a few deep shuddering breaths, gasp a bit, tremble as if gripped by rippling spasms . . . groan 'take me' or something like that and at least show some team spirit.[52]

So it is all down to good manners, to 'making other people' (tired male lovers) feel 'comfortable'. Lest this advice gets the columnist condemned as 'a disgrace to liberated womanhood', she hastens to add that she only advocates faking it 'in the case of occasional orgasmic blips'.[53]

The faking-it fad was shortlived. By April 1993, *New Woman* was advising women that faking orgasm was 'not just ok, it's good for you' and suggested that they set up a neighbourhood orgasm faking circle. Yet that very month, *Cleo* proffered advice on how to achieve 'the best orgasm of your life', and how to have an orgasm 'as often as you want' – for 'the truth is that virtually all women are capable of reaching orgasm whenever they want to'. All you need do is follow simple instructions, most memorably, 'forget about him'.[54] Not to be outdone, the April 1993 issue of *Cosmo* promised help on how to have an orgasm '*every* single time'. A feature article, 'Everything you always wanted to know about orgasm', set out the new sexual truth: 'Yes, you have orgasms, but does that mean you know all there is to know about them? When it comes to orgasms, the truth really sets you free!'.[55] This new liberating truth about sex points to the possibility of achieving 'extragenital' orgasms, multiple orgasms, simultaneous orgasms and 'male' orgasms, in which a woman emulates a male orgasm. Some hurdles needed to be overcome, however. Surveys suggest that no more than a third of women can experience an 'intercourse orgasm', and women wanting to experience multiple orgasms had to be 'sufficiently comfortable with her body and highly aroused by her partner'. Also, some women, oblivious to the new performance imperative, were still faking it. Indeed, some did so as a '*way of life*', believing their men expected it.[56]

While women had a fairly clear picture of the truth about heterosexual sex in the 1990s – that it was what men want – a feature article on why men go to prostitutes in *Cosmo*'s February 1994 edition complicated that picture somewhat. One man said he went to prostitutes because it was like having sex with 'a rubber tyre' which made him come 'like a fucking train'. Another went because he could not ask his girlfriend to do 'the things I really want'. However – and this is where it starts to get complicated – 'if she did want to do them, I don't think I'd love her any more'.[57] Obviously, women needed

52 Feltz, 1992b, p 80.
53 Feltz, 1992b, p 140.
54 Swift, 1993, pp 98–100.
55 Bakos, 1993, p 111, original emphasis.
56 Bakos, 1993, p 114, original emphasis.
57 Campbell, 1994, pp 71–3.

to walk a fine line between a permissible performance of enjoying sex acts men wanted and an impermissible display of liking them too much. Throughout the mid-1990s, women were also expected to heed 'shock' surveys in which men expressed their sexual desires, and still more advice about the '6 steps to Joygasmic sex'. Still, a call for sexual 'honesty' and a plea for women to learn from the 'hard times', suggests that things had moved on since the injunction of the early 1990s to fake orgasm – for whether you are 'lying out of politeness, shame or guilt, you are only cheating yourself and your partner out of real intimacy and real pleasure'.[58] By 1996, the new truth about sex was that you had to be truthful.

Bringing to a close this swift sampling of late twentieth-century magazine sex talk, *Cleo*'s August 1999 Australian edition set out 'things that go through a man's mind' before, during and after sex. The things, presented by a male writer, ranged from wondering whether there had been enough 'foreplay', to worrying whether she might be 'faking' it, to pondering whether he could 'accidentally slip it in her bottom'.[59] While it does not appear to have occurred to him that if he did so, he could be prosecuted for rape under Australian criminal law, the inclusion of the accidentally-on-purpose anal penetration thought in his wish-list was not that surprising. In his list of '20 really dirty things all men want you to do in bed but are too scared to ask', published in *Cleo* four months earlier, number 11 was 'let us have sex with your bottom'.[60] Avid readers of *Cleo* and *Cosmo* may not have found anything amiss in the quick shift from a spoken desire for consensual anal sex to an unspoken desire for nonconsensual anal sex. After all, male sexual desire for anal sex with women is a constant refrain in women's magazines.

Sex in the new millennium – we've come a long way, baby

Well, have 'we'? Have we come a long way with the liberating of sexual desire and our understanding of the truth about sex? Did late-twentieth century popular sex talk usher in an era of sexual enlightenment for women, delivering us from sexual repression with its orgasmic-centered discourse – the truth that will set us free? Or has it had the opposite effect, regulating every aspect of our sexuality, right down to the last detail of our sexual performance? Recall that Foucault rejected the 'repressive hypothesis' in favour of an interpretative framework that focused on the proliferation of discourses about sexuality and, closely related, the policing of sex and bodies through public discourses. What would he have made of the discursive

---

58 Krizanovich, 1996, p 93.
59 Fennell, 1999b, pp 96–101.
60 Fennel, 1999a, pp 59–60.

ferment about sex – the drive to find liberation in incessant discourse about sexuality – that gathered momentum in women's magazines in the 1990s?

I picture him laughing in his grave, delighted that the great process of transforming sex into discourse that he had traced from the eighteenth through to the late twentieth century was still alive and well 30 years after he dissected it in *The History of Sexuality*. Here was further proof that Western societies, far from being sexually repressive, are overwhelmed by a desire to tell the truth about sex:

> ... to utter truths and promise bliss, to link together enlightenment, liberation and manifold pleasures: to pronounce a discourse that combines the fervour of knowledge, the determination to change the laws and the longing for the garden of earthly delights.[61]

How amused he would be to see that the 'great sexual sermon' lived on.[62] But would he have even noticed a new trend, a focus on reports on violence against women in women's magazines at the turn of the new millennium? While the March 2000 issue of *Cosmo* featured an article on men's sexual assaults on women, the March 2000 issue of *Cleo* reported on 'male rape' – men's sexual assaults on men – perhaps to 'balance' its August 1999 *Cleo* report on women who rape other women. By describing woman-on-woman rape as 'a lot more common than you may think',[63] the magazine gave expression to that stubborn urge – which, as we shall see in Chapter 2, afflicts some male 'family violence' researchers – to find women equally, if not more violent than men. By contrast, in October 2002, *Cosmo* launched its *Stop in the Name of Love* domestic violence campaign as a response to UK research indicating high levels of men's violence against women. Those research findings and feature stories about men sexually assaulting their women partners are juxtaposed with standard feature articles on 'modern sex' that report that fellatio, one of men's 'deepest desires', has now been elevated to a 'spiritual experience'.[64] At least, it has for men – pleasing your man remains a dominant theme in new millennium discourses on sex, as is evident in feature articles titled 'Blow his mind', 'Four secret things' and, in the October 2001 edition of *She*, 'The Top Ten Male Sex Fantasies'. To cut a familiar story short, he really wants more blow jobs, although how this could possibly count as a secret after a decade of enlightenment from *Cosmo* about the sex acts men want women to perform is a mystery.

It would have been neat to take as our final example of early twenty-first century sex talk an article published in May 2003 in the *Guardian Magazine*

---

61 Foucault, 1979, p 22.
62 Foucault, 1979, p 7.
63 Elder, 1999, p 80.
64 Kelly, 2002, p 170.

on Britain's 'bum fetish'. Mainstream global culture, we are told, is pre-occupied with 'the aesthetic and sexual properties of the bottom' which extends to a 'frenzied arse appreciation' of celebrity bottoms. The 'next natural step' is of course the country's 'fascination with anal sex'. A national survey of sexual attitudes and lifestyles is cited that indicates a big increase in the practice of heterosexual anal sex between 1990 and 2000, including stories of teenage girls being pressured into anal sex. The 'truth', it suggests, is that it would be madness to see this 'backdoor mania' as 'an empowering function of feminism' however much fashion editors try to dress up the current obsession with celebrity bums. After all, 'many women don't like it', apparently. Moreover, men's demands for anal sex are just another way of telling women that their pleasure is 'secondary, if not irrelevant'. It might be 'fine' to succumb to his demand 'once in a while (on your birthday?)'; but it is not 'if the whole sexual culture is driving in that direction'. Sadly, the author suspects that it is; and that is not the only problem. First, 'arse-centricity' is highly racialised. J-Lo's 'sticky-out arse' might be coded as black, but Kylie's 'timid behind' is a conduit for a very Anglo-Saxon message, namely that 'defined arses are unarguably nice, but you don't have to be strident, or rapacious, or voluptuous, or black, to constitute a perfect model of feminin-ity'. Second, the 'cultural' fixation with bottoms has homoerotic over-tones, conjuring up an image of men's desire to penetrate women as if they were men. So, all in all, 'the rise and rise of anal sex' is hardly a strike for 'sexual liberation'. It might be 'a nice theory' that arse-centricity is liberating, but there is a 'crack in it'[65] – or perhaps more than one.

Tempting though it is to 'end' our study of popular sex talk here, with a feminist challenge to what women's magazines repeatedly identify as one of heterosexual-identified men's most desired sexual practices, we would surely be left aching for more, for news of what came next. Where did sex stray after 2003? Not that far, as it happens. A brisk romp through a compilation of various 2006 and 2007 editions of *Cleo*, *Cosmo* and *New Woman* reveals that magazine sex advice columns are still trying to get inside his head to discover what he wants, still advising women how to please their men. Sadly, 'Surgery saved my sex life' was torn out of my library copy of the April 2006 edition of *Cleo*, but it does have a list of '67 lusty moves he'll crave', includ-ing 'all-day foreplay', a 'warm-up so good', if you follow the instructions, 'you won't even want to move onto the real thing'. Interestingly, though, 'too many blokes define foreplay as a slurred "You awake, love?" '. We find, too, that there is still more homework to be done by the properly prepped sexed-up girl about town. Just when you thought you had 'the whole G-spot thing sussed', the December 2006 *Cosmo* publishes 'Hello! The new G-spots every girl oughta try and find', listing her A-Spot, C-Spot, P-Spot and U-Spot,

65 Williams, 2003, p 22.

and not forgetting his M-Spot – 'practise until you know them by heart'. Most remarkably, however, the magazines are still telling and selling secrets. There are secrets from a men's magazine editor and from 'the one woman who really knows how to exude single-girl sexiness' and how to 'tap into your inner sex kitten' – one of *Cosmo*'s editors-in-chief. Then there are *Cosmo*'s '69 secrets of sexed up couples' and *New Woman*'s test to discover the secret to sexual satisfaction – 'Where are you on the sex scale?'. But best of all, the February 2007 *Cleo* features '46 surprisingly hot sex secrets even we'd never heard of', including this: 'everyone should give anal sex a go', although how they could never have heard of that defies belief. Still, it is satisfying to find still more proof that Foucault's judgment some 30 years ago that what is 'peculiar to modern societies' is 'not that they consigned sex to "a shadow existence", but that they have "dedicated themselves to speaking of it *ad infinitum*, while exploiting it as *the* secret" ' has stood the test of time.[66] It seems that when it comes to sex, we are still constrained and condemned to confess our secrets in order to discover our truth.

Let us now return to our starting point – those creeping doubts expressed in the October 2003 edition of *Cosmo* about the transformative potential of its own sex talk. Recall the worried editor's concerns about the coming of 'soul-less sex'. Her concerns spill over into a feature article, 'Say No to soul-less Sex' published in the same issue:

> *Cosmo* has fought for over 30 years for your right to express your physical and emotional sexual desires without shame. Yet more of you are having a series of encounters that fail to meet your needs. Feminism taught us sex should be on equal terms for both partners, whether it's for one night or for life. But this sexual liberation has been reinterpreted as an imperative to get sex, whatever the emotional cost . . . This is why *Cosmo* says it's time to love yourself enough to say no.[67]

It might be time to say 'no', but where else did young women learn that sexual liberation equated to 'the imperative to get sex', if not from outlets for popular sex talk such as advice columns in magazines like *Cosmo*? After 30 years, by their own reckoning, of telling women readers to say yes and please their man, *Cosmo* now changes the tune to 'love yourself and say no'. What had prompted this change of heart was the rising incidence of casual sex and, its corollary, the well-publicised increase in sexually transmitted diseases. The English had become 'a nation of binge drinkers', unable to recall who they had sex with the night before. For all the talk about sexual freedom, the reality is not living up to the hype, as women fall into soul-less

66 Foucault, 1979, p 35, original emphasis.
67 Borno, 2003, p 65.

sex practices that cannot but fail to meet their needs. And what of the 'much-vaunted gourmet sexual experience' promoted by magazines like *Cosmo* for decades? It is proving to be elusive, leaving young women to endure 'McSex – flat, lukewarm, with a nasty aftertaste'. Not that the magazines wish to take any responsibility for propagating the hegemonic heterosexual sex talk that has produced women like 'Janine' who, 40 unsatisfying men later, is still 'on a mission' to get an orgasm. Everywhere it is the same, apparently: women are having casual sex, but 'perhaps not getting the orgasms they deserve'. Sex for these young women is 'never as good as you think it's going to be. And that's a fact'.[68]

It is precisely this 'fact' that has *Cosmo*'s agony aunts and former champions of women's sexual freedom wondering whether 'sex', as they have defined it, is 'now failing to meet our sexual needs'. If young women feel they have to have drunken casual sex each weekend, it is because sex is 'the new black' – sex sells – and sex is being 'sold hard to women'. Naturally, their own pivotal role in getting young women to 'fall for the new aggressive female sexuality', in selling them the vision of post-faking-it orgasmic bliss, is glossed over. While they would not want to advocate a return to 'the constraints of pre-sexual liberation days', they believe it is time, finally, for their readers to think for themselves and do 'what is right for you' because if 'you do it and if it feels wrong, then you do not ever have to do it again'.[69] That might be a relief for some women, but for those still keen to see one-night stands as 'a pleasure mission', it is difficult to see how advice about knowing what 'you want in bed' can assist, as so little of the new 'soul-less sex' appears to take place there. Advice about how to convince yourself that you can find sexual fulfillment in a toilet cubicle at a local bar might be more practical for the sexually 'free', active girl about town today. As for sex itself, it has become, as one journalist bemoans, 'the least sexy thing anyone can think of', swamped as it is by a cultural climate of sex talk overload where the adjective 'sexy' is applied to everything from mobile phone ring tones to sexed-up governmental policy.[70]

Radical versus Foucauldian feminisms

Some feminists believe there is a fine line between consensual sex and forced sex. Radical feminists, as we have seen, questioned whether there is any line at all. MacKinnon, for example, famously compared women's reports of sex with victims' reports of rape and with pornographic representations of sex, declaring that they 'look a lot alike'.[71] In her view, 'women's

68 Borno, 2003, pp 65–7.
69 Borno, 2003, p 68.
70 P Vernon, 'The Guide', *Guardian*, 11–17 August 2001, p 52.
71 MacKinnon, 1989, p 336.

victimisation by apparently extreme practices' is indistinguishable from 'the nonactionable experience of living every day as a woman in a sexist society'. The point, she said, is not to 'redraw the boundary between transgression and ordinary social behaviour so much as to question whether any line' can be drawn in a 'patriarchal' society.[72] Women's experience 'blurs the lines between deviance and normalcy', obliterating 'the distinction between abuses *of* women and the social definition of what a woman *is*'. From MacKinnon's radical feminist perspective, 'being *for* another is the whole of women's sexual construction'. It follows that sexuality is the basis of sex inequality. Women's personal lives are governed by the 'substantive principle', no less, of 'pervasive powerlessness to men, expressed and reconstituted daily *as* sexuality'. Heterosexuality, she insists, 'institutionalises male sexual dominance and female sexual submission, making sexuality "the lynchpin of gender inequality" '. Indeed, for MacKinnon, sexual objectification is 'the primary process of the subjection of women' or, more graphically, 'Man fucks woman; subject verb object'.[73]

It becomes absolutely crucial at this point to explain why MacKinnon's opinion that consensual is indistinguishable from coercive heterosexual sex – an opinion already aired earlier in this chapter – bears repeating here. Why give any more space to the view that heterosexuality is 'the structure of the oppression of women' when such claims have been pummeled by feminist analysts since the moment they were first uttered in the 1970s?[74] Why reprise her outmoded line that the 'more feminist view' is that sexuality is 'a social sphere of male power of which forced sex is paradigmatic'.[75] Why bother at all with MacKinnon's belligerent 'feminism unmodified' when it has been drastically modified or outright rejected within the feminist movement over the past 30 years? I do so for two very good reasons. First, despite intense feminist criticism, radical feminist claims about men's sexual domination of women are still widely misrecognised today as *the* feminist view of sex. The insistence that heterosexual sex is forced sex, that all men are potential rapists, has also led to the commonplace view that feminists are anti-sex. To take just one example, the author of a recent best-selling book about how to make sex-less long-term relationships sex-active again told an interviewer that she had expected 'the feminists' to 'come after' her for writing the book because 'desire is not politically correct'.[76] This casually expressed though well-drilled ignorance of the rich and diverse body of feminist work on sexual desire typifies the non-feminist understanding of feminism that remains pervasive today. Second, those who should know better, critical social

72 MacKinnon, 1982a, p 705.
73 MacKinnon, 1982b, p 541, original emphasis.
74 MacKinnon, 1987, p 60.
75 MacKinnon, 1983, p 646.
76 Esther Pearl quoted in the *Guardian's Observer Woman*, 10 October 2006.

thinkers who lay claim to holding counter-hegemonic perspectives on the social, frequently present radical feminist views as feminism *tout court*. Postmodern feminist theories, as we shall see, are lucky to find a place in the footnotes, even in self-defined 'critical criminology' texts. Reclaiming them from oblivion, I will discuss some of postmodern feminism's most significant contributions to the sex/violence problematic in Chapter 5. Here, however, where we need to keep the focus firmly on sex, or rather, on discourses about sex, all that is required from MacKinnon's numerous critics is enough to distinguish a radical feminist from a Foucauldian feminist framework.

We might begin by noting how quickly feminists moved to contest radical feminism's cavalier annihilation of female sexual desire. As long ago as the 1980s, Judith Vega, one of the first to take MacKinnon to task for failing to take into account 'the actual reality' of women's consent to sex, dismissed her rhetorical style of argument as 'characterised by a conjuring certainty', in which women's sexual agency miraculously disappears – 'all women are and will be victims at all times'. She also rejected MacKinnon's 'global and static image of coercion' that relied on universalising and essentialist non-social and non-historical categories of men and women, thereby fore-shadowing a host of poststructuralist feminist critiques of global feminist frameworks. But it was MacKinnon's denial of consent that really vexed Vega. Moreover, it was not only the radical feminists who got it wrong. By insisting on drawing a firm distinction between sex and rape, liberal feminists who assumed it to be 'a natural matter that women consent to sex with men' deny 'the confusion between coercion and consent that women can experience'. It followed that neither the radical nor the liberal feminist understood that consent is 'a moment of the social construction of the female subject'; consent is context-dependent, taking on many meanings ranging from pleasure to avoidance of violence, contempt, manipulation, boredom, revenge, sin and ecstasy. In Vega's view, then, women's consent to sex is not identical to coercion, as the radical feminist maintained, but it is not quite independent of it either, as the liberal feminists believed.[77]

Feminists influenced by poststructuralist theories started developing this more nuanced feminist approach to the complexities of heterosex as long ago as the 1980s. For example, in her now classic Foucauldian feminist text, *Feminism and the Power of Law*, Carol Smart identified legal feminism's problem not as men or 'male violence' as the radical feminists did, but as 'phallocentrism', a term which implies a culture 'structured to meet the needs of the masculine imperative', but which 'takes us beyond the visible, surface appearance of male dominance to invoke sexuality, desire and the subconscious psychic world'. In a phallocentric culture, men's experience of sexuality prevails inasmuch as sexuality is understood to be 'the

---

77 Vega, 1988, pp 84–6. For more on the complexities of consent, see Duncan, 1995.

pleasures of penetration and intercourse – for men'. This, Smart was at pains to point out, does not mean that sex with men was not pleasurable for women, but rather that 'the focus on phallic pleasure does not inevitably coincide with the potential of female sexuality'.[78] Addressing the 'thorny question' of whether rape is a question of violence or of sex that preoccupied white Western feminism at the time, Smart acknowledges that MacKinnon had identified an important problem for feminist analysis and strategy – taking the sex out of rape by calling it a crime of violence as the liberal feminists did, overlooked what was problematic about heterosexuality. But it did not follow for Smart that we should condone a strategy that calls rape violence on the ground that heterosexual sex is violence. In her view, the reason we need to be hesitant about calling rape violence was that it could mislead us into ignoring the much larger problem of 'phallocentric sex'. Smart was happier with Liz Kelly's notion of a 'continuum of sexual violence' that reveals that rape and heterosexual sex had 'common ingredients', but which, crucially, did not suggest they were 'the same thing'.[79] It could not be emphasised enough: they were *not* the same thing. Framing penetrative heterosex as an essentially violent relation between the sexes, conceding 'to the penis the power to push us around, destroy our integrity', could not be more anathema to radical feminism's feminist critics.[80]

Phallocentric sex then, is not forced sex. It is sex performed under conditions of what Bob Connell famously called 'hegemonic masculinity'. Borrowing directly from Gramsci, Connell defines hegemonic masculinity as 'a social ascendancy' or dominance achieved by men 'in a play of social force that extends beyond contests of brute power into the organisation of private life and cultural processes'.[81] Put simply, hegemonic masculinity is the gender order in which we live – an order in which masculinist perspectives pass as 'truth'. Borrowing from Gramsci again, we might say that phallocentric sex is hegemonic sex, performed under conditions of 'hegemonic heterosexism', a sexual status quo supported by a pervasive commonsense understanding that men's sexual demands of women are as 'natural' as women's desire to comply. Or drawing on Foucault, we might say sex is performed according to the rules of 'heteronormativity', a process of normalisation to which he 'attributes so much of modern sexuality'.[82] In this sexual order, 'normal' women 'spontaneously' consent to sex. Importantly, they do so through the discourses available to them.

---

78 Smart, 1989, pp 27–8.
79 Smart, 1989, pp 43–4. See also Teresa de Lauretis' critique of MacKinnon's 'absolutist emphasis' on the (hetero)sexual monopoly of 'male power' unmitigated by any possibility of resistance: de Lauretis, 1990, p 127.
80 Gatens, 1996, p 88.
81 Connell, 1987, p 184.
82 Berlant and Warner, 1988, pp 552–3.

Reading *Cosmo* take 2 – a Foucauldian feminist reading strategy

How, then, do different feminists read *Cosmo*? Rather than searching for proof that heterosexual sex is forced sex, Foucauldian feminists problematise discursive productions of exemplary heterosexuality in order to denaturalise technologies of the self that create our 'true' selves. For example, in a superlative study of women's experience of coercion in heterosexual relationships, Nicola Gavey identifies the dominant discourses through which women negotiate their sexual encounters with men and constitute their own sexual subjectivity. While the 'permissive sexuality' discourse provides the subject position of a 'sexually liberated' woman, the 'male needs' discourse creates the subject position of a woman who is responsive to and takes responsibility for male 'needs'. Gavey argues that these two discourses 'in conjunction' can 'render a woman almost "unrapable" '. For when a woman says in the same breath that sex is 'no big deal' to her, but means 'a hell of a lot to him', non-consent becomes 'almost inconceivable'. While she is not being coerced, the whole notion of consent becomes problematic. Just as importantly, Gavey demonstrates how subjectivity is produced through contradictory discourses. This is a complex process. As she shows, the unsatisfactory sexual experiences of her interviewees were not constituted solely by their positioning in dominant sexual discourses. There is rather a discursive struggle between the 'permissive sexuality' discourse and other discourses not yet fully articulated, including a feminist discourse about women's right to mutually enjoyable sex, expressed by one interviewee as, 'really, I would have been better off to have found the right words to say no'.[83]

Gavey's study, undertaken in the 1980s, was based on interviews with women recalling sexual experiences from the early 1970s, a time of so-called sexual revolution for women. Turning to the women's magazines published in the late twentieth and early twenty-first centuries, we find the permissive sexuality and male needs discourses not only thriving, but merging in the frequently reiterated imperative to 'please your man'. *Cosmo*'s sexually liberated woman pleases her man even if it involves compromising her own sexual desires. Recall the *Cosmo* feature article about the two sex acts men desire most, which advised women who did not like performing oral and anal sex with men to compromise. What MacKinnon might call coercive sex, *Cosmo* calls 'arousal variations'. It is all a question of compromise – hers not his. The message was clear: too many women were refusing to compromise, failing to come across with the sexual goods at the right frequency. Occasionally, there was a resistant voice. Recall the woman who

83 Gavey, 1989, pp 467–71.

described the sex acts men want more of as 'unappealing', 'sickening' or even 'threatening', and confessed that she felt like vomiting during one of men's most desired sex acts and that this was the 'consensus' amongst her women friends. This counter-discourse was short-lived, however. Within a few months she was telling *Cosmo*'s women readers to give their men a break during sex, to fake it, shudder, groan and tremble and at least show some 'team spirit'. The male needs discourse was firmly back in place.

How, though, would a Foucauldian feminist read *Cosmo*'s shift in emphasis in the 1990s, from telling women to do what men want to telling them to pursue their own sexual pleasure? Was this a great step forward or was it yet another instance of what Foucault described as 'a discourse in which sex, the revelation of truth, the overturning of global laws, the proclamation of a new day to come, and the promise of a certain felicity are linked together'?[84] For all their emphasis on sexual freedom – 'when it comes to orgasms, the truth really sets you free!' – sex advice columns urging women to meet certain performance requirements read more like the imposition of a new tyranny. Take the frequent injunctions to women to fake their way through heterosexual sex, or better still, accomplish orgasmic sex for real. What a delicate balancing act the perfect heterosexual orgasmic performance is: do not be too eager (he does not want a slut), but do not hold back either (he does not want a prude). Here, surely, is a perfect instance of Foucault's thesis that late modernity's incessant talk about sexual freedom, far from being liberating, merely embroils us further in its discursive web.

Of course, while starting from a very different premise – that women are 'systematically and structurally positioned for exploitation by men' – radical feminists like MacKinnon join Foucault in challenging conventional discourses of sexual liberation.[85] Radical and Foucauldian feminists would agree that the arrival of 'soul-less sex' signals the predictable failure of the truth-telling project that was supposed to set women free. Three decades earlier, feminists had problematised the notion of women's sexual freedom. As Susan Sontag put it in 1973:

> The question is: *what* sexuality are women to be liberated to enjoy? Merely to remove the onus placed upon the sexual expressiveness of women is a hollow victory if the sexuality they become freer to enjoy remains the old one that converts women into objects . . . This already 'freer' sexuality mostly reflects a spurious idea of freedom: the right of each person, briefly, to exploit and dehumanise someone else. Without a change in the very norms of sexuality, the liberation of women is a

84 Foucault, 1979, p 7.
85 Brown, 1995, pp 20–9.

meaningless goal. Sex as such is not liberating for women. Neither is more sex.[86]

Three decades on, sex as such does not appear to have become any more liberating for women, at least if hegemonic sex talk is anything to go by. Consider, for example, a report by a science editor, published in *The Observer* in September 2002, about tests being carried out on 'the seducer's ultimate dream', a nasal spray designed to send 'healthy, normal women' into states of high sexual arousal. While the spray would not assist the 40 per cent of women who 'suffer from "female sexual dysfunction" – they are interested in sex but cannot reach orgasm' – it still had a massive potential market. It could assist women who lack libido, 'while at the same time providing hope for a lot of unsatisfied men'. There was a down side to the new drug, however. It could only be administered as a nasal spray which 'isn't good news for seducers'. It could not be put in a drink and 'sticking it up a girl's nose is hard to do surreptitiously, after all'. And there was more bad news for men: even if a pill could be produced, it would not 'turn on a woman who was previously uninterested in a man or in having sex. She has to be halfway there already'.[87]

While a radical feminist might seize on this report as evidence that all men are potential rapists, a Foucauldian feminist sticks to the job of problematising the discursive construction of sex and desire. She might begin by querying why inability to reach orgasm is described as a 'dysfunction' when it is said to be experienced by nearly half of the 'female' population, thereby making it sound more like a norm. Next, she might also ask why it is her 'dysfunction', and not his, despite his manifest failure to bring her to orgasm. She would surely also register how quickly a device designed to enhance *her* sexual experience is transformed into one for enhancing *his*. She might note too that the plight of 'dysfunctional women' who have no use for the spray as they are already interested in sex is of absolutely no consequence to the science editor, immersed as he is in phallocentric culture. But at the same time, a Foucauldian feminist would problematise phallocentric constructions of male sexual desire, pointing out that it is not only women who get short-changed in discursive constructions of sexual desire. Men lose out too, especially when male sexuality is discursively produced in palpably reductive ways that assume an eternal naturalness to men's sexual drive. From time to time, oral and anal sex might drop a few places on lists of the 'Top ten male sex fantasies' in sexual advice columns directed at women, but the constant reiteration that men desire sex acts they never seem

86 Quoted in MacKinnon, 1982b, pp 533–4, original (Sontag's) emphasis.
87 R McKie, 'Nasal Spray for Women who are Sniffy about Sex', *Observer*, 29 September 2002.

to get enough of leaves little room for men themselves to challenge the tedious reproduction of a sexuality structured to meet the needs of a male imperative.[88]

Tragically though, women appear to have even less room to manoeuvre when it comes to expressing counter-hegemonic heterosexual desire. Consider the case of a woman who, under the cover of anonymity, wrote a book – *The Bride Stripped Bare* – revealing her distaste for several hegemonic heterosexual sex acts. Being 'outed' as the author was most distressing for her. This was one section she did not want her husband to read:

> I can't stand giving blow jobs, but I have never said that to a lover; for years I have dutifully kneeled. Many girlfriends feel the same. One describes it as a chore in the same way she describes defrosting the fridge. Yes, of course, she has never told her husband this.[89]

Puzzled about why it was 'still so hard for women, basking in the glow of so many feminist advances, to be more honest about sex', she nevertheless continued to lie about her own desires, and was mortified when exposed as the author of a book describing how she really felt. It had left her husband feeling 'raw and vulnerable'.

Such is the power of hegemonic heterosexuality, a sexual regime where his feelings still matter most despite 'feminist advances', where lying to save his pride and compromising herself remains the path of least resistance for many women. Occasionally, the 'truth' that women can find sex acts that men demand distasteful breaks through the confining boundaries of hegemonic sex talk policing women into pleasing and performing for their man, but it has yet to do so in a way that fundamentally challenges the terms of heterosexual negotiation. This is not to say that there have been no changes in the discursive constitution of women and sex. Most obviously, women are not always being fucked in today's advice columns – they are no longer perennially positioned as object in the 'gendered grammar' of popular sex talk.[90] On the contrary, women are being advised to become sexual agents who must perform certain types of acts. Today's sexually active girl about town is now constituted as a subject, a somewhat restrained and precarious load-bearing subject, compelled to be attentive to the demands of the male needs discourse and alert to the dangers of being too attentive to them, but a subject nevertheless.

---

88 Much has been written about the discursive policing of female sexual identity (e.g. Lees, 1986) and female sexual desire (see, e.g. Coward, 1987). Meanwhile, the question of how male heterosexual desire is represented in popular culture is a relatively unexplored field of research, but see Reekie, 1988.

89 N Gemmell, 'What do Women Really Want in Bed', *Guardian*, 10 July 2003.

90 Marcus, 1992, p 392.

To conclude there however, would be to miss the whole point of reading *Cleo* for this chapter. That point again, was certainly not to suggest that heterosex is not pleasurable for women. Nor was it to endorse the radical feminist view that heterosexuality and the way that it is policed is 'the root cause of women's problems in the realm of sexuality'. Bringing it all back to an underlying cause is, for Foucault and Foucauldian feminists, 'too reductive an explanation of all the operations of power around sex'.[91] After Foucault, power is no longer understood as held by one group over another. Rather, power produces truth, or rather, 'effects of truth' through discourses of sexuality. Accordingly, the focus shifts to how men and women get enmeshed in regimes of 'power-knowledge-pleasure' that create intimate relationships between power and pleasure and normalise heterosexual sexual desire in the process.[92] We can agree with the radical feminists that bringing sex into discourse does not liberate sexual desire; that for all the immense and intense verbosity on sex and orgasm, the truth about sex has not set us free. But that is not the same as saying that women are forced into heterosex. It is simply to say, with Foucault, that sex is not a domain of nature; that sex, far from being instinctual, is an activity swathed in cultural meanings, prescriptions and constraints, and that discourses on sex are operations of power that constitute our subjectivities and most intimate desires. Reading *Cleo* and *Cosmo*, one discovers that women are not simply passive clones of male desire; but they are not fully independent sexual agents either. One discovers too that consenting to heterosex in a phallocentric culture is still today a very complex business – at least it is for women.

A brief note on having *a* sex

Before moving on from sex to sexed crime, I should acknowledge, albeit with some trepidation, that 'sex' has other meanings, most obviously, sex as in having *a* sex.[93] What it means to have a sex might appear to be straightforward. Filling in the 'F' or 'M' box on bureaucratic forms, making a statement about what sex one *is*, seems simple enough. Only two answers are permissible – 'female' or 'male'. 'H' for hermaphrodite will not do, nor will 'T' for transsexual, and certainly not 'U' for uncertain or 'I' for irrelevant. But it turns out on close inspection that a sex is one of the most complicated things you could have, let alone be. Indeed, being sexed or being a sexed

91 Bell, 1993, pp 24–7.
92 Foucault, 1979, p 11; Duncan, 1995, pp 329 and 339.
93 Foucault identifies three ways in which has been defined:

> . . . as that which belongs in common to both men and women; as that which belongs *par excellence* to men, and hence as lacking in women; but at the same time as that which by itself constitutes woman's body, ordering it in terms of the function of reproduction: 1979, p 153.

being became one of the most densely theorised social phenomena of the late twentieth century.

Foucault had no time for bureaucratic forms. Nor did he have much interest in what it might mean to be sexed specifically as 'a female' as opposed to 'a male', beyond a tantalisingly brief reference to the 'hysterisation of women's bodies', a process involving the saturation of the 'feminine body' with sexuality.[94] He thus missed the chance to use the requirement to fill in the F/M box on bureaucratic forms as a prompt for querying the self-evidence of the F-or-M answer. Others have paid closer attention. Over the past 40 years, feminists and other critical analysts have asked a great many questions about the sex/gender problematic – that is, about the relationship between sex, gender and sexuality. Commencing with challenges to the received notion that sex is clearly distinguishable from gender, that we are born a sex and then socialised into gender roles, critics have demanded to know where sex stops and gender begins.[95] As Judith Butler mused:

> . . . perhaps this construct called 'sex' is as culturally constructed as gender; indeed, perhaps it was always already gender, with the consequence that the distinction between sex and gender turns out to be no distinction at all.[96]

From here Butler proceeded to develop her controversial theory that sexed being is not, as used to be assumed, a biological given. Rather, it is a consequence of a constantly reiterated performance – we learn how to perform as properly gendered men and women. And importantly, our sexed/gendered identities are performed in thoroughly sexed and sexualised bodies that are culturally saturated from birth.

For many feminist analysts, the dismantling of the sex-gender distinction and querying of what it means to be *a* sex has brought about a 'highly desirable gender trouble'. Sex had been 'subsumed into gender' for too long.[97] Far too much attention had been paid to gender, and far too little to sexed bodies, not all of which are clearly articulated to gendered identities.[98] The reduction of sexual politics to gender difference, the 'positing as primary the relations obtaining between gender and power, gender and discourse, or gender and class' had trivialised feminist struggles, proceeding 'as if women's bodies and the representation and control of women's *bodies* were not a

---

94 Foucault, 1979, p 104.
95 The debate in Australia was sparked by the publication of Moira Gatens's now classic critique of the sex/gender distinction in 1983 (since republished in Gatens, 1996, pp 3–20). See Edwards, 1989; Lloyd, 1989; Thompson, 1989.
96 Butler, 1990, p 7.
97 Murphy, 1997, pp 37–9.
98 See Smart, 1994 and Hubbard, 1996.

crucial stake in these struggles'.[99] At the same time, work needed to be done on how experiences of race and class 'transform the experience of gender' – what was needed was a feminist theory of embodied subjectivity that took account of race, class, sexuality and other forms of difference without insisting that gender and sexual difference were 'foundational in some sense, either as categories or sets of relations'.[100] Outside feminist and cultural studies courses, however, the rich body of work devoted to unpacking the sex/gender problematic has become, effectively, a buried subjugated knowledge. Here is not the place to desubjugate it. All we need take from this brief encounter with late-twentieth theories of sexed being is that as soon as you start to talk about sex, as in having a sex, you get into trouble – 'gender trouble', no less.[101]

Moreover, just about *everyone* gets into trouble. Foucault got into trouble on several counts. He has been widely criticised for suggesting that the 'rallying point for the counter attack against the deployment of sexuality' is bodies and pleasures.[102] First, he seems to assume, against the whole thrust of his thesis, that bodies and pleasures exist in a realm outside of discursively constituted regimes of truth. Second, he overlooks that fact that sexual pleasures are experienced by specifically sexed bodies. Yet elsewhere he appears to be suggesting that 'sex' can be read as 'gender' in his texts. That, at least, is how a feminist analyst has read the following passage from one of his interviews:

> How is it that sexuality has been considered that privileged place where our deepest 'truth' is read and expressed? For this is the essential fact: that since Christianity, Western civilisation has not stopped saying, 'To know who you are, know what your sexuality is about'. Sex has always been the centre where our 'truth' of the human subject has been tied up along with the development of the species.[103]

In shifting unproblematically from 'sexuality' to 'sex' as if they were synonymous and equally central to who we are, to 'our deepest "truth" ' – Foucault, so it has been argued, covertly introduces gender as 'the essence of sex/uality'. He 'only appears not to be dealing with gender'.[104] Whatever one makes of this intriguing argument, it is clear that Foucault paid little explicit

---

  99 Gatens, 1996, p 17, original emphasis.
100 Moore, 1994a, pp 83 and 90.
101 Butler, 1990.
102 Foucault, 1979, p 157. See for example Haug *et al*, 1987, p 204.
103 Foucault, 1989a, pp 137–8.
104 McCallum, 1996, pp 84–91. In her analysis of Foucault and the 'desexualisation' of rape, Bell sets out three different meanings of 'sex' – sex as anatomy, as sexuality and as gender: Bell, 1991, pp 91–3.

attention to the question of having or being a sex in his three-volume history of sexuality.

Feminists, on the other hand, have devoted a great deal of thought to this question, but they too can get into trouble when tackling the sex/gender problematic, most notably when they declare, as MacKinnon once did, that forced sex 'constitutes the social meaning of gender' – that to 'be rap*able* . . . defines what a woman *is*'.[105] There is no need to rehearse any of the host of feminist objections to this highly contentious notion that woman's essential identity is tied to unwelcome sex with men. We need only record that gender has travelled a long way since radical feminists tried to pin it down to a woman's always already unpleasant sexual encounter with a man. Sex and gender have been troubled every which way, and now find themselves trans-formed into multi-purpose adjectives as in – gendered or sexed identity, gendered or sexed violence. For now, having familiarised readers with Foucault's method of discourse analysis; with his ideas about sex, power and truth and with a Foucauldian feminist reading strategy, it is time for some light relief. So let us turn to the question of how 'sex crime' is put into discourse.

105 MacKinnon, 1983, pp 650–1, original emphasis.

Chapter 2

Sex, violence and criminology – from sex to sex killers

Shifting our attention from sex to sex killers via criminological studies of various forms of interpersonal violence, Chapter 2 investigates how criminologists and other crime 'experts' respond to the problem of men's violence against women. As examples of the failure of mainstream criminology and related disciplines to come to grips with the sheer scale of that violence abound, the discussion will be confined to examples from my undergraduate teaching materials. These texts, taken at random from journals and textbooks, are certainly as 'staggering' and inane as the ones Foucault ridiculed in 'Prison Talk'. But while we might laugh with him at their stupefying banality, there is also a much more serious side to my critique which deploys an engaging type of discourse analysis that I call spotting discursive manoeuvres. It is borrowed from Hilary Allen's brilliant analysis of the 'discursive manoeuvres' deployed in British social work and psychological reports on women charged with serious offences in the 1980s. As she shows, these discursive manoeuvres have the effect, albeit unintentionally, of erasing women's guilt and their responsibility for their violent acts and their potential dangerousness, thereby 'rendering them harmless'. Interestingly, Allen found that the kinds of discursive constructions made in reports on women offenders – for example, that they were mothers and therefore, presumed to have loving, maternal and 'harmless' personalities – were 'absent or untypical in cases involving males'.[1] While not wishing to deny the problems raised for feminism by Allen's examination of the sanitation of violent women defenders in professional reports, I intend to draw on her insights about the operation of discursive manoeuvres for a very different purpose – that of exploring the stunning erasures that occur inside and outside the criminology discipline when the problem of men's violence is addressed.

---

1 Allen, 1987, p 82. It would be interesting to compare reports prepared for court hearings of women charged with violent offences today. Women's incarceration rates have increased dramatically since Allen did her study, suggesting that women offenders are no longer rendered harmless in official discourses.

Some of the discursive strategies that enable these erasures are well-known, none more so than the victim-blaming narratives routinely invoked in criminal courts, in the media and in supposedly 'objective' criminological texts to excuse men who kill 'provocative' women.[2] But there are others, notably 'strategies of recuperation' which channel resistant voices into 'non-threatening outlets', for example, by labelling feminist speech about men's violence as 'extreme' or dismissing as hysteria women's allegations about violent men.[3] Unravelling these discursive strategies and unpacking the 'regimes of truth' about 'sex crime' that they support, should be good clean fun for readers initiated into Foucauldian discourse analysis in Chapter 1.

Disappearing acts – un-naming men's violence

Our first text is 'Violence: Criminal Psychopaths and Their Victims', an analysis of the police reports on 101 incarcerated men in Canada published in 1987. These men are divided into two groups, one comprised of 55 'psychopaths (Group P)', the other of 46 'nonpsychopaths (Group NP)' selected on the basis of a 22-item 'psychopathy checklist (PLC)'. The details of this checklist are not provided. We are told only that the PLC is a 'reliable and valid instrument' for assessing psychopathy in prison populations – so reliable that it was not necessary to interview the research subjects. Their PLC scores were determined on the basis of parole files and psychiatric, psychological and social work reports. While some of these entries were deemed to be 'subjective', there was enough 'hard data' to identify 55 Group P men and 46 Group NP men, with mean PLC scores of 32.1 and 15.4 respectively. What were the findings? Cutting a convoluted story short, the study's hypotheses that the Group P offenders – the psychopaths – 'seldom commit violent crimes coloured by intense emotional arousal' and that their victims are likely to be strangers were supported by the research. By contrast, most of the murders committed by Group NP occurred 'during a domestic dispute or during a period of extreme arousal'.[4] Moreover, whereas Group P's violence was 'callous and cold-blooded' and committed against male strangers, Group NP had 'understandable motives' for their violent acts and they knew their victims, most of whom were women. This difference is explained by the fact that Group P men, being nomadic and without long-term attachments, were 'less likely to find themselves in violent domestic disputes, most of which involved females'. These results were

2 See also Allen's (1988) equally superb analysis of law's spectacular betrayal of a sex-neutral standard in the operation of the provocation defence, a betrayal favouring male defendants.
3 Alcoff and Gray, 1993, p 268.
4 Williamson *et al*, 1987, pp 454–6.

thought to make 'theoretical sense', although a bigger sample was required to draw firmer conclusions.[5]

Many questions are left begging by the research. First, what is gained by dividing prison populations into separate groups on the basis of an unspecified psychopathy checklist? What knowledge is produced that could possibly prevent criminal violence or assist victims? How could it ever matter whether men commit violent crimes in an emotionally aroused state? Why would the victims of sexual assaults – committed by an almost equal number of Group P men and Group NP men (nine and 10 respectively) – care less whether their assailants were cold-blooded or not? Second, given that Group NP committed three times the number of murders committed by Group P (19 and six respectively), why is the research focus not on their violence and their victims, 66 per cent of whom are women (compared to 39 per cent of Group P's victims)? More particularly, on what basis is Group NP's violence – which includes 12 'family' murders – described as understandable? The reason is taken to be self-evident. After all, these men – ordinary, normal, family guys – lived with women. That could make them angry. No wonder they 'found themselves' hurting and killing them.

Finding themselves in violent situations with women and children appears to be an occupational hazard for family men. While researching the Cleveland child abuse scandal in the UK in the late 1980s, MacLeod and Saraga discovered a case study about a child rapist in a pioneering book about the use of therapy with 'abusive families'. Brian, it said:

> ... when paying hide and seek with his daughter's friend of four years of age ... *found himself* sexually abusing her, and during the act was convinced the little girl was encouraging him, unlike his wife.[6]

MacLeod and Saraga draw the obvious parallel: 'I found myself robbing a bank, and during the act was convinced that the bank teller was encouraging me'. Bank tellers do not encourage violence, but women and children do, and they are so powerful and manipulative that they leave men without the ability to stop themselves. They continue:

> There is, we are aware, quite a long history to this way of talking about male sexuality – as driven and uncontrollable. It is surely not too much to ask that people theorising about sexual violence – above all against

---

5 Williamson *et al*, 1987, pp 460–1.
6 MacLeod and Saraga, 1988, p 18, original emphasis.

children – should begin to examine their assumptions about male sexuality, and respond to the research that is available.[7]

Unfortunately, it has proven to be too much to ask. Two decades after MacLeod and Saraga despaired of conventional ways of talking about male sexuality, non-feminist commentators on sex and sex crime have still not learnt to think carefully about how they put men's violence into discourse. They still respond defensively to reports of its pervasiveness, and they still talk about it in ways that deny men agency. Not that they consciously try to conceal the reality of men's violence. It cannot be emphasised enough that there is no need to invoke a conspiracy of silence or denial on the part of non-feminist commentators hell-bent on shifting the focus from male perpetrators to their provocative or otherwise faulty victims. There is no plot afoot to airbrush men out of the history of domestic violence, leaving nothing but an agent-less 'cycle of violence' in their place. It is not a question of malicious, deliberately obfuscating intent. Analysis, as Foucault advised, should not concern itself with power 'at the level of conscious intention', but should concentrate instead on power's effects.[8] What matters is the effect of editing out men and masculinity from analyses of forms of violence in which women have been hurt by men. The effect, to be clear, is that men are 'disappeared' from narratives and explanations of men's violence.

Such extraordinary disappearing acts have become, if anything, more common and more complicated today. Consider, for example, what happened after an 'explosion' of sexual assault allegations against footballers in Australia in 2004. The women complainants found themselves not merely deprived of a voice, but as one feminist analyst put it in an astute reading of the events, 'deprived of the insignia of citizenship, and both the symbolic and corporeal materials that would enable them to testify to injury' committed by sporting heroes. Crucially, this 'dereliction' took place at the textual level, on the 'symbolic surface' of the events.[9] The women were 'literally deprived of a grammatical position from which to speak or act'. Sports commentators and other apologists for the footballers figured the women – and not the men – as sexual predators. With the women elided in the commentaries so as to become 'unmarked' actors, the footballers were discursively constituted as the victims of the women's sexual aggression, an aggression that was then discursively erased so that the women complainants no longer occupied 'an actual subject position'. Grammatically speaking, the women were 'structurally absent from the event they are nonetheless

---

7 MacLeod and Saraga, 1988, p 18. A recent Australian research report found that 44 per cent of men believe that rape results from men not being able to control their need for sex: www.aic.gov.au/publications/tandi2/tandi344.pdf.
8 Foucault, 1980c, p 97.
9 Philadelphoff-Puren, 2004, p 37.

responsible for', and once again, we find men 'putting themselves' in compromising positions. Spokesmen for the footballers bemoaned how 'players can put themselves in this position'; one was fined for having 'put himself in a position of risk', and one club chairman announced that his club was 'not going to be put into a compromising situation where such a thing could happen again'.[10] In this grammatical construction, men are positioned as 'potential recipients of women's negative actions', and not as violent agents, and nothing is said about the women themselves or the question of sexual assault. On the one hand, the women are discursively rendered incapable of 'credible speech about sexual violence' when the perpetrator is a sportsman. On the other hand, he benefits from tactful 'not seeing' on the part of the audience of spectator-fans who 'readily accept the excuses offered' for his 'slip'. This recalls Erving Goffman's observation some 30 years ago about the role played by the audience in the self-presentation of team identity – at moments of crisis for the performers, 'the whole audience may come into tacit collusion with them in order to help out'.[11] Tacit collusion, as we continue to see, is a formidable barrier to dealing fairly and openly with women's sexual assault allegations against men.

Returning to criminological texts, nothing surpasses a study of the 'intersexual nature of violent crimes' in the United States when it comes to showcasing the ethical bankruptcy of the discipline's handling of the issue of men's violence against women. The avowed aim of this study is to 'determine the extent to which violent crimes occur within or between the sexes'. Two hypotheses are tested. The first is that 'men commit violent crimes against other men more often than (statistically) expected'. That is, male offending is hypothesised to be an 'in-group phenomenon'. The second hypothesis is that 'F-M' violence (women's violent acts against men) occurs relatively more often than 'M-F incidents' (men's violent acts against women). That is, women's violence is hypothesised to be 'less of an in-group phenomenon than male offending'. In plain English, it is hypothesised that women are more violent towards men than they are towards women, and men are more violent towards other men than they are towards women. It is a very convoluted path the researcher follows. Most notably, he has to put to one side – or 'control' for – what he acknowledges is 'the greater propensity of men to commit violent crime'.[12] Using his preferred baseline 'Model 2' – which assumes that there is 'no propensity for men or women to be the *victims* of criminal homicide', and which sets 'the proportions of men and women in the *offender* category' equal to the proportion of male and female offenders (if this makes any sense) – he finds support for his

10 Philadelphoff-Puren, 2004, pp 41–2.
11 Cited in Philadelphoff-Puren, 2004, pp 48–9.
12 O'Brien, 1988, p 154.

hypotheses.[13] To do so, he has to ignore his statistical tables indicating that men committed 85.49 per cent of the 11,410 homicides in his sample, and 88.85 per cent of the 5,119 aggravated assaults. Given this startling statistical asymmetry, it is not surprising that he feels the need to control for men's greater propensity to commit violence:

> Model 2 shows that men murder men, and women murder men more often than expected; and men murder women, and women murder women less frequently than expected. These findings support hypotheses 1 and 2: M-M violent incidents occur more often than expected, and F-M violent incidents occur relatively more often than M-F violent incidents (*once the greater propensity of males to assault has been controlled*).[14]

With that propensity controlled, the researcher is more able to come to the 'interesting' conclusion that 'females' – (positivistic code for women) – use violence in simple assaults against men 'less often than expected', but for aggravated assaults they resort to violence against men 'more often than expected' – that is, of course, if you control for men's greater propensity to commit violence. So for women, 'intersexual violence is associated with more serious forms of violence, but for men, intersexual violence is associated with less serious forms of violence'. Why is this so? Men, he speculates, 'threaten women into compliance with minor assaults', and as long as women 'comply', men 'may not *need* to escalate violence'.[15] Women, on the other hand, because of their physical size, will not be able to threaten men with 'minor' violence and so may be forced to end the 'cycle of violence' by resorting to serious violence. The researcher's agenda soon becomes clear, a lone footnote giving the game away. He is responding to feminist research on battered women who kill their husbands. But far from being concerned with exposing, let alone condemning, the violence endured by women forced to kill in self-defence, his aim is to confirm his hypotheses that serious violence is mostly an 'out-group phenomenon' for women and mostly 'in-group' for men. That men use 'minor threats to gain compliance from women' is as unproblematic for this researcher as the notion that there are 'routine activities of males and females' that structure the rates of intersexual violence in Western societies. After all, men spend more time away from home, interacting with same-sex rather than opposite-sex individuals, while 'women spend more time at home, where there is less segregation on the basis of sex, and where a large proportion of violent incidents occur'.[16]

13 O'Brien, 1988, p 156, original emphasis.
14 O'Brien, 1988, p 160, emphasis added.
15 O'Brien, 1988, p 166, emphasis added.
16 O'Brien, 1988, pp 165–7.

Thus does this criminologist un-name the pervasive social problem of men's violence against women which was put onto the political and criminological agenda by feminist activists and researchers over the last three decades of the twentieth century. Following the standard non-feminist script, he begins by transforming the lived experience of women who are battered and killed by male partners into aggregate data. Next, he translates the data into a location, say a 'home', a place where violent 'incidents' occur. Finally, he blames women for the violence that takes place there. Women who do not 'comply' with and 'submit' to men's demands spark off that perennial favourites with positivists – a 'cycle of violence' – and end up receiving 'minor' violence. Women might then end the cycle by resorting to 'serious' violence. Whether or not they do, men's responsibility for their own violence against women disappears down a deep tunnel of aggregate data, base models and reality-defying verbal gymnastics.[17]

Paradoxically, this study of 'intersexual' violence ends up de-sexing and de-gendering the very intersexual violence it set out to explore. De-sexing sexed violence is an occupational hazard for criminologists who never stray across disciplinary boundaries to the 'new' theorisations of sexed subjectivities and sexed violence developed by feminist scholars in a range of disciplines.[18] Variations of the discursive strategies discussed above still saturate turn-of-the-century criminology journals and textbooks. In standard textbooks, 'Masculinities' but not 'Men' may occasionally show up in the index, but they do not make an appearance in the chapter on violent crime. Expect men's violence against women and children to be re-classified as 'spouse or partner abuse', a safely un-gendered sub-category of similarly un-gendered 'violent offences'. Unsurprisingly, spouse or partner abuse can take up less than two pages and men do not even need to be mentioned when criminologists resort to 'controlled studies' revealing that a majority of non-gendered 'abusers' have 'experienced violence in childhood or witnessed violence between their parents'.[19] This is what passes as 'truth' or objective analysis in mainstream criminology. Putting men's violence into discourse in this way, deleting the agents who are the bearers of masculinity and rendering spouses and partners genderless, remains *de rigueur* for non-feminist criminologists tackling the vexed problem of men's violence against women and children.

17 O'Brien, 1988, pp 166–7.
18 This is so even when criminologists are asked to research violence at the national level, as they were in Australia in the late 1980s. The country's first National Committee on Violence was given a brief to examine 'the contemporary state of violent crime in Australia', including 'related social, economic, psychological and environmental aspect' and 'gender issues in violence': National Committee on Violence, 1990, p xxi. See the discussion of its findings in Howe, 2004a.
19 Jones, 1998, p 377.

Diversions – women (and feminists) are worse

Feminist scholars have been alert to the diversionary effects of non-feminist approaches to the question of men's violence for some time. Consider, for example, what Mary McIntosh had to say about the formulation of the question of child sexual abuse in the public domain in Britain in the 1980s:

> Perhaps its most remarkable feature is the absence of the perpetrator as a recognizable character in the drama. There are 'parents', ungendered and acting in couples, readily endowed with all the rosy lineaments of the myth of modern classless parenthood, and there are 'children', also often ungendered, and of indeterminate age.[20]

For MacLeod and Saraga, the failure to discuss the gender of the perpetrators of child abuse 'amounts to a deceit'. They provide by way of example the frequently recycled 'theory' of 'a cycle of abuse' that is transmitted from one generation to the next in which the abusers are parents rather than adult men, and the problem located in a 'deviant' or troubled family.[21] As we have seen, the notion of a 'cycle of abuse', or 'cycle of violence', is also used to describe the man's experience in an abusive relationship. His anger builds up until he explodes violently. Then he is remorseful and a quiet phase ensues until the 'cycle' starts again. In both versions of 'the cycle', the abuser is a victim of forces beyond his control and he usually ends up disappearing altogether behind a cloud of obfuscation. In some criminological quarters however, abusive, violent men have re-emerged, re-packaged as victims, not simply of the genderless cycles of violence ruling their lives, but of women's violence.

The women-are-more-violent-than-men school of thought is predominantly a North American development. However, its foundation texts – Straus and Gelles' family conflict studies suggesting that women's assaults on their husbands constitute a social problem comparable in nature and magnitude to that of men's assaults on their women partners – have been cited favourably elsewhere, notably by a small but vocal group of researchers in the UK.[22] In one such study, emphasis is placed on the 'causal influences that are common to both men and women' in order to provide a 'meta-analysis of partner violence'.[23] Here a distinction is made between aggressive actions and the consequences of such aggression in order to equalise

---

20 McIntosh, 1988, p 6.
21 MacLeod and Saraga, 1988, p 18.
22 Straus and Gelles, 1986. Women-are-more-violent-than-men research has been reported in the Australian, British and American press. See, e.g. S Goodchild, 'Women Are More Violent, Says Study', *The Independent*, 12 November 2000.
23 Archer, 2000a, p 651.

the number of aggressive acts committed by men and women against each other. Laughing derisively at such a tactic might seem like good sport, but for the fact that it is women's violence against men that is one of the new hot items on the criminological agenda in Britain today.[24] Postgraduate programmes in some leading universities are encouraging doctoral students to write dissertations 'proving' that the feminists were wrong to focus on men's violence because women are as violent, if not more violent than men. In the near future, expect to see the publication of British dissertations taking a similar tack to a North American study of 'gay and bisexual male domestic violence victimisation' presented as a 'challenge to contemporary feminist domestic violence theory'. The study suggests that feminist work on domestic violence – with its 'doctrine of male victimisers and female victims' – has 'contributed to the invisibility of gay and lesbian domestic violence because it precludes the possibility of such violence occurring'.[25] Amongst other problems – well-documented elsewhere – with the women-are-more-violent-than-men thesis mounted on behalf of the 'invisible legion of assaulted husbands',[26] this kind of transparently anti-feminist analysis makes for bad history. Its advocates would do well to brush up on genealogies of the discovery and rediscovery, by first and second-wave feminist activists in the United States, Britain and Australia, of widespread domestic and sexual violence committed by men in the private realm.[27] Blaming feminism for obscuring violence within queer relationships is like blaming feminist campaigns against men's sexual assaults of girls for obscuring men's sexual assaults of boys. Let the historical record stand: since the late nineteenth century, it has been feminist campaigners and their allies who have exposed high levels of men's violence in the home against women and against children of both sexes. By bringing those issues into the public arena in the face of immense obstacles, notably male-dominated legislatures and the legal profession, feminist activists and researchers have given a voice and a discourse – 'survivor discourse' – to *all* victims of sexed violence.[28]

Nothing however, stops non-feminist positivists from pursuing the women-are-more-violent-than-men line of research – not national surveys of violence that show that the problem is in the reverse order, and not the medical records of pregnant women or the accounts of so many survivors, men as well as women, testifying to the massive and incalculable physical and psychic harm inflicted by violent men on women and children. At the turn of the new millennium, after three decades of Derridean deconstructions of dualistic modes of thought, family violence researchers still parade a

24 Archer, 2000b, pp 697–8.
25 Letellier, 1994, p 95.
26 Dobash *et al*, 1992, p 74.
27 See Chapter 6.
28 Smart, 1999; Alcoff and Gray, 1993.

spectacularly mind-numbing array of naive binary oppositions – science/ politics; empirically-based or evidence-based analysis/'politically-motivated analysis' – and there are no prizes for guessing on which side of these great divides feminist research falls.[29] The recent British amplification of the 'family conflict' strain of thought is also remarkable for its well-drilled ignorance of theoretical developments in feminism over the last 30 years. How, in particular, could it be maintained, again in 2000, that there are 'two conflicting viewpoints about partner violence' – the 'family conflict' view and '*the* feminist view' – and that the latter 'regards partner violence as a consequence of patriarchy'?[30] Anyone reading the feminist literature would have discovered a great diversity of feminist opinion on men's violence. They would find too that feminist invocations of 'patriarchy' to explain anything are hard to find outside of radical feminist texts post-1980, and scarcer than hen's teeth in postmodern-inflected texts where the emphasis has shifted to the discursive constructions of truth under conditions of hegemonic masculinity. Researchers informed about the minority and Third World feminist critiques of universalising and essentialising white feminisms that we shall discuss in Chapter 5, would never have suggested that in modern secular liberal Western nations where women are 'emancipated', there will be 'a greater impact of the norm of disapproval of men's physical aggression toward women and a lesser impact of patriarchal values'.[31] They would have known that such a racialised construction of an emancipated west and a patriarchal 'non-west' has been massively critiqued in the postcolonial literature. Also, for the record, women and children subjected to men's violence in Western societies on a daily basis have yet to register any 'norm of disapproval' or the supposed decline of 'patriarchal values' – they are too busy surviving men's physical assaults, sexual assaults and homicidal fury.

Next up for consideration is a chapter on violent crime in a criminology handbook. It does not take long for 'violent crime' to meet some definitional hitches. Pondering whether he should include rape and indecent assault as violent crime when criminal statistics classify them as 'sexual' crimes, the author – who has strayed far outside his own criminological field – decides to focus on what he refers to as 'the risks of non-domestic "sexual" and "non-sexual" (in form) violence', whatever that is.[32] Why make these distinctions? Why refer to 'non-domestic' violence? Why declare that the existing data from the British Crime Survey suggests that '*in England and Wales as a whole, actual* violence in the home is *not* a common experience for a

29 Archer, 2000b, p 697.
30 Archer, 2000a, p 651, emphasis added.
31 Archer, 2000a, p 668.
32 Levi, 1997, p 843.

large *proportion* of women'?[33] And why place almost the entire sentence in italics? While the twin spectres of 'female on male violence' and 'feminists' rear their heads suspiciously throughout the chapter, it is only towards the end that the agenda becomes clear: the feminist focus on risks and fear of crime has led criminologists astray. Not only has the discipline lost sight of the causes of violence; worse, the feminist-forced etiological focus on masculinities has led to an over-emphasis on men, thereby failing to account for 'the non-violence of all males most of the time', and 'the non-violence of the majority of adult working-class and middle-class males all of the time'.[34] What is most striking about these discursive twists and turns is that the problem is no longer men's violence, or even violent crime. It is feminist research exposing the prevalence of men's violence. The whole point of the study finally becomes clear: without avid anti-feminist gatekeepers, feminists might derail the criminological enterprise altogether with their irritating practice of naming men as the perpetrators of most forms of violence, and making 'non-violent' working-class and middle-class men feel bad in the process.

While some non-feminist apologists for men's violence are keen to protect men's reputations from feminist attack, others are too busy sympathising with violent men to notice. Few could be as besotted with his interviewees as Elliot Leyton who, when he embarked on 'his journey into the souls of modern multiple murderers' in the United States, could not understand the 'profound personal fulfilment they seemed to derive from their killings'. After four years of total immersion in their diaries, confessions and interviews, he emerged with a clearer picture: 'I see their motives as so obvious and their gratifications as so intense that I can only marvel at how *few* of them walk the streets of America'. Evidently, Leyton had come to understand only too well the fulfilment that comes from serial homicide. These men were not 'freaks'; they were simply the 'logical extension' of dominant cultural themes, notably 'manly avenging violence'.[35] Another researcher, a counselling psychologist who worked on defence and appeal teams for multiple killers in the United States, found that university staff involved in devising creative therapy programmes for the prevention of violence became fascinated by his death row stories. Not only could they talk for hours about multiple homicide – they had, he said, an *'almost intuitive understanding* of this unique prison population'.[36] Such is the seductive appeal of criminal violence that, as we shall see in Chapter 4, even self-defined 'critical' criminologists can get caught up in the excitement of tales of men's lethal assaults

---

33 Levi, 1997, p 852, original emphasis.
34 Levi, 1997, pp 880–1.
35 Leyton, 2003, p 12, original emphasis.
36 Norris, 1988, p 2, emphasis added.

on women, abandoning critical insight for a defensive emotional attachment, even to convicted rapists. For now, let us turn to a burgeoning criminological industry: the production of texts on so-called serial killers or sex killers.

Murderous texts – lusting to kill in the age of sex crime

The arrival of the serial sex killer or lust murderer has proved to be a very exciting event for sections of the criminological fraternity in the last third of the twentieth century, providing a new lease on life for criminology's compulsion to search for the forces bearing down on the killer, causing his lust to kill. He – for these killers are almost exclusively male – has spawned a huge criminological industry. The following section examines some representative but once again randomly selected texts from the subgenre of what might be called murderous texts about these 'new' criminal types. What knowledge do they provide about the homicidal violence known today as 'serial sex killing'? How do these texts discursively constitute lust killers? What assumptions are made about what counts as criminological knowledge about a form of killing which involves the mutilation and often sexual violation of women, young men or children? Serial sex killing might be one of the least prevalent forms of interpersonal violence, but it is a useful case study for contrasting two radically different methodological approaches to the question of the intersection of sex and violence. On the one hand, positivistic criminology, still posturing as the science of crime, hauls out its gargantuan 'scientific' data-collecting apparatus, replete with classification systems, measuring devices, psychological expertise and criminal profiling in order to get 'inside the criminal mind' and find the 'truth' about sex killers.[37] On the other, Foucauldian discourse analysis dissects criminological 'scientific truths', paying particular attention to how experts discursively constitute 'sex killers'.

Criminologists and psychologists usually begin with definitional and classificatory issues, taking pains to distinguish serial or episodic killers who kill over a period of time, perhaps months or even years, from mass killers who murder their victims in a single episode. Matters get more complex when the label 'serial killer' is used interchangeably with that of 'sex killer' or 'lust killer', inasmuch as a 'sexual element' is thought to be present for most serial killers. Consider, for example, Joel Norris's description in *Serial*

---

37 The positivist's measuring fetish surely reaches its nadir in research using a penile plethysmography to monitor erectile responses of convicted rapists and university student 'non-rapists' to audiotapes of verbal descriptions of consensual sex and rape: Barbaree *et al*, 1989.

Killers: The Growing Menace, published in 1988, of a 'newly identified class of criminals called serial murderers' as 'motiveless killers, recreational killers, spree killers or lust murderers'.[38] Claiming there has been an alarming increase in the number of these killers since 1961, Norris provides a celebratory list of some of the most active serial killers in the United States – a kind of Who's Who of American Serial Killers for the period 1961–84. The most striking things about the list are that over 95 per cent of the known killers in the list are men, and most fit into the sexual murder category which, for Norris, includes any who killed to satisfy their lust. Serial killers, he informs us, are 'different in kind from any type of criminal', different even from mass murderers. The serial killer is 'an entirely different criminal', so different that he is not even a man – he is 'simply a biological engine driven by a primal instinct to satisfy a compelling lust', a 'single-celled creature reacting to an overpowering chemical stimulus'.[39]

To take another example, in *Serial Homicide*, Holmes and De Burger emphasis 'the need for classification', arguing that classification of 'pertinent data' is a 'fundamental' step in developing 'adequate knowledge' about serial murder or 'profiling' that can be 'utilised in dealing with this threat to society'. To this end, they develop a 'four-category typology of serial murders that reflects dominant motives in their homicidal behaviour' to help correct misconceptions – for example, that the serial killer is 'a raging psychotic' or that 'every serial killing is a lust murder', although many are, apparently. As for lust killers, those motivated by 'a quest for sexual gratification', they can be differentiated into 'disorganised asocial' and 'organised nonsocial' types.[40] With the typographies in place, what do criminologists have to say about the sex of sex killing? The sexed nature of sex killings might seem to be self-evident inasmuch as it is commonly taken to mean rape followed by murder. Even if we start with the broader phenomenon of 'sex crime', it seems that what counts as sex crime is usually taken as given in criminology texts. It means rape, and usually more specifically the rape of women and children. In Soothill and Walby's *Sex Crime in the News*, for example, 'sex crime' is used interchangeably with 'rape' or 'sexual violence'.[41] But a closer reading of expert accounts and media reports of 'sex crime' shows that the sexual nature of sex crime, and especially of sex killing, is far from obvious. According to a 'leading' forensic psychologist, an Australian backpacker murderer was a typical serial killer, one motivated by 'a confused view of sex and power':

38 Norris, 1988, p 12.
39 Norris, 1988, pp 17 and 23.
40 Holmes and De Burger, 1988, pp 47 and 97–100.
41 Soothill and Walby, 1991. See Howe, 1998, pp 1–2.

Getting power from his victims and perhaps making them plead for their lives or torturing them first made him feel better about himself. It's probably the commonest basis for serial killings – the involvement of sexuality and power.[42]

Leaving aside the fact that this killer did not sexually assault all his victims – three of whom were men – notice how the expert assumes that overpowering and torturing people has something to do with sexuality. Moreover, if pronouncing that serial killers are 'sexually motivated' and that the 'ultimate thrill is killing the victim' has zero explanatory value, declaring that in the final analysis they are all 'evil' puts the final full stop to any further inquiry. Media and police reports also trip up over 'sex crime'. Reporting the murder of a young woman, an Australian newspaper suggested it was a 'sex attack', despite the fact that the police had no evidence that she had been raped. It appears to have been sufficient for the murder to qualify as a 'sex attack' for the victim's body to have been 'only partly clothed'.[43]

Occasionally, criminologists register a problem with their accounts of 'sex attacks'. In *Sexual Crimes and Confrontations*, eminent British criminologist DJ West had trouble pinpointing what exactly was sexual about 'sexual homicide'. While he was not surprised to learn that 'murders of women are more often sexually-motivated than murders of men' – in one study of 306 murders of women over 16, 14 per cent were 'thought to be sexually-motivated' – ascertaining 'what sorts of incident to regard as sexual murders' was 'surprisingly problematic'. Homicide in the furtherance of a sexual assault was 'the main criterion' for West, but he would also include cases where the victim is killed to escape detection 'rather than to satisfy a lust already appeased'. He also wanted to include killings by jealous or spurned lovers because although 'sexual activity does not take place at the time' of these homicides, 'the emotions generated by frustrated lust may be the root cause'. Including so-called *crimes passionels*, which he claims are 'less exclusively male offences than are murders directly linked to sexual arousal', enables him to single out Ruth Ellis, the last woman hanged in England, rather than name one of the thousands of men who have killed their wives in a jealous rage over the centuries. As for serial homicide, the murder of 'a succession of women strangers, even without prior sexual assault' was, in his view, 'usually so closely connected with abnormal sexual preoccupations on the part of the male offender' that it warranted inclusion as a sex crime. Rape murders committed by 'lone offenders of markedly deviant sociopathic disposition' also certainly fitted the bill. In the final analysis, West's

---

42 Quoted in B Walsh, 'What Drives a Man to Kill Again and Again – Sex and Power', *Herald Sun*, 26 May 1999.
43 See Howe, 1998, pp 41–2.

argument, such as it is, boils down to a simple assertion that a man who shoots dead eight young women over a year 'without warning and without prior sexual molestation', can claim the mantle of serial killer *and* of sex killer because he clearly shot them 'with an underlying sexual motive'. The observation that most of the victims were killed 'when they were with their boyfriends inside parked cars at night' stands in for an explanation, leaving unexplained why seeing people in parked cars at night could provide a 'sexual' or any other motive for homicide.[44]

If West was puzzled, at least initially, about what made sexual homicide sexual, other experts have no difficulty at all with recognising which incidents to include as sexual murder. Consider the following statement from *Sexual Homicide*, a study undertaken by Federal Bureau of Investigation (FBI) researchers working at the national centre for the analysis of violent crime in the United States who claim to have coined the word 'serial killer' in the mid-1970s:

> It is theorised by the FBI that placing foreign objects into dead victims may be a form of regressive necrophilia. This act therefore is a substitute for actual sexual intercourse.[45]

While some might struggle to grasp how placing an object in a butchered dead body is equivalent to having sex, the FBI investigators see it clearly as a sexual act, even when the killer leaves no 'conventional evidence of a sexual crime' – presumably semen – for the homicide investigators. Serial homicide may appear to be 'motiveless and random', but it takes place 'in a context of power, sexuality and brutality'.[46] How then do criminologists account for this 'new' form of killing? How, in short, do they put sex killers into discourse?

Serial sex killers as their mothers' sons

Let us start with the FBI study, *Sexual Homicide*. Deploying criminal profiling to build a composite picture of the kind of person most likely to become a sex killer, the investigators interviewed 36 convicted, incarcerated 'sexual murderers' who killed a total of 118 victims, 'primarily women'. The interviews give them insights into the 'formative events' in the killer's life. Moving swiftly past the opening line – 'All male and almost all white, they were usually eldest sons' – they pass over, in just one quick sentence, two key factors in the making of the serial sex killer, namely his maleness and his

44 West, 1987, pp 179–83.
45 Ressler *et al*, 1988, p 51.
46 Ressler *et al*, 1988, pp 1–3.

whiteness.[47] More recently, non-feminist criminologists have started to add 'female' serial killers to the very long lists of male serial killers, but leaving aside, for now, such pockets of criminological resistance to the overwhelming statistical evidence that serial killers are usually white men, let us linger a bit longer with *Sexual Homicide* which arrives very quickly at the 'root cause' of sexual homicide. It is 'family dysfunction'. Almost immediately, we learn that 'inadequate' mothers are responsible for 'family dysfunction'. Indeed, 'family dysfunction' is code for faulty motherhood.

The testimony of the killers interviewed bears this out. Some had observed 'indiscriminate sexual behaviour by the mother'. One had seen his mother going out with other men; another was upset when his mother left his father, who had served time in an institution for the criminally insane, for a new man; still another believed that 'the break-up of the family' was part of his downfall – 'I had no male supervision'. Somehow, the absence of the father is the mother's fault, and so is the son's subsequent sexual violence. As one killer explained:

> I believe what caused the rapes on the street was when I was a kid I never had a dad around. He was gone. My stepdad and me never got along. My half brothers and sisters could do things that I'd get whipped for because he said my mother was setting a bad example for me. That made me hate him. If those women weren't by themselves, that would stop a lot of rapes and murders.

Tracing the source of his homicidal violence towards women back to his mother's choice of partner might seem strange, but this is what passes as 'scientific' explanation in positivistic criminology. Wallow around long enough in an offender's background and an expert will find a woman, invariably his mother, to blame for her son's subsequence violence. Mums emerge in criminological accounts as the principal or root cause of the serial killer's killings. The mother is the formative event in the early life of the serial killer; she is the key to enabling criminologists to erase men's responsibility for their own violence. Moreover, maternal culpability is not restricted to biological mothers, and nor is mother-blaming restricted to criminologists. Their 'virulent conceptions of motherhood' pass over effortlessly into the media and popular culture.[48]

Consider, for example, the case of the man dubbed the 'Granny Killer' for murdering six elderly women in Sydney, Australia in the 1990s. According

47 Ressler *et al*, 1988, p 15.
48 For an account of the 'virulent conceptions of motherhood' pervasive in North American culture in the mid-twentieth century that found their way into the Warren Report on Lee Harvey Oswald, see Simon, 1998, pp 94–105.

to newspaper reports, this 'polite, quiet father of two' could 'yet be shown to be Australia's worst serial killer'. Psychiatric evidence given at his 1991 trial revealed that he hated his mother because she was a 'driven woman' and had 'fast and loose morals', and when she developed the breast cancer which had killed her, it was 'almost as if she was reaching out from the grave and striking him once again'. So naturally his fatal attacks had 'strong elements of rage against a "look-alike mother" and sexual gratification'. He also had 'hostile feelings' towards his mother-in-law, whom he found 'domineering', and nursing home staff, it was reported, shared his perception of her as a 'tyrant'.[49] A photo of her as a young woman appeared in one newspaper report as if it had some kind of explanatory force. To take another Australian example of the penchant for blaming mother figures for their sons' violent crimes, a psychiatrist testifying at the 1993 Melbourne trial of a man charged with serial rape said the offender had a 'deep-seated hatred for his mother' because she failed to protect him from sexual and physical abuse by his father.[50]

Such mothers, it seems, can cause men to grow up to be rapists or serial killers. Criminological accounts frequently feature serial killers with a taken-for-granted 'revenge against women':

> Jerry's relationship with his mother was neither warm nor accepting. In fact, it could be accurately stated that Mrs Brudos was rejecting. For example, Jerry was forced by his mother to move out of the home into a backyard shed when his brother came home from college.[51]

No wonder he was driven to sexual violence against women. Describing a man who killed eight women as having 'acted under pressure of sexual frustration and pent-up rage against women', another criminologist moves straight to this explanation of his homicidal fury:

> His relations with mother figures, which so often set the tone for a man's subsequent attitudes to women, had been fraught. He was adopted and reared as an only child. He was jealous of his parents' closeness to each other and notably cool towards his father . . . He was deeply attached to his indulgent mother, but she could never do enough to satisfy his craving for attention.[52]

As mothers go, this one would surely have been a candidate for the 'good

49 M Whittaker, 'The Cunning Killer Never to be Released', *Australian*, 30 December 1991.
50 H Kennedy, 'Hunt for Armidale Rapist', *Sunday Herald-Sun*, 14 March 1993.
51 Holmes and De Burger, 1988, pp 108–10.
52 West, 1987, pp 184–5.

enough' category in most spheres of inquiry, but like so many others, she could not escape censure by her homicidal son and, by extension, the criminologists accounting for his crimes.[53]

Other predisposing factors

While the FBI investigators dwell for some time in *Sexual Homicide* on what their interviewees had to say about their dreadful mothers, they have very little to say about their frequent disclosures of sexual abuse. Child sexual abuse is identified as the first factor contributing to 'the formative events component' of their 'motivational model'.[54] But we are not told who abused the interviewees, only that most reported a poor relationship with their fathers and that killers with histories of sexual abuse were more likely to report a 'reconstituted family structure'. The investigators do not question why the relationship failed; whether, as is so often the case, the mother left because of her male partner's violence. The problem for the killer beset with 'formative events' is simply the failure of his parents' marriage which, naturally, sets off the causal chain leading to serial killing:

> One begins to see how an early fantasy pattern used to cope with childhood abuse and unsatisfactory family life might turn a child away from reality and into a private world of violence where the child can exercise control.[55]

Having replicated the standard criminological moves of tracing the 'root causes' of violence back to the mother in order to blame her for the son's subsequent violence, and then obfuscating the killers' reports of sexual victimisation by men in their families, the researchers promptly disavow the background factor approach:

> Whereas psychological motives for violent behaviour are usually conceptualised . . . as having roots beginning with trauma, insult, and/or overstimulation in early childhood, our thesis is different. We theorise that these men are motivated to murder by way of their thinking.[56]

But just how different is their thesis? What differentiates taking account of the role played by thought and fantasy in the formation of the sex killer and

53 For an enthralling account of the 'remarkably persistent line of thought' in Western cultures that 'monstrous progeny resulted from the disorder of the maternal imagination', see Huet, 1993, p 1.

54 Ressler, *et al*, 1988, p 71.

55 Ressler, *et al*, 1988, pp 24–8.

56 Ressler, *et al*, 1988, p 34.

noting that his thinking pattern emerged from his early life experiences from a psychological explanation grounded in background factors? Hypothesising that fantasy drives sadistic actions and supplies the motivation for sexual murder does not take us very far. After all, not all children who have troubled childhoods have violent fantasies, and those who do rarely act on them, let alone grow up to be sex killers. Still, the idea that 'these men murder because of the way they think' is one that might have opened up a fertile line of inquiry into the dominant cultural scripts that make facile links between violent fantasies in troubled heads and the acting out of those fantasies in homicidal rage.[57]

The FBI researchers do not make these connections. Instead, they turn their attention to the 'pre-crime stress or precipitating factors' leading to sexual homicide. The first is 'conflict with females', said to have set the stage for murder in over half the murder cases considered in Sexual Homicide. Another key precipitating factor was 'marital problems'. Learning that his wife was having an affair intensified one killer's fantasies of rape and murder. Cutting short a long story about crime scenes and profiling characteristics of 'organised and disorganised murders', let us jump straight to the FBI investigators' conclusion. They end up endorsing a 'psychosocial framework' which they say should be expanded to include 'measurable behavioural indicators from analysis of crime, such as presence or absence of a weapon, or injury to a victim'. They also call for further research into 'biochemical hormonal sensory levels' of people to determine whether there is 'a basis of hormonal release addicting the person to violent fantasy and violent acts'. Thus, despite all the hype about providing a different kind of analysis, Sexual Homicide ends up endorsing the idea of a biological basis to violent fantasy and sex killing, and reinforcing the case for biological and 'psychosocial' explanations of this homicidal type.[58]

A book that attempts to meet the challenge of demonstrating the biological basis of sex killing is one we have already encountered – Joel Norris's Serial Killers: The Growing Menace. Norris, a counselling psychologist who has advised defence teams acting for serial killers in the United States, argues that serial murder is a form of disease which has engulfed American society, 'the most progressive society ever known to mankind'.[59] This disease can be detected by 'key behavioural patterns' that include evidence of genetic defect, brain damage, severe chemical imbalances brought about by chronic malnutrition and substance abuse, and 'an absence of a sense of self which is the result of consistently negative parenting or non-parenting'. Norris's hypothesis, informed by scientific studies on the causes of violence, is that

57 Ressler, et al, 1988, p 43.
58 Ressler, et al, 1988, pp 47 and 214–16.
59 In the 20-year period from 1968 to 1988, the United States produced 120, or 75 per cent, of the 160 convicted serial killers in the world: Norris, 1988, p 19.

'episodic aggression, which involves child and family abuse, rape and serial murder, is inherently a disease and therefore treatable and preventable'.[60]

Basing his finding on a study of 260 serial killers, Norris provides a spectrum of biologically-based causes of the disease. His episodic killer is shaped by the old standbys – agent-deleting discursive manoeuvres such as 'patterns of child abuse' and 'pathologically negative parenting' – as well as brain injuries, inherited neurological disorders, chronic malnutrition, drug use and toxic poisoning caused by pollution. Norris's main findings are presented in his chapter on 'The New Criminologists', a 'new category of neuropsychiatric specialists' who 'go much further' than previous experts in linking organic, psychiatric and social symptoms in order to predict dangerousness with a 90 per cent accuracy rate. Not to be confused with the New or Critical Criminologists who tried to break with positivistic criminology's over-determined criminal type in the 1960s and 1970s, Norris' 'New Criminologists' are most definitely old-style correctionalist criminologists, the sort who revel in positivistic paradigms making the mother the first or primal cause and the wife a contributing or precipitating factor in a man's subsequent violence. For example, one convicted serial killer is portrayed as having:

> . . . a deep-seated hatred of women that had started with his mother and continued with his wife – hatreds which helped to push him almost like a watermelon seed into committing murders that repelled him and that he now claims he never wanted to commit.[61]

Moreover, while all mothers are worrying, 'a seriously psychiatrically impaired' one is especially problematic as she is 'likely to contribute to a child's violent behaviour in several ways', leaving him or her with 'a sense of loss, a pervasively inconsistent home life, and errant nurturing'. Unwell or not, mothers of 'homicidally aggressive children' have other wayward habits, most notably, that of marrying violent men. When the problem becomes the mother who married the violent man and not the violent man himself one begins to suspect that Norris' 'New Criminologists' will not add any new knowledge beyond the standard mother-blaming criminological narrative.[62]

Take their claim to be able to predict dangerousness with the help of a 'critical mass of symptoms'. These symptoms – signs of mental disorder that can be detected by doctors and school guidance counsellors – include loose or illogical thought patterns, profound feelings of isolation, episodic periods

60 Norris, 1988, pp 36–9.
61 Norris, 1988, p 171. To support this allegation, Norris reproduces a photo of this killer with his mother and wife – the two women the killer blamed for his 'untempered hatred of women'.
62 Norris, 1988, pp 173–5.

of deep sadness and crying, bedwetting, sleepwalking, suicidal fantasies, extreme cruelty to animals and 'deviant sexual behaviour' such as exposing genitals.[63] The combination of these factors and poor parenting can be lethal. In sum, in homes where the child has 'a congenital neurological defect' *and* was raised by criminal or violent parents, it is 'logical to assume that the child could emerge as an episodically violent criminal, and possibly a serial murderer'.[64] Within a few pages, the problem is narrowed down to the single-parent home – 'an entire generation of children will soon emerge for whom there are no normal, supportive parental relationships'. This impoverished and malnourished generation 'will in turn give birth to a succeeding generation of children out of control, who will carry the disease of generational violence well into the next century'. Serial murder, which is a disease or syndrome, has symptoms that are identifiable long before the first murder. Behind that 'mask of sanity', the serial killer is searching for help, or suffering from 'deviate sexual behaviour and hypersexuality', or perhaps from a head injury or drug use. He might have abusive parents, or be the result of an unwanted pregnancy or the product of 'a difficult gestation period for the mother'. Perhaps he suffers from feelings of powerlessness or inadequacy or presents with the symptoms of neurological impairment said to be displayed by most serial killers, including dyslexia, confusing left and right, 'grandiosity', incontinence, sleep disorders and poor muscular co-ordination. Signs of genetic disorders include 'abnormalities' such as bulbous fingertips, fine hair, malformed ears, pliable ears, and gaps between the toes. Not that any of these things are 'absolute predictors' of future criminal behaviour – they are 'simply the synthesis of the combined symptomatology of hundreds of serial killers'.[65]

Predictably, Norris concludes by confirming his hypothesis – serial killing is a generational disease, 'passed on through child abuse, negative parenting and genetic damage'. He notes, in passing, that domestic violence is 'the foremost cause of injury to women', but instead of seeing this as evidence of the prevalence of men's violence against women in Western societies, domestic violence becomes yet another symptom of a diseased society, one that can be cured by experts like Norris himself.[66]

Sex crime – surface of (re)-emergence for biological positivism

Serial Killers: The Growing Menace is symptomatic of another disease – the disease of biologically-based criminological positivism which for over a

---

63 Norris, 1988, p 176.
64 Norris, 1988, p 184.
65 Norris, 1988, pp 193, 215–16 and 240–2.
66 Norris, 1988, pp 243–4.

century has searched for the causes of crime in the bodies and minds of convicted offenders. Variants of the same themes have been trotted out since Lombroso, the 'father' of criminology, thought he spotted tell-tale signs of criminality in the physiologies of men imprisoned in late-nineteenth century Italy. This is not the place to recapitulate all the arguments for and against biologically-based criminology.[67] All we need note is this: whether crime is biologically or socially induced is a question that throughout the twentieth century taxed positivists searching for the magical mix of hereditary and other 'background' factors that can explain, and therefore, predict criminal behaviour. Remarkably, that question is still today over-determining how criminologists put sex, violence and crime into discourse. So overwhelming is the drive to discover all the factors bearing down on badly-mothered men causing them to commit crimes that not even the devastating critiques of all forms of positivistic criminology launched by self-defining 'New' or 'Critical Criminologists' in the 1960s could halt the positivist juggernaut. Associated with the names of Foucault in France, David Matza in the United States, and Taylor, Walton and Young in Britain, critical criminologies attempted to forge a radical epistemological break with positivism and its etiological obsession with individual criminals and what drove them to crime. Their aims, broadly speaking, were to shift the criminological focus away from individual offenders to the criminalisation process and to hold the state responsible for producing alienating criminogenic conditions such as poverty in which crime flourishes. Critical criminologists also famously challenged taken-for-granted positivistic distinctions between criminals or 'deviants' and non-criminals, as well as the carefully-erected classification systems of supposedly different criminal 'types'. Criminality, critical criminologists insisted against the positivists, is not something inherent in individuals, but rather a label imposed by the state. In short, criminality was a matter of social definition.[68]

Undeterred by all the criticism, biological positivists cling on to the highly versatile Lombrosian paradigm of the constitutionally-disposed criminal. While few today would defend the discredited notion of a 'criminal mind', the notion that biology is criminal destiny lives on defiantly in mainstream criminology textbooks. But what a strange trajectory biologically-based criminological positivism has followed, starting with Lombroso's search for the criminal mind by measuring skulls; moving through so-called studies of 'somatotypes' based on male physiologies, and ending up either in the criminogenic uterus of the drug-addicted, 'inadequate' mother, or in the biochemical hormonal sensory levels of inadequately-parented men. Studies

---

67 See the critique of the 'genetic fundamentalism' of the 'gene hunters' in Schwartz, 2005–6, pp 20–1.
68 Taylor, Walton and Young, 1973; Young, 1981.

of serial sex killers have, as we have seen, provided the spark for a whole new spate of biological explanations of violent crime. Moreover, these studies have allowed biological positivism to reinsert itself as a key analytical player – a resurgence that is perhaps nowhere better illustrated than in Wilson and Herrnstein's massively controversial *Crime and Human Nature*. Here, 'human nature' quickly transmogrifies into 'male' nature, while biological and social factors are produced to explain why young men are the most likely social group to become criminals:

> It is likely that the effect of maleness and youthfulness on the tendency to commit crime has both constitutional and social origins. That is, it has something to do both with the biological status of being a young man and with how that young man has been treated by family, friends and society.

While Wilson and Herrnstein concede that there is no such thing as a crime 'gene' or a born criminal, and that 'constitutional factors' are not necessarily genetic, biological factors nevertheless triumph over social ones in their account of crime and 'human nature'. Indeed, some traits, including criminal traits, are inherited and some individuals are 'biologically predisposed to criminality'. It follows that 'an individual's anatomical configuration is correlated with criminality' – not that anatomical features cause crime; they are merely 'correlated with criminal behaviour'. Notwithstanding this slippage between correlations and causes, Wilson and Herrnstein were ready to assert, in 1985, that 'the case for constitutional differences in criminality is strong' and to predict that it has a 'future'.[69]

While their prediction that biologically-based criminology would continue to flourish has proved correct, the case presented in *Crime and Human Nature* is far from strong. Its so-called 'modern evidence' – somotypes (or body shapes), twin studies, adoption studies and the XYY chromosome – had all been utterly discredited by the time the book was published.[70] No wonder it created a furore. Sociologically-minded criminologists wanted to 'strike back' on behalf of the mesomorphs – men with the body type most likely to place them in criminally compromising positions, according to biological positivists.[71] Others, sensitive to the 'pariah status of biological or genetic approaches to crime', strove to defend the book from attacks on its 'putative biologism'.[72] Many were outraged that discredited, and frequently racist, biologically-based 'theories' had resurfaced to taunt

---

69   Wilson and Herrnstein, 1985, pp 69–70.
70   See for example, Jenkins, 1987, pp 333–4.
71   Braithwaite, 1987, p 52.
72   Adelson, 1986, p 44.

sociological criminology in the name of 'science'. Our specific concern here however, is what biological positivists have to say about the sex or gender of crime.

In *Crime and Human Nature*, looking at 'gender' means looking at women's offending, or rather, 'female crime', the 'maleness' of most crime having been taken for granted in the stunningly vacuous and, as it turns out, exculpatory claim that the criminality of young men has constitutional and social origins. People (read: men) who are constitutionally and socially bound to commit crime cannot be held to account as they are not responsible agents. While Wilson and Herrnstein try to distance themselves from Lombroso's biological positivism, insisting that no one 'subscribes to Lombrosian biology any more', they still believe that crime is genetically determined. Tellingly, this is most apparent in their understanding of 'gender'. The gendered asymmetry of crime and the entire 'sexual division of labour in human society', may not be 'rigidly fixed in the genes', but 'their roots go so deep into the biological substratum that beyond certain limits they are hard to change'.[73]

That was as far as Wilson and Herrnstein were prepared to take their case for constitutionally-based criminality in 1985. A decade later, Moir and Jessel cast caution and dissembling to the wind to embrace full-throttled neo-Lombrosian biological positivism in *A Mind to Crime*, a book that attempts to build on the 'evidence' presented in *Crime and Human Nature* that socio-economic factors are '*incidental* to crime'.[74] Moir and Jessel re-assert a biological basis for criminal violence in the starkest terms, focusing on the 'chemistry and neurophysiology of the criminal mind' and berating criminologists for not taking biology more seriously. There is 'very strong evidence', they insist, that many criminals have disordered minds, and are 'not like the rest of us' – the brain structures of the paedophile, the violent criminal and the serial killer are different from each other but, most importantly, are different from 'normal people'.[75]

Once again, we find a series of unsubstantiated assertions about 'the evidence' for the theory that biology is criminal destiny. A bold declaration that there is 'no "gene for crime" (except one – the gene that makes us male'), is followed immediately by a claim that 'a whole array of genetic influences' predispose some to non-violent property crime and others to violence. The biggest biological predisposing factor is 'gender', which for Moir and Jessel is interchangeable with 'sex', as in having a sex:

Sex is the strongest human distinction . . . Sex differences in crime has

---

73 Wilson and Herrnstein, 1985, pp 122 and 125.
74 Moir and Jessel, 1995, p 20, original emphasis.
75 Moir and Jessel, 1995, pp 1–3.

been so clear and bright that most studies have been blind to it. When it comes to crimes of violence, men have a near monopoly.

This is so because the 'male mind' is 'wired and fuelled to be more criminal': men are 'born with a greater number of crime cards up their sleeves, predisposing them to criminality – cards that the female simply does not have'.[76] So, once again, men's responsibility for their 'near monopoly' of violent acts is elided, disappearing under a fuse box and a pack of crime cards that make them genetically male and criminally predisposed.

As for the 'sexually deviant criminal', the one with a 'truly sexually deviant mind' who is 'sexually aroused by inappropriate needs', he is 'probably born, not made'.[77] Interestingly, not all sexually violent men have a truly sexually deviant mind. According to Moir and Jessel, the 'non-violent paedophile' has 'a distinct brain abnormality, a mind lacking the normal pattern for sexual arousal'. By contrast, the violent paedophile has additional abnormalities in the frontal lobes and in 'the animal area of the brain', while schizophrenics who kill – 'and there is often a sexual element to such killings' – suffer from brain abnormalities which bring on their delusional paranoia, and which 'may be an underlying genetic disorder'. As for rapists, some – especially date rapists – 'differ little from "normal" men who keep their sexual impulses under control'. Significantly, date rapists are not criminal types – they simply misread 'social clues' that the sex they are having is not consensual. They are then, very different from the stalking rapist who plans his attack. He has a mind that is wired differently. Furthermore, 'he often has an effeminate personality, and is sometimes homosexual', and suffers from hormonal imbalances and 'abnormalities in the sexual control centres of the brain'. Researchers 'at the forefront of knowledge' have proved all this apparently, and criminologists need to catch up with 'the evidence'.[78]

Interestingly too, Moir and Jessel stick to the idea of innate biological differences, knowing full well that it has been massively critiqued because of its 'tarnished' historical association of the notion of biological inferiority with genocide in the name of racial purity. They respond to this criticism recounting a story about a criminologist who submitted a paper on biological and physiological theories of crime to a leading journal but was rejected as a 'right-wing zealot'. Such a 'perversion of science by political psychopaths' could not withstand the power of 'scientific truth' – the truth

---

76 Moir and Jessel, 1995, pp 3–4. Only women suffering from premenstrual tension have 'a pattern of neurotransmitter abnormalities similar to those of the violent male' and that makes some of them 'regularly and disastrously run emotionally amok'.

77 Moir and Jessel, 1995, pp 6 and 189.

78 Moir and Jessel, 1995, pp 6–7.

revealed over 'four decades of study' that there is a massive gap between the intelligence scores of offenders and non-offenders.[79] In fact, science has revealed no such thing, and not surprisingly, 'evidence' for this and most of the other claims in *A Mind to Crime* fails to materialise. It is nevertheless illuminating to note how the authors illustrate the versatility of biologically-based criminological positivism. Biology – which for them means being born a male and acquiring a mind wired to be more criminal and having more cards up your sleeves – can explain and thus rationalise, any violent act, including 'family violence'. There is even 'an underlying biological cause for family violence'. It is located in a 'special mind which perpetrates this vile sort of behaviour', principally 'the aggressive psychopathic mind, and the explosively disordered mind'. So, contrary to the findings of the first study discussed in this chapter – that it was non-psychopathic 'normal' men who assaulted women – Moir and Jessel claim that psychopaths constitute 'a significant proportion' of wife batterers, and that most of them have significant head injuries.[80] They even conjure up a biological basis for jealousy inasmuch as 'the male is constitutionally jealous'. The 'Othello syndrome' is 'a compulsive disorder', and while brain scans have yet to uncover 'the seat of jealousy', they have no doubt it will be discovered soon – in 'abnormalities in the emotional areas of the brain'.[81]

There is no need to summarise the chapter on 'sexually deviant minds' in *A Mind to Crime*. We already know what is coming. An abnormal mind leads inexorably to sexually deviant acts. That is biological positivism's standard operating procedure. Take a violent crime, attribute it to an individual's 'biology', rely on a host of unsubstantiated assertions about 'scientific evidence' to divest biologically-driven men (and premenstrual women) of responsibility for their violent acts – their hormones, head injuries, wired brains made them do it – rename deeply engrained cultural scripts entitling men to kill 'their' women if they suspect adultery as the 'Othello syndrome', and finally, for good measure, throw in a bad mother, preferably one with a disordered mind and, hey presto, you can find a biological 'explanation' for each and every violent crime.

The merest reflection reveals that positivistic criminology begs far too many questions when it attempts to explain the link between sex, gender and violence. Getting back to our murderous texts, we might opt to join feminist analysts like Cameron and Frazer who, flabbergasted by criminology's 'thoroughgoing individualism', have challenged the discipline to notice that when it comes to violent crimes like serial homicide, the killers are 'mostly male, victims mostly female'. Why, they ask in their book, *Lust to Kill: A*

79 Moir and Jessel, 1995, pp 8 and 20.
80 Moir and Jessel, 1995, pp 208–22.
81 Moir and Jessel, 1995, p 273.

Feminist Investigation of Murder, do criminologists focus on individual killers when there is a clear pattern emerging of killers from one social group killing members of another?[82] Following Cameron and Frazer's lead, we might query criminological accounts in which men are transformed into biological engines or watermelon seeds driven by a primal instinct to satisfy a lust that compels them to kill. More, we could read these accounts, as well as the accounts which killers give of themselves, as 'constructed texts' which depend on cultural codes to give them meaning and – after Foucault – as 'controlling discourses' that enabled the new category of 'sex murder' to 'come into being'.[83] Violent men are either presented as born criminals or, more usually, placed within a multi-factorial framework that gives biological factors pride of place. This framework combines 'psychogenic' explanations that account for crime in terms of individual psychological factors with 'biogenic' explanations focusing on biological disorders such as brain tumours or neurological dysfunction. Tacked on to these are much less-developed 'sociogenic' explanations that look perfunctorily at the effects of the environment and social structures in order to understand all the factors that 'influence' the development of, say, 'the typical serial killer'.[84] In short, the sex killer is the product of a slick retrospective arithmetical equation that looks something like this. His defective genes, plus his head injury, plus his experience of sexual abuse, plus his peanut butter sandwiches plus – and this, of course, is directly connected to the unsatisfactory provision of such sandwiches – his bad mother, plus his absent father, plus his poor schooling, plus his poor socialisation, plus his feelings of alienation, plus his pornography collection and his polluted environment, plus his rejection by a woman, plus his sighting of a woman who reminds him of his mother or his wife equals a serial killer, or, for that matter, a mass murderer, a serial rapist or any episodically violent man the positivist criminologist wants to account for. He is the sum of all these disparate parts.

The controlling discourses which produce sex killers take their place in a long line of positivistic criminological texts that search for the holy grail of background factors and reproduce them in an ever expanding multi-causal frame. So powerful is the etiological force informing this research that it sweeps up all in its wake, including Jack Katz who in his book *Seductions of Crime: Moral and Sensual Attractions in Doing Evil* famously proposed that criminologists should focus not on background factors but on the foreground, on the actual experience and 'seductive appeal' of committing violent crime. We shall return to the strange case of the analyst who turned his ear to the 'seductive appeal' and 'involving aesthetic in the sounds and

82 Cameron and Frazer, 1987, pp 30–1.
83 Cameron and Frazer, 1987, pp xii and 22.
84 Holmes and De Burger, 1988, pp 42–3.

rhythms of repeatedly slapping another person' – say an American soldier interrogating peasants during the Vietnam war – and got lavishly praised by self-defining critical criminologists for doing so.[85] But one key point should be registered here. Katz called for a 'systematic empirical theory of crime' that 'explains at the individual level the causal process of committing a crime' and that also 'accounts at the aggregate level for recurrently docu-mented correlations with biographical and ecological background factors'. In doing so, he remained attached to the perverse correlation-proves-causality logic of the positivists.[86] He also planted himself firmly in the camp of those positivists attempting to link foreground or precipitating factors to the background and supposedly predictive variables predisposing indi-viduals to crime.[87] It follows that his putatively post-positivistic theory about the seductive quality of crime still ends up smacking of 'multi-causation', that all-embracing analytical mode that David Matza, one of the founding fathers of critical criminology, dismissed as long ago as the 1960s as 'a powerful force for intellectual inertia'.[88] It is far from being the only analysis to do so. Nor, as we shall see in Chapter 4, is it the only one to end up de-sexing, in the sense of de-gendering sex crime, thus losing sight of the 'Man' question – the question of the discursive place vacated by men within conventional framings of sex crime.

Re-sexing sex crime (to be continued)

The 'relentless banality' of the proliferating serial killing literature has not escaped criticism. Its profiling of the man most likely to succeed as a serial or lust killer has been ridiculed as cliché-ridden, as loaded with commonplaces, 'disconnected factoids' and tautologies. As for profiles of men who kill women that refer to 'mother hatred' or 'hostility towards women', they display no irony or awareness of how stunningly reductive an insight like 'hostility' is in the context of repetitive sexual murder.[89] It is clear however, that trenchant criticism of the proclivity for profiling the killer's mother rather than the killer himself has not registered with profilers and other 'experts'.[90] Nor do they appear to be aware of feminist problematisations of the sex of sex killing. The substitution of the idea of a 'continuum' of men's sexual violence for the positivistic assumption of a clear demarcation

85 Katz, 1988, pp 3–5.
86 Katz, 1988, pp 311–12.
87 See Steven Katz's excellent but so rare critique of the positivism of *Seductions of Crime*: Katz, 1989.
88 Matza 1964, p 23.
89 Seltzer, 1998, pp 125–31.
90 For examples of the predilection for profiling the killer's mother, see Caputi, 1987, pp 65–75.

between violent and non-violent men has simply passed them by.[91] Their positivistic criminological gaze remains fixated on individual killers, occasionally diverting attention to their mothers and their wives.

Feminists have been troubled by the discursive construction of male sexuality in non-feminist portrayals of 'sex crime' for some time. In a now classic study of the 1981 Yorkshire Ripper trial, Wendy Hollway reveals how the men in the courtroom 'refused to recognise the way in which the killer's acts were an expression – albeit an extreme one – of the construction of an aggressive masculine sexuality and of women as its objects'.[92] Sharing an assumption that 'normal' male sexuality contained 'an important element of aggressiveness' to which 'the female' submits, the lay, legal, psychiatric and journalistic discourses figured the defendant as abnormal, as different from normal men. At the same time, his victims were said to have provoked his desire for 'sexual revenge', the killer having committed his first murder after a prostitute allegedly accused him of being 'fucking useless' when he was slow to get an erection. Naturally – in the eyes of the male commentators – he felt a 'seething rage' and attacked and killed her. To them it was a 'classic' case of provocation and understandable sexual revenge. As Hollway observes, by blaming the victims, they not only avoid 'the threatening recognition that a man will kill when mocked about his sexual potency'; they fail to ask what he was revenging and on whom. They also failed to question the idea that 'a bit of aggression in men's sexuality' is 'natural'. [93]

Some feminists have taken the critique further. In *The Age of Sex Crime*, published in 1987, radical feminist Jane Caputi describes the sex of sex murder as 'patriarchal and pornographic' – it is 'political sex'. For her the violence, force, humiliation and domination that characterise sex killings are on a 'continuum' with normal heterosexual sex. Rape-murders, serial murders and recreational murders are all 'crimes of political, patriarchal domination'. As such they are not psychotic aberrations but rather 'an eminently logical step in the procession of patriarchal roles', or simply the 'latest expression' in a misogynist tradition of 'gynocide'. Contrary to the assumption made in standard criminological accounts then, these killings are neither motiveless nor random – the motive is gynocide, and the victims are not random, but rather women and children.[94] By contrast, Cameron and Frazer's analysis is informed by Foucault's questioning of expert discourses and is therefore more attuned than Caputi's to the idea of the discursive constitution of sex killing. A decade after Foucault expressed amazement at criminology's 'garrulous' discourses, it was Cameron and Frazer's turn

91 Kelly, 1987.
92 Hollway, 1981, p 33.
93 Hollway, 1981, pp 37–38.
94 Caputi, 1987, p 3.

to be astonished, this time by criminologists' accounts of 'the lust to kill'. Particularly puzzling to them was the criminological fixation with 'why *this* individual kills *that* one', ignoring the 'prior question, why members of some *groups* kill members of others'.[95] They were perplexed too by criminological definitions of sex killing as murder following rape or sexual assault. Despite its 'clarity', they found this definition problematic because it excluded so many crimes they would 'intuitively want to describe as "sexual"', including killers who stabbed women victim's genitals and breasts, thereby leaving 'little doubt of a sexual motive', and those who achieved orgasm by killing:

> It seems that rape and sexual assault are neither necessary nor sufficient to make a murder 'sexual'. What is important is the eroticisation of the act of killing in and for itself. Bearing this in mind, we shall define sexual murder as including all cases where the killer was motivated by sadistic sexual impulses – 'the lust to kill'.[96]

In standard criminology texts, sex killing is defined as a type of serial killing. Turning the definitions on their head, Cameron and Frazer classify serial or 'Ripper' killings as a variant of 'sexual murder', a category created by influential discourses such as psychiatry, sexology and criminology in late nineteenth century Western societies.[97]

Lust to Kill was a very significant intervention, paving the way for critical inquiries into the discursive construction of sex crime, including 'the strange cultural industry devoted to popular representations of serial killing' known as 'Ripperology', or 'the lore of Jack the Ripper'. His 1988 centenary was 'celebrated' with blood red cocktails and even the publication of a hoax diary purportedly written by the unknown killer himself. The diary became the occasion for Cameron to examine conceptions of serial killing at the close of the twentieth century. What struck her was not only the 'pseudoscientific ineptitude' that marks popular and expert discourses on the subject, but also the way that standard accounts 'obscure the connection between the utterly deviant and the thoroughly ordinary'. While the profile is 'meant to underscore the radical otherness of the killer', it actually 'ends up stressing his radical normality'. Killers are frequently depicted as quiet family men who, 'apart from their proclivity for murder', are 'rarely out of step with the social and sexual mores of their cultural milieu'. As for sex, and especially the sex of 'sex crime', it spells trouble for 'lumpen positivists', be they criminal investigators or criminologists. The sex of serial killing – like the

95 Cameron and Frazer, 1987, p 30, original emphasis.
96 Cameron and Frazer, 1987, pp 17–18.
97 Cameron and Frazer, 1987, pp 17–18 and 22.

masculinity of the killer – is 'wilfully obfuscated' by experts like the one who suggested that 'hatred not sex' was Jack the Ripper's motive. Cameron gets to the heart of the problem with contemporary positivistic approaches to 'sex crime':

> In the minds of today's so-called experts, it would appear that sex and hatred are separate by definition. If so, one wonders how sex by itself could *ever* be a motive for murder. (For necrophiles perhaps? Even then, how free from other motives – hatred, for instance – is a desire that your partner be, specifically, *dead* at the moment of coitus?).[98]

Expert discourses miss the point of the murderous act, 'which is violence *as* sex, desire *as* hatred'. Indeed, the fusion of sexual desire and hatred, and of lust and loathing, 'ought to be impossible to overlook when it is pushed to the limit of murder'. Moreover, it should 'force us to think about an extraordinarily unpalatable aspect of the masculine subjectivities/sexualities our culture has produced'.[99]

Clearly, the project of re-thinking so-called 'sex crimes' has become a very complex business. There is so much more to be said about feminist critiques of the discursive construction of sexed violence and also about the responses of non-feminists to their work that the discussion spills over into the next three chapters. There we shall develop the feminist critique of the conventional links made between sex, violence and crime, and, in the process, highlight the limitations of Foucault's and other non-feminist 'critical' approaches to the question of men and sexed violence. Until then, it is to be hoped that this chapter has helped to instil a practice of critical attentiveness to 'expert' discourses on 'sex crime'.

98 Cameron, 1994, pp 147–52, original emphasis.
99 Cameron, 1994, p 153, original emphasis.

Chapter 3

Pierre Rivière – a postmodern case study

In his famous 1975 interview, 'Prison Talk' – the one in which he expressed astonishment at the staggering inanity of criminological texts[1] – Foucault was asked about his latest book, *I, Pierre Rivière, Having Slaughtered My Mother, My Sister and My Brother*. The book, an edited collection of historical documents and commentaries by Foucault and his research team, brought to light the case of a nineteenth-century French peasant who killed three members of his family in a Normandy village and then, while imprisoned awaiting his trial, wrote a memoir explaining his actions. Asked why a barely literate peasant would write such a memoir, Foucault replied that it was a 'totally strange story'. Getting prisoners to write their memoirs was, he said, indicative of 'the first great burst of curiosity' about the criminal mind, a curiosity that took the form of an emergent medical and criminological obsession with a new question: 'What is this individual who has committed this crime?'. The new impetus to encourage offenders to speak about themselves could not, however, explain how Rivière had come to write his memoir as he had planned to write it before he committed his crimes. In any event, Foucault and his research team were not really interested in the killer or his memoir. Declining to conduct 'any kind of analysis of Rivière, whether psychological, psychoanalytical or linguistic' – a task left to psychoanalysts and criminologists – they focused instead on exposing 'the medical and juridical mechanisms that surround the story'. Not that this was a respectful division of intellectual labour – Foucault was contemptuous of criminological and psychiatric analyses of offenders. He was therefore pleasantly surprised that Rivière's memoir, which had left the experts 'silent at the time', had 'struck them equally dumb' when it was published 140 years later.[2]

Foucault was somewhat disingenuous when he said that he did not want to hear what modern-day experts had to say about the case. In another

1 Foucault, 1980a, p 47.
2 Foucault, 1980a, p 49.

interview, he confessed that it had been his 'secret desire' to hear criminologists and 'shrinks' discuss this 'magnificent case' in 'their usual insipid language'. When they declined to do so, he congratulated them on their prudence, for it was his belief that there was nothing to be said about the case itself inasmuch as the killer's memoir was so powerful that it precluded the possibility of comment of any kind about his crime. As he put it, the killer's own discourse on his act 'so dominates, or in any case so escapes from every possible handle, that there is nothing to be said about this central point, this crime or act, that is not a step back in relation to it'. So, not only did Foucault have nothing to say about Rivière's crime, he did not believe anyone else could speak about it either – interpretation was simply out of the question. Even more remarkably, he maintained that the crime was accompanied by 'a discourse so strong and so strange that the crime no longer existed'. It had escaped 'through the very fact of this discourse held about it by the one who committed it'. Foucault was emphatic on this point: Rivière's memoir was so 'extraordinary' that his crime 'ended up ceasing to exist'.[3]

What then, *was* Foucault's interest in the case and why was he so ecstatic when he came across the trial documents in the archives? It was for him a splendid event, one that provided a fascinating 'intersection of discourses' – of the legal and medical personnel at the trial, of the villagers and of the murderer himself. Together these discourses formed 'a rather strange contest, a confrontation, a power relation, a battle among discourses and through discourses' that was played out at Rivière's trial. At the heart of this discursive contestation was a dispute over the evidence, especially the medical evidence, as to the defendant's mental state. Should the nascent idea of taking into account the extenuating circumstances of disordered offenders apply in this case, or should the defendant be executed as a parricide? While the prosecution presented the memoir as proof of his rationality and hence grounds for condemning him to death, the defence argued that it was a sign of madness, and hence grounds for confining him for life. Foucault and his colleagues had little interest in this debate, however. Their reason for publishing the documents was rather to 'draw a map' of the courtroom disputes in order to plot the interaction of the discourses as 'weapons of attack and defence in the relations of power and knowledge'.[4]

Most importantly, for Foucault and his research team, the case demonstrated how a particular kind of knowledge, that of the emerging discipline of psychiatry, was formed and how it interacted with law. Here was an early instance of lawyers inviting medical experts to pronounce on the sanity, and thus, responsibility, of the accused for his crime. More broadly, the case

3 Foucault, 1989b, pp 131–3.
4 Foucault, 1982a, pp x–xi.

provided 'a key to the relations of power, domination and conflict within which discourses emerge and function', thereby providing excellent material for Foucauldian discourse analysis. In short, it was a perfect postmodern case study, not that Foucault would ever have called it that, such was his opposition to labels. As for the killer's discourse, he was adamant that he was not going to interpret it. Not for him 'the trap' of interpretation, a trap that would have enmeshed him in the 'power relation' established by 'expert' discourses, notably criminology. It could not be emphasised enough – he had nothing to say about the killer or his memoir.[5]

Overture – more notes on creating a usable Foucault

His disclaimers notwithstanding, Foucault did in fact have an opinion about Rivière and his crime. Moreover, while the case has not, as he says, attracted much criminological attention, what has been said – and more crucially what has not been said – about this nineteenth-century Normandy killer is very revealing for anyone interested in seeing what happens when masculinist scholars, even one of Foucault's stature, make instances of men's violence against women the starting point for critical inquiry. Before proceeding to the case itself though, there is still so much more to be drawn from his interview, 'Prison Talk'. First, there is his 'methodological precaution' against the teleological or 'progressivist perspective', which assumes that history has reached its proper modern end in the present moment. Then there is his ground-breaking exposure of the articulation of knowledge and power and with it the relinquishing of the utopian, humanist dream of 'a time when knowledge will cease to depend on power'. For knowledge, he insists, is always already implicated with power. And finally, it is in 'Prison Talk' that Foucault counsels us to utilise the writers we like. Foucault himself liked the German philosopher Nietzsche, but his point is that it does not matter whose ideas one cherishes, even Foucault's, for that matter. All that matters is that ideas get used:

> The only valid tribute to thought such as Nietzsche's is precisely to use it, to deform it, to make it groan and protest. And if commentators then say that I am being faithful or unfaithful to Nietzsche, that is of absolutely no interest.[6]

And that advice, as it happens, is followed in Chapter 3, which takes the form of a postmodern case study of interpersonal violence that is at once *for*

5 Foucault, 1982a, pp xi–xiii.
6 Foucault, 1980a, pp 49–54.

and *against* Foucault. My working assumption is that the best way to pay tribute to Foucault's ideas about power, truth, knowledge and violence is to use them, to make them groan and protest, and if purists protest that we are not being true to the Master, that is of absolutely no interest. All that concerns us is how men's violence is discursively constituted – this time by the theorist who made the discursive constitution of truth and the relationship between truth and power central to his work – in a case study that has attracted relatively little close historical, criminological or feminist attention.

It is well to have Foucault's imprimatur for taking a cavalier, even 'unfaithful', approach to his and other authoritative voices, for he is at first blush, a strange choice for feminist adulation. As Meaghan Morris famously put it, 'any feminists drawn into sending Love Letters to Foucault would be in no danger of reciprocity'.[7] So, why pimp for Foucault? Why make him an object of feminist desire? Why urge folk to let themselves be seduced by his work; why ease them down the Foucauldian way, especially when there is no turning back once that path is taken? He was, after all, a profoundly masculinist thinker, one moreover, who could not see the psychic injury of rape, even when the harm of sexual assault was spelled out to him by French feminists.[8] Such a man is surely a very strange bedfellow for a feminist project focusing on men's violence against women. How could anyone, it might be asked, who is intent on subverting masculinist knowledge claims about that violence, countenance Foucault, even for a moment?

The answer is that, paradoxical though it may seem, his methodologies and insights are pivotal for challenging criminological and other 'expert' discourses that serve to legitimate men's violence today. It was Foucault, after all, who exposed how criminology works as a controlling discourse, one with an extraordinary capacity to pass as truth about crime and violence. It may have been Gramsci who bequeathed to us the gift of understanding how hegemony works – how subordinated people 'consent' to, or become submerged by, dominant conceptualisations of the way things are. But what greater shadow could be cast over dominant ideas themselves, particularly criminological ones, than that of the great French theorist who traced the articulation of power with knowledge? It was Foucault, after all, who demonstrated that power was implicated in the production of 'knowledge' and 'truth' in a range of fields, including medico-legal and criminological explanations of 'the criminal'. Where else but from him did Cameron and Frazer get the idea that killers' accounts of their murders are no more than 'constructed texts', texts constructed from the discourses available to them? Where else, but from Foucault, and especially from *Discipline and*

---

7 Morris, 1988, p 55. See Howe, 1994, pp 110–11.
8 See his famous debate with French feminists in Foucault, 1988a, pp 200–5.

Punish, did we learn to problematise criminological discourses by unpacking the way in which they become part of our normal everyday framework for understanding criminality?[9]

So much for the overture. Let us get on with the business of creating a usable Foucault that we commenced in the first two chapters for those interested in continuing the challenge to commonsense understandings of sex, violence and crime. Foucault's most usable parts, as it turns out, are not his observations about interpersonal violence, which, unlike the institutional violence of prisons and psychiatric hospitals, was *never* one of his focal concerns. Making Foucault an object of postmodern feminist desire involves returning to his early 1970s work on 'power/knowledge' theorising the relationship between power, knowledge and the production of 'regimes of truth'. Along the way, we might do some violence to Foucault, making *him* groan and protest, a process I began by classifying him as a poststructuralist, even though he was adamantly against classification, either of people at risk of criminalisation or of his own thought, and he specifically refused the poststructuralist label.[10] I want to return now to his analysis of the crucial constitutive link between power and truth, ignoring the fact that in his final years, Foucault was to say that his main concern all along had not been with power, but with the question of 'subjectivation'. That Foucault was to form the view that the knowledge/power articulation, far from being his fundamental problematic, was merely an instrument for analysing the formation of the subject, is of no concern whatsoever.[11]

How to study power (and sex and violence)

Chapter 1 set out Foucault's instructions about how to study sexuality as well as a few pointers about how to study power. Elaborating on his methodical advice about how to study power, we might usefully begin by introducing 'power/knowledge', a concept with which he is uniquely identified. Power/knowledge is shorthand for indicating that power produces knowledge and vice versa. For Foucault, they are inextricably connected and, crucially, discourse is the place where they meet. As he says in 'Prison Talk', the 'mechanisms of power' have 'never been much studied', and what had been studied 'even less' was the relationship between power and knowledge. Yet understanding this relationship was essential because the exercise of power 'perpetually creates knowledge and, conversely, knowledge constantly induces

9 Cameron and Frazer, 1987, pp xii and 22.
10 See Chapter 1, n 14.
11 By the early 1980s, the self-formation of the subject, and the processes by which the human subject enters into 'games of truth' had become his focal concern See Howe, 1994, pp 103–4. For the way in which his work has influenced feminist poststructuralist work on the constitution of female subjectivity, see McNay, 1992 and Probyn, 1993.

effects of power'.[12] He therefore set about devising a method for studying power; but not power as it had been traditionally conceived, not power understood as 'juridical', as power in the domain of law. His analytical problem was not sovereignty and obedience, but rather 'domination and subjugation'.[13] Inasmuch as domination and subjugation are central to this book's analysis of discursive productions of 'men's violence', his methodology for studying power warrant a closer look.

Foucault's method for studying the interrelationship between power and knowledge and for undermining dominant knowledges is set out most clearly in two famous lectures he gave in 1976 called, simply, 'Two Lectures'. There he proclaimed his preference for 'local criticism', a form of criticism whose validity is 'not dependent on established regimes of thought', one which involves *an insurrection of subjugated knowledges*.[14] He identified two kinds of subjugated knowledges. One was a buried historical knowledge, an erudite knowledge that enables us to rediscover conflicts and struggle, and that can only be revealed by critique and scholarship. The other kind of 'subjugated knowledge' was to be understood as something quite different, as a whole series of low-ranking, 'naïve', 'popular' or local knowledges, such as those of the psychiatric patient or the sick person or the delinquent, that have been disqualified by expert scientific discourses. This local 'popular' knowledge, far from being a 'general commonsense knowledge', is 'particular, local, regional', and 'owes its force only to the harshness with which it is opposed by everything surrounding it'. What both forms of subjugated knowledge – the erudite and the disqualified popular kind – have in common is a 'memory of hostile encounters', one hitherto confined to the margins, and a concern with a forgotten or marginalised 'historical knowledge of struggles'. The critical work they perform can be brought together in a 'genealogy', a term Foucault gives to 'the union of erudite and local memories which allows us to establish a historical knowledge of struggles and to make use of this knowledge tactically today'.[15]

Genealogies, he explained, have 'nothing to do with' positivism. They are not 'positivistic returns to a more careful or exact form of science'. They are 'precisely anti-sciences'. That is, genealogies are not conducted 'in the name of some kind of scientism'. On the contrary, they oppose the 'effects of the centralising powers' linked to the institutionalisation of organised scientific discourses. Instead, genealogies 'emancipate' or 'desubjugate' historical knowledges, rendering them capable of opposing 'the coercion of a 'unitary,

---

12 Foucault, 1980a, pp 51–2.
13 Foucault, 1980c, pp 94–5.
14 Foucault, 1980c, p 81, original emphasis. This phrase is italicised in this translation of 'Two Lectures', but not in the translation of this lecture in Foucault, 2003, p 7.
15 Foucault, 1980c, pp 81–3.

formal and scientific discourse' that orders its claims in the name of 'truth'. That is, genealogies reactivate local or 'minor' knowledges 'in opposition to the scientific hierarchisation of knowledges and the effects intrinsic to their power'.[16] To study the relationship between knowledge and power, Foucault proposed a 'non-economic analysis', one which did not rely on a narrow conception of power as repression, but was concerned instead with 'the *how* of power'. This entailed studying the effects of power exercised through discourses of truth. The mechanisms of power, the effects of truth, in other words, 'the rules of power and the powers of true discourses', were his focal concerns. He wanted to work out how to study 'the fact of domination', focusing not on the 'global kind of domination that one person exercises over others', but on the 'manifold forms of domination that can be exercised within society'.[17]

To assist with this new way of studying power, he drafted five 'method-ological imperatives and precautions'.[18] The first shifts the focus from 'legit-imate forms of power in their central locations' to power at 'its extremities, in its ultimate destinations, with the points where it becomes capillary, that is, in its more regional and local forms and institutions', where it is 'less legal in character'. Second, we should not be concerned with power 'at the level of conscious intention', but rather, at its point of application, where it pro-duces its 'real effects'. Do not ask who has power or 'why certain people want to dominate', what their aims and strategies are. Ask instead 'how things work at the level of on-going subjugation, at the level of those con-tinuous and uninterrupted processes which subject our bodies, govern our gestures, dictate our behaviours'.[19] In other words, look at how we are constituted as subjects 'as a result of the effects of power'. It is, after all, one of the 'prime effects of power that certain bodies, certain gestures, certain discourses, certain desires, come to be identified and constituted as indi-viduals'. Third, power should not be thought of as the property of an individual or a class, as domination of an individual or group over others. Do not conceptualise power as something possessed by some people and not others, but rather as 'something which circulates' through a network that threads everywhere. Individuals are always 'simultaneously undergoing and exercising' power. Fourth, do not study power starting from 'its centre' or from the top down. Rather, conduct an '*ascending* analysis of power', start-ing from the local level, noting how power mechanisms operate at, say, 'the effective level of the family'.[20] Identify the 'real agents' of power – his

16 Foucault, 1980c, pp 83–5. 'Emancipate' is translated as 'desubjugate' in Foucault, 2003, pp 8–11.
17 Foucault, 1980c, pp 92–6, original emphasis.
18 Foucault, 1980c, pp 89 and 94–6.
19 Foucault, 1980c, pp 96–7.
20 Foucault, 1980c, pp 98–9, original emphasis.

examples are parents and doctors – and do not 'lump them under the formula of a generalised bourgeoisie'. Identify how techniques of power operate in everyday life, especially the mechanisms of exclusion, the apparatuses of surveillance, 'the medicalisation of sexuality, of madness, of delinquency, all the micro-mechanisms of power' that operate at the pivotal local level. Fifth and finally, while major mechanisms of power have been accompanied by ideologies, Foucault suggests that it is better to focus on the production of 'apparatuses of knowledge', including methods of observation and other 'apparatuses of control'.[21]

From 'regimes of truth' to 'social hegemonies'

By way of summary, Foucault suggests that an analysis of power be based not on juridical power and state institutions, but on 'the study of techniques and tactics of domination' at the local level. He was particularly interested in the techniques or mechanisms of power which he says first emerged in the seventeenth and eighteenth centuries and which operate on bodies by means of a continuous surveillance and a 'tightly knit grid of material coercions'. This power he called 'disciplinary power', a power exercised over bodies by means of constant surveillance.[22] The exercise of this power has led, he says, to the establishment of 'our' modern or disciplinary society – a *society of normalisation*. In this process, the human sciences, for example psychology, played an important part by producing apparatuses of knowledge that establish procedures of normalisation. Furthermore, the medicalisation of behaviours, discourses and desires which has taken place since the ninenteenth century is also exemplary of disciplinary power masked as neutral science.[23] While Foucault's elaboration of disciplinary power lies outside the ambit of this book, his ideas about the medicalisation of modern Western societies are most germane to the Pierre Rivière case.[24] For Foucault, this case illustrated perfectly the emergence of psychiatry and its power to discursively constitute particular individuals as dangerous, a process he called the 'psychiatrisation of criminal danger'.[25] The 'interweaving of effects of power and knowledge' could, he felt, be grasped easily 'in the case of a science as "dubious" as psychiatry', a 'regime of truth' that especially intrigued him.[26]

Fascinated by the rules determining which statements are accepted as

21 Foucault, 1980c, pp 100–2.
22 Foucault, 1980c, p 104. He uses the term 'bio power' to refer to the production, regulation and control of bodies and of whole populations: Foucault, 1979, pp 81–102.
23 Foucault, 1980c, pp 102–7, original emphasis.
24 See Howe, 1994, Chapter 3.
25 Foucault, 1988b, p 128.
26 Foucault, 1980d, p 109.

'scientifically true', Foucault isolated 'the politics of the scientific statement' as a key analytical focus. Crucially, he saw this problem as first and foremost a discursive question. To determine what 'effects of power circulate among scientific statements', it was necessary to focus on the 'discursive regime' and the effects of power peculiar to the 'play of scientific statements' therein.[27] He was particularly interested in psychiatric and the other self-proclaimed scientific discourses, notably psychology, criminology and sexology that started to develop in the nineteenth century. How, he asked, did these emergent disciplines set about establishing 'regimes of truth' about social problems such as crime? Every society, he claims, has 'its regime of truth' in which those who are 'charged with saying what counts as true' claim a scientific status. Indeed, in modern Western societies, 'truth' takes the form of scientific discourse. It follows that the key to understanding how power operates is to decipher the operative scientific 'regime of truth'.[28]

In the final analysis, what matters is not changing people's consciousness, or 'emancipating truth from every system of power (which would be a chimera, for truth is already power)'. For Foucault, the important task, as we saw in Chapter 1, is to detach the power of truth from the forms of hegemony within which it operates. Power, he said, must be understood as a 'multiplicity of force relations' that are embodied not only in 'bourgeois hegemony', but in 'the various social hegemonies'.[29] It is precisely at this point that Foucault's analysis of regimes of truth meets, or rather borrows from, Gramsci's notion of 'hegemony'. As Renate Holub notes, the influence of his Marxist predecessor is unacknowledged in Foucault's work, but their understanding of power bears many resemblances. For both, power is not imposed from above, but dependent on consent from below. And for both, 'power is produced and reproduced in the interstices of everyday life, and for both, power is ubiquitous'.[30] There are also important parallels, especially in their methodology and political aims. Methodologically, both recognised the importance of the local or micro level for understanding how power operates. Politically, both wanted to undermine their societies' regimes of truth by, as Gramsci put it, forging counter-hegemonies, or as Foucault put it, by staging an insurrection of subjugated knowledges. While Gramsci had in his sights the dominant ideas of the ruling bourgeoisie class in twentieth-century Western societies, Foucault focused on expert or controlling discourses, especially psychiatry, psychology and criminology. It is the reality-forming power of the emergent nineteenth-century discipline of psychiatry that returns us to the Pierre Rivière case.

27 Foucault, 1980d, pp 112–13.
28 Foucault, 1980d, pp 131–3.
29 Foucault, 1979, pp 93 and 125.
30 Holub, 1992, p 29.

For Foucault – the medicalisation of criminal violence

Several questions may have been plaguing readers from the outset of this chapter. First, how does a memoir written by a French peasant explaining why he decided to murder his mother, his sister and his young brother one summer's day in 1835 assist our project of understanding how sex, violence and crime are put into discourse today? Second, what light do Foucault's methodological directives for studying power at the local level throw on the Rivière case? Third, how does an analysis of this case rate as a 'postmodern' case study? Answering the last question first, the case can be labelled as postmodern inasmuch as it exemplifies Foucault's argument about the centrality of discourse to the operation of power and the production of truth. As he shows, the case provided an intersection where powerful discourses, notably law and newly emergent medical discourses about the dangerous criminal confronted each other and engaged with the discourses of the villagers and of the killer himself. No wonder Foucault became so excited when he came across the case in the archives. He was especially interested in the 'medico-legal opinions' formulated about the offender – the medico-legal discourses in which doctors fought over the meaning to be given to Rivière's killings. This battle would determine his fate – execution or committal to an institution for the criminally insane. As for the killer's memoir, we shall leave it hauntingly in the background, at least for now, just as Foucault did, and turn instead to consider what he saw as significant about the case. Recall that his stated intention in publishing the book was to expose the interaction of all the discourses battling it out for the 'truth', discourses that operated as 'weapons of attack and defence in the relations of power and knowledge' surrounding the case.[31]

Indicted for murder, Rivière stood trial at the assize court at Caen in August 1835. The prosecution argued that it was a case of parricide and ought to be punished like regicide with execution. The defence argued that he was insane. Medical opinion was divided on this issue. The prosecution's medical expert testified that the defendant showed no signs of insanity. He had not fallen on his head, he did not suffer from any illness that may have impaired his brain and he had answered the doctor's questions cogently before returning to complete the writing of his memoir. There were, the doctor said, simply no signs of 'mental derangement'. In his view, Rivière was a melancholic, but in full control of himself. By contrast, Dr Vastel, the doctor for the defence, claimed it was a case of 'true mental alienation'. In fact, he had 'never seen a more manifest case of insanity among the hundreds of monomaniacs' he had treated – 'so manifest indeed that one's heart feels

31 Foucault, 1982a, p xi.

pity far rather than horror for this wretched being'.[32] But the defendant's memoir was a major stumbling block to determining his state of mind. Was it proof of rationality or a sign of madness? In all, six doctors were called to give evidence at the trial on the question of his sanity. Three found him to be sane, three insane, creating a difficult decision for the jury. Finding themselves caught up in the discursive battles being waged between the lawyers and the expert medical witnesses, the jurors took three hours to return a unanimous guilty verdict. But six jurors considered that extenuating circumstances should be accepted. Then, after the sentence of death was passed, 10 jurors effectively washed their hands of their decision by petitioning the king to show the condemned man mercy on the following grounds:

> We realise that all the ills he suffered in the person of his father, whom he cherished to the extent of sacrificing himself for him, must have powerfully contributed to the disturbance and derangement of his mental facilities, which were never wholly sound.[33]

The Caen doctors who had testified for the defence also drew up a memorandum in favour of the accused man, declaring him to be prey to a 'singular monomania', namely *aversion to women and female animals*.[34] Several Paris doctors agreed. They sent a report to the king agreeing with the defence doctor's report, and criticising the prosecution's doctor for believing Rivière to be sane simply because he was unable to fit him into any of the known categories of madness. In their view, he was delusional and therefore not fully responsible. As such, he should be committed to an institution – he was 'too ill to be left at large'.[35] In the end, that view prevailed. Acting on the recommendation of the minister of justice, the king commuted his death sentence to life imprisonment.[36]

The outcome of the trial, however, was of little interest to Foucault. For him, the case was simply an 'excuse' to examine psychiatry presenting itself as a scientific discourse as it moved into the area of pronouncing on criminality in the court room. Importantly, Rivière's trial took place at a time when medical opinion was divided over the question of how to deal with the problem of the disordered offender. Accordingly, the trial's significance lay in the way it helped to crystallise a new power dynamic based on scientific pronouncements about the disordered criminal. The 'real purposes' of the doctors became apparent in their attempts to 'pathologise a sector of

32 Foucault, 1982a, pp 122–31.
33 Foucault, 1982a, pp 166–7. According to the presiding judge, reading his memoir had had a considerable effect on them: p 146.
34 Foucault, 1982a, p 167, original emphasis.
35 Foucault, 1982a, pp 163–6.
36 Rivière hanged himself four years later.

criminality in which Rivière's case is a very significant episode'. What was at stake in the discursive battles between the legal teams and their medical authorities was nothing less than 'the partial replacement of one method of control by another'. Thus for example, the report by the Paris experts demonstrated 'the power to annex' the case to the new 'medical apparatus', the new power/knowledge which would fundamentally challenge the way that serious crimes were dealt with in the courts. More ambitiously still, the report indicated that the new science of 'mental medicine' was trying to 'erect a new apparatus', an intervention based on a knowledge 'capable of *anticipating the possibility* of criminal behaviour' before it occurred.[37]

Herein lies the strength of Foucault's analysis of the case. It was, as he and his research team show, an exemplary case demonstrating the critical importance of the intervention of psychiatry in the field of law. This marked the beginning of a new kind of hegemony in which medical experts would become the arbiters of meaning in cases involving violent offenders, pronouncing on their level of responsibility for their actions. Elaborating on this argument in his analysis of the emergence of the concept of 'the dangerous individual', Foucault explained how during the nineteenth century the emergent discipline of psychiatry developed and refined the notion of madness to include individuals who did not exhibit behaviour previously described as insane. One key strategy was to focus on 'monstrous' crimes – cases of homicidal fury where the otherwise seemingly normal person explodes in an inexplicable and apparently motiveless homicidal rage. In such crimes, which consisted entirely in an insanity which was manifested in nothing but the crime, some medical experts started labelling perpetrators 'monomaniacs', as we have seen Dr Vastel did when he declared Rivière to be a classic case of monomania. Despite his sounding authoritative with this diagnosis, the concept did not feature strongly in the case. The trial was important for a far more important development – that of the idea of limited or diminished responsibility.

This notion was applied by medical experts to behaviour that was not insane but could nevertheless be defined as pathological, an idea that led to the development of a theory of limited or various degrees of insanity and the legal doctrine of diminished responsibility. The medical conflation of criminal acts with pathological mental states produced what Foucault referred to as 'a psychiatric and criminological continuum', enabling the medical profession to redefine criminality as a psychiatric category. This in turn gave medical experts a capacity to claim expertise, and thus power – the power to define, to diagnose, to determine criminal outcomes and, ultimately, to predict dangerousness. The Rivière case was at the heart or 'confluence' of all these developments that were paving the way for greater psychiatric

37 Castel, 1982, pp 251–2, original emphasis.

intervention in the courts. But more that that, Foucault and his team believed that the introduction of extenuating circumstances into criminal courts opened the way for introducing 'all the social and human sciences' into the judicial procedure. It was the beginning of a veritable invasion of experts of 'various kinds' that reduced judicial power and transformed the way criminal trials were conducted.[38]

All in all then, the courtroom drama in the Rivière case provides a very revealing window for Foucault, illustrating the 'how' of power. More specifically, it shows how criminality and criminal insanity began to be constituted in discourse. It is a classic study of emergent psychiatry carving out a space for intervention and deployment of power – the power of dominant or 'expert' discourses to constitute social problems, in this case, that of the criminal personality. Above all, the case demonstrates clearly how power is exercised through expert discourses, here medico-legal discourses that constituted the killer in conflicting ways: mad and so not responsible for his homicidal fury, or bad and criminally responsible according to others. Given all these riches, none better to Foucauldians than the opportunity to explore important transformations in the deployment of power by dominant groups at the crucial local level – at the level of a French provincial courtroom – how is it possible to use the case against Foucault?

Foucault's promise – dissipating the familiar

Of all that has been said for and against Foucault, the most inspired tribute to him is surely Keith Gandal's brilliant defence of his work against the criticism that it was nihilistic. Foucault, he insists, did not deny 'the possibility of a meaningful political practice'. Paradoxically, however, Gandal's wonderful tribute can be used to show just how problematic Foucault's reading of the Pierre Rivière case is. According to Gandal, what had been mistaken for nihilism in Foucault's work was his 'sense that articulating a set of values inhibits effective and ethical political action'. Questioning 'our most familiar practices without providing value-systems or alternatives', Foucault's project was not to provide solutions, but rather 'to identify and characterise problems'. He wanted 'precisely to bring it about' that we 'no longer know what to do', that we question everything previously taken for granted:

> His project was not to consider and set forth the Good, but rather to explore, make problematic and stop the Unbearable. 'For him', says Deleuze, 'to think meant to react to the intolerable'.[39]

38 Foucault, 1988b, p 141 and Moulin, 1982, p 215.
39 Gandal, 1986, p 123.

Resisting any 'totalitarian' impulse to 'lay out a blue print for society', he preferred to pursue 'local' problems, such as the incarceration of the mentally ill. As Gandal puts it:

> Foucault's method was to grasp a situation, an experience, in its specificity and its history, in the particular *conditions* that produced it and maintained it, in order to change it.

And:

> He believed that a progressive politics needed not a vision of what should be, but a sense of what was intolerable and an historical analysis that could help determine possible strategies in political struggles.[40]

Interestingly, Gandal notes that one of the many things that Foucault found intolerable was 'the power of men over women'. Describing his work as part of a 'series of oppositions which have developed over the last few years', Foucault included 'opposition to the power of men over women' in his list as well as opposition to the power 'of parents over children, of psychiatry over the mentally ill, of medicine over the population, of administration over the ways people live'.[41] But he was reluctant to speak for subjugated groups – he wanted them to speak for themselves, drawing on their subjugated knowledges to instigate a politically-informed practice of criticism which did not rely on expert opinions. Gandal defends this respectful silence on Foucault's part. If he 'remained silent about his values', if he was reticent about providing answers or principles, it was because he was concerned that articulating an ethics as a set of principles 'would pre-empt a task of questioning and telling new truths'. For Gandal then, Foucault's 'radicalism consisted in his dedication to questioning just what seemed most obvious and least open to question'.[42] His very laudable goal was to assist in:

> ... wearing away certain self-evidences and commonplaces about madness, normality, illness, crime and punishment; to bring it about, together with many others, that certain phrases can no longer be spoken about so lightly, certain acts no longer, or at least no longer so unhesitatingly performed, to contribute to changing certain things in people's ways of perceiving and doing things, to participate in this difficult displacement of forms and sensibility and thresholds of tolerance.[43]

40 Gandal, 1986, p 124, original emphasis.
41 Foucault, 1982b, pp 211–12.
42 Gandal, 1986, pp 122, 129 and 133.
43 Foucault, 1981, pp 11–12.

Understandably, Foucault hardly felt capable of much more than that.

As I have acknowledged elsewhere, Foucault's work has had the desired effect of disrupting and dissipating much that is familiar and accepted.[44] Not only did he disrupt conventional ideas about madness, normality, crime, punishment and sexuality, he also challenged us to confront all accepted ideas and to rethink our very being – to consider 'straying afield' of ourselves, no less. Who could not be stopped in their tracks by his stunning suggestion that:

> There are times in life when the question of knowing if one can think differently than one thinks, and perceiving differently than one sees, is absolutely necessary if one is to go on looking and reflecting at all.[45]

And yet, although he singled out the power of men over women as one of his focal concerns, nowhere is there any evidence that he ever seriously turned his mind to it or felt the need to think differently about it. Nowhere does the king of dissipating the familiar pause to problematise one of the most familiar relationships of them all – that of men and women. Nowhere does he stoop to breach the self-evidence of the masculinist frames of reference that blind non-feminist scholars to the power dynamics involved in relationships between men and women and crucially, in the discursive representations of those relationships. His subscription to the heroic interpretation of Pierre Rivière is a classic case in point.

Against Foucault – spell-bound and speechless

Recall Foucault's claim that there was nothing to be said about Rivière's crime or his memoir. Recall too that he saw the book he compiled about the case as 'a trap', one designed to trick 'the shrinks' and other experts into analysing the case in their usual asinine way. Given his strenuous opposition to any kind of interpretation at all, one might have expected Foucault to have been against the making of a film about the case centring on the idea of a peasant seizing the opportunity for speech. Instead, he said that he subscribed to the idea 'completely'. He was especially pleased that the film memorialised the tragedy of peasant life – that it gave them 'their tragedy':

> Basically, the tragedy of the peasant until the end of the eighteenth century was still hunger. But, beginning in the nineteenth century and perhaps still today, it was, like every great tragedy, the tragedy of the

---

44 Howe, 1994, pp 120–1.
45 Foucault, 1985, p 8.

law, of the law of the land. Greek tragedy is a tragedy that recounts the birth of the law and the mortal effects of the law on men.[46]

The Rivière case then, was a 'drama about the law'. It was not simply a case about the intervention of psychiatry in the field of law – it was a case about a new civil code which had been imposed on the daily life of the peasant 'as he struggles in this new juridical universe'. Asked whether it was problematic that the peasants get to speak 'only through such a monstrous story', Foucault was unconcerned. In his view, the crime 'posed no problem' for the peasants given roles in the film:

> On the contrary, instead of becoming an obstacle, it was a kind of space where they could meet, talk and do a whole lot of things which were actually those of their daily lives. In fact, instead of blocking them, the crime liberated them.

As for as the danger of focusing too much on 'the indiscreet violence of the peasantry', that was not a problem for Foucault either inasmuch as the film showed 'none of that lyricism of violence and peasant abjection' that the interviewer seemed to be hinting at.[47]

Speaking of the lyricism of violence, Foucault confessed that the real reason why he and his colleagues spent over a year reading the documents relating to the case, was 'simply the beauty of Rivière's memoir'. Indeed, 'its beauty alone' was 'sufficient justification' for reproducing it – the beauty, that is, of a text explaining why the author decided to hack to death his mother, sister and brother one summer's day in France in 1835.[48] Indeed, it was 'owing to a sort of reverence' for the memoir, that Foucault and his research team were unwilling to superimpose their own interpretation on it, for as they readily admitted, they had fallen 'under the spell of the parricide with the reddish-brown eyes'.[49] Several questions immediately spring to mind, especially to the mind of anyone trained in Foucauldian discourse analysis and thereby accustomed to asking who does the speaking and registering the positions from which they speak. From whose perspective is this a beautiful text? How is it possible for a theorist attuned to the discursive construction of truth to be spell-bound by a self-justifying account of murder? Under what discursive conditions is it feasible to feel reverential towards such a bloody text? Does Foucault's commentary give rise to methodological questions that we might fairly have expected him to raise

---

46 Foucault, 1989b, pp 132–4.
47 Foucault, 1989b, pp 135–6.
48 Foucault, 1982a, p 199.
49 Foucault, 1982a, p xiii.

himself? Patricia O'Brien believes so. In a brief but incisive commentary on the case, she notes that although Foucault 'sees deviance as a product of power, he enshrines individual criminal action'. Moreover, elevating the memoir to a work of beauty that is beyond interpretation implies that it has 'an underlying authenticity' that somehow transcends and is thus untouched by the discursive battles going on around it, and in which it played a central part. Exempting it from interpretation implies 'there is a validity to the document that exists some place outside' power relationships. O'Brien suggests too that the avoidance of the 'trap' of interpretation, the refusal to interpret it, is 'based on a mystical sense, a terror, of the inviolability of the document'.[50] In attempting to avoid the 'trap' of interpretation, Foucault not only ignores his own methodological rules for studying power; just as strangely, he appears to be oblivious to one of his own central premises, namely that there are no actions or texts outside of discourse. It is therefore not possible for the memoir to stand on its own, like some kind of non-discursive entity. The memoir played a key role in the battle between conflicting interpretations of the killer, his crime and his victims. By the same token, it is not possible for Foucault to stand outside these power relations in order to avoid the 'trap' of interpretation. For, according to his account of the power of discourses, no one can escape their constraints, let alone allow themselves to be spell-bound and thus silenced by their author, no matter how dazzling and enthralling the prose.

There is a second and related problem with Foucault's analysis of the case. Despite his disclaimers, Foucault and his research team do in fact interpret the crime and the memoir. In their account, the killer is enshrined as a peasant hero fighting against domination and resorting to violence as an act of speech against an unjust social system. The first 'Note' compiled on the case by Foucault's research team elaborates on this interpretation, describing the crime as 'an event':

> The event was freedom; it cut like a blade, perturbed, thwarted, or took every sort of institution in the rear. An exemplary event, murder, here aimed, in a frozen world, at the timelessness of oppression and the order of power.[51]

So enthralled were they by the supposedly universalising themes invoked by the heroic and tragic interpretation of the case that they overlooked a crucial empirical detail. The blade on the murder weapon (a pruning bill) was actually aimed with deadly force at three hapless members of the killer's family and not at any 'frozen world' of oppression. Equally puzzling, finding

50 O'Brien, 1978, p 514.
51 Peter and Favret, 1982, p 186.

'beauty' in a text that explains and justifies the exercise of such deadly violence betrays a staggering blindness to the 'fact of domination', the very same fact Foucault said should be at the heart of any study of power relations.

This blindness on the part of a theorist dedicated to specifying how power operates and how bodies are subjugated at the local level bears further scrutiny. We might begin by noting that the murderer as hero is a common theme in masculinist accounts of murder.[52] Enraptured by his master's account, Foucauldian John Rajchman declares that 'our culture finds works like Pierre's to be strangely beautiful', belonging to 'a counter-tradition including such heroes as Artaud and Sade which our outmoded literary culture has suppressed'. In refusing to comment or to judge Rivière, Foucault – like the killer himself – stakes out a position of 'radical freedom', no less.[53] By contrast, historian Richard Cobb dismisses the 'Notes' compiled on the case by Foucault and his team as 'pretentious twaddle', the product of a 'fashionable French form of analysis'. Yet he too subscribes to a heroic reading of Rivière, although it is not his murderous rampage but rather the walk he embarked on immediately afterwards which Cobb admires, elevating it to 'poetry and beauty'. This walk, on which Rivière covered about 500 km, averaging about 20 km a day for a month, was for Cobb 'the culmination of his unhappy life, his last achievement, his groping to poetry and beauty, a pathetic attempt to escape . . . from a cruelly observant rural society'. As for Foucault's interpretation of the crime as an 'act of social protest', and the suggestion in the Notes that the killer's mother was 'something of a feminist before her time', Cobb rejects this as 'a lot of rubbish,' as a 'prostitution of history' and a 'betrayal of evidence'. He does however, accept Rivière's account of his mother, an account revealing his 'deep, physical repugnance for women'. In Cobb's view, it was:

> . . . abundantly clear that his mother was an abomination who, from the day of her marriage, set out to make her husband's life hell, taking away his pillows and nagging him at night so that he could not sleep, putting foul weeds into his soup, attempting to ruin him financially, even at cost to herself, so that she could have the satisfaction of seeing him reduced to working as a *valet de ferme*, engaging him in costly lawsuits and, above all, doing everything in her power to make him ridiculous and to deprive him of his honour and esteem in the eyes of an attentive and closely observant peasant community.

After all, Rivière was 'eloquent on this subject': his mother delighted in

52 Cameron and Frazer, 1987, Chapter 2.
53 Rajchman, 1985, pp 69–72.

humiliating his father, she deliberately insulted him in public, was 'probably a little mad, though always meanly calculating'. She even managed to become ill after each confinement, and it is clear she had 'detested her husband from the day of her marriage, and that what kept her going was making his life miserable'. Furthermore, 'she seems to have had a daughter worthy of her in Victoire', whereas the villagers all agreed that the father was a 'peaceable, patient, long suffering man'.[54]

Foucault, of course, refused to comment on the case, so we cannot know whether he would have shared Cobb's views on members of the Rivière family. Nevertheless, it pays to note that a complacent, unquestioning acceptance of a killer's description of his mother as an 'abomination' – the converse side of the heroic interpretation of the killer – is common in non-feminist accounts of men's homicidal fury against women. The killer's story quickly becomes a criminological account of the woman's violent death: she deserves to die because she was a bad wife, a bad mother, a bad woman. Cobb's review is not exceptional in this regard. Other reviewers of *I, Pierre Rivière* also follow this trajectory. According to one, he wrote a memoir 'of striking beauty and insight' that shows how his 'shrewish mother' was 'the bane of his father's existence' and that they were 'only nominally married since they lived apart most of the time'. He kills her to 'relieve his father' and 'eliminate the source of the pain'.[55] Another claims it to be 'generally known' that she was 'an insufferable shrew who made his father's life abjectly miserable' throughout their unhappy marriage. Understandably then, her son had to 'deliver his father from the misery which his mother and his sister created with calculating viciousness'.[56]

Forgetfulness and the power of masculinist hegemony

It takes a more careful reading to notice that not everyone thought that Madame Rivière 'could have driven anyone insane'.[57] It takes an even more astute reading to notice who shared the killer's view of his mother, and who did not think she deserved to die. More usually, Rivière is said to have written, as Jack Katz puts it, an 'emotionally compelling account' of his crime that refers to 'a long series of deceits and monetary exploitations by his mother against his father'. Interestingly, though, it is Katz – who we met in Chapter 2 and who, as we shall see in Chapter 4, does so much to promote

---

54 Cobb, 1978, pp 551–2.
55 Klee, 1976, p 193.
56 It was also understandable that he killed his younger brother – 'an innocent child he and his father loved dearly'. He wanted to ensure his father did not grieve for him on the scaffold: Bittner, 1976, pp 257–8.
57 Kurzweil, 1977, p 412.

the idea of the seductiveness of criminal violence – who notices that Rivière glossed over the details of the killings, the brutality of his lethal attacks, the number of blows 'which extended beyond what was necessary to accomplish death', and his mother's advanced state of pregnancy at the time. As he points out, omitting these details enabled the killer to continue 'his attack on his mother before a new, larger audience'. Furthermore, commentators, Foucault included, have also discounted these 'situational details' in favour of broader sociological and historical themes. In doing so, they have all 'literally rationalised' the killings, a 'viciously cruel, extremely messy act', interpreting them as 'the logical outcome of an ongoing family injustice' or of the class positions of French peasants, thereby missing 'the gruesome lived reality' of the homicides.[58]

Katz himself does not dwell on what it might mean to confront that gruesome reality, other than to express regret that another opportunity to track 'the lived mysticism and magic in the foreground of criminal experience' has gone begging.[59] Having got so close to the heart of the problem with Foucault's analysis, namely that it has the effect of rationalising and erasing the vicious and messy homicides, he retreats from a line of thought that might have led him to problematise masculinist readings of the case that identify with the killer and provide him with understandable motives for homicide, notably mother-hatred. Far from identifying with the gruesome lived reality of the victims, he wants to get emotionally close to the killer, to get into 'the foreground', the moment of frenzied homicidal violence in order to experience its lived magic. It follows that he has no interest in questioning Foucault's notion that the homicides were 'liberating'. He does not ask, as we do here, liberating for whom? How could a text explaining, and thus justifying, the killing of three members of his family be interpreted as 'liberating'? How could Foucault have been blinded to what his methodological precaution about studying 'local' power should have made palpably obvious, namely power within the Rivière family? After all, his stated aim was to detach the power of truth from forms of hegemony operating at any given time. Yet when he waxed eloquent about Rivière's 'liberating' crime and confessed to having fallen under his spell, he succumbed to what Renate Holub calls – referring to Gramsci – 'a forgetting', a forgetting of 'his own powerful analytical tools in the demystification of power'. What Gramsci forgot – interestingly, when he addressed the question of women's emancipation – was 'the ubiquitous operations of hegemony', the operation of certain ways of seeing and validating relationships in the public, but above all in the private sphere, 'in the cultural, in the micro-spaces of everyday

58 Katz, 1988, pp 310–11.
59 Katz, 1988, p 311.

life'.[60] What Foucault forgot when he analysed the Rivière case, was not only his commitment to studying power at the local level and to unpacking the discursive constitution of hegemonic truths; he also forgot almost all of his methodological rules for studying the operation of power.

Being blinded by hegemonic masculinist perspectives on gendered relationships is not something that is confined to men and non-feminists. Consider, for example, the case of Chris Weedon, author of the influential feminist exposition of poststructuralist theories that we drew on in Chapter 1. Strangely, Weedon adopts an unquestioning passive tense to summarise Foucault's interpretation of 'Rivière's deed'. That deed, she says, 'is interpreted as a protest against the intolerable conditions of everyday life in the French countryside, in which poverty, disease and exploitation deprived the peasants of their humanity'. She continues:

> . . . Rivière, it is argued, was making a bid to speak out through his deed . . . Pierre Rivière is interpreted as a questioner of the system without the right to speak. Rivière's deed is not only a bid to speak, but in speaking, to change the social power relations in which the exclusion of the peasantry from the social nexus . . . led to their occupying no social position at all.[61]

Weedon views this version of history as one with 'much explanatory power' inasmuch as it demonstrates the implications of discursive contests over meaning for individual groups and classes and 'the effects of silencing on a class which had been led to believe that it now had a right to be heard'.[62] That this peasant hero, this rebel questioner of the system, killed two peasant women and a little boy, depriving them of *their* right to be heard somehow eludes her. But Weedon is by no means the only feminist to have been caught short. In the course of developing a feminist jurisprudence – a poststructuralist feminist jurisprudence, no less – Marie Ashe praises Foucault for showing, in his reading of the Rivière case, that 'the master narratives of a culture are susceptible to the challenge and resistance expressed by first person narratives in the voice of individual subjects'.[63] Once again, what is overlooked is that far from resisting his culture's master narratives about

---

60 Holub, 1992, p 198.
61 Weedon, 1987, pp 115–16.
62 Weedon, 1987, pp 115–17.
63 Ashe, 1995, p 106. In a book about 'sexing the self', Elspeth Probyn finds nothing problematic about Foucault's decision to let Pierre's discourse 'stand alone without any detracting commentary'. Nor does Moya Lloyd see anything odd in Probyn's interpretation of his memoir as exemplifying the confessional production of the self, a process that might be a means of 'refiguring feminist notions of experience': Lloyd, 1996, p 261. Neither has anything to say about how the lives and deaths of the victims in this case might be reconfigured.

subordinating gendered relationships, Pierre reinforced them, and while he is left to bask in the glory of heroic subjectivity, his hapless victims are reduced to annihilated objects. Such is the power of hegemonic masculinist discourses to pass as truth and catch nearly everyone out.

A counter-hegemonic reading

But not absolutely everyone. In a rare counter-hegemonic reading of the case, Julie Marcus takes Foucault to task for failing to take account of gender in his analysis of the trial documents. It is an audacious, heretical reading, one that strives to understand 'the difference gender makes'. Simply put, Marcus argues that Foucault and his followers have failed to notice that the killer was a man and his victims were women and a young boy who lived with them. But there is much more to her critique than that. Taking up what she calls 'an engendered and non-patriarchal position', Marcus begins by noting the gender of the killer and his victims and returning to what she refers to as the 'facts of the matter'. They are that Pierre was aged 20 at the time of the murders, and the eldest child of his mother, Victoire Brion Rivière. She was aged about 40 and was 7 months pregnant when she was murdered. Five of her children were alive, but at least one had already died. Pierre also slaughtered his 18-year-old sister Victoire and his 8-year-old brother Jules. Each was severely hacked and bashed about the head and his mother's head was nearly severed from her body. Madam Rivière lived apart from her husband and the children were spread across the two households, Pierre living with his father, while his victims lived with his mother. As Marcus puts it, Pierre killed 'the mother-led family in its entirety'. She also takes note of his virulent hatred of women, and even of female animals, and his strange fear of an incestuous encounter with the women in his family. Desubujating the subjugated local knowledges overlooked in the case, she spots the evidence in the documents *for* his mother, the evidence that the courts supported her in her legal battles with her husband over property distribution. When Pierre's memoir – the document Foucault famously refused to analyse – is read 'from an engendered and non-patriarchal position', the standard representations of the wife as 'shrewish and disputatious and those of the husband as gentle and forbearing, at once become suspect'.[64]

Shaking us out of a complacent acceptance of the killer's self-justifying account of his homicidal solution to his father's matrimonial problems and of his crimes as liberating and heroic, Marcus single-handedly breaks the strange spell cast over Foucault and his followers by a mother-hating parricide. Catapulted back to the other court documents by her counter-hegemonic reading of the case, we find what he missed – ample material for

64 Marcus, 1989, pp 67–9.

challenging the hegemonic view of Pierre as a peasant hero and, more importantly, for conducting a genealogy of the local subjugated knowledges and power relations at the most local, most immediate level – that of the family. Contrary to the impression created in masculinist readings of the case, the villagers were divided in their opinions of the family. While prominent local men described Pierre's father as 'the mildest of men', claiming it was 'the general opinion' that the wife was 'in the wrong', others villagers, including widows and farmers' wives, spoke of Pierre's strange habits and aversion to women. One neighbour recalled an incident at his grandmother's house. The neighbour's arrival at the house had apparently caused him to see the devil in the fireplace. But this was not an isolated incident – he 'had often behaved in the same way towards other women'.[65] Again, while medical witnesses in the case referred to the murdered woman's 'self-willed, imperious and shrewish disposition' which for years had made her husband's life burdensome, and while the local press played up her reputation as 'something of a shrew', Pierre himself admitted, much to his chagrin, that the courts considering the financial disputes between his parents supported his mother against his father.[66] Indeed, it is from his doting son that we learn that his father – the man whose honour Pierre wanted to protect – was a violent bully who battered and raped his wife. In his Memoir, he catalogues Rivière senior's attacks on his mother, including an incident when he held her captive while grain was loaded onto a wagon against her wishes. His sister's desperate efforts to protect her mother from her violent father are also recorded. Yet in Pierre's victim-blaming and self-justifying ramblings, it is his mother who had 'sinned against God', his sister and brother who had sinned by remaining with her, and all three were 'in league to persecute my father'. And it is this incoherent story – that he had planned to kill them all to avenge his father, or because he 'saw God who ordered me to do it', or to help his father out of 'his difficulties' and to 'deliver him from an evil woman who had plagued him continually ever since she became his wife' – that has been transformed, with Foucault's blessing, into the tale of heroic peasant rebellion.[67]

Rejecting this the received view that the violence in the Rivière family originated in peasant unrest, as Foucault and his followers suggest, Julie Marcus argues that it originated in the 'gender hierarchies' in the family. More precisely, she sees Pierre's 'deed' not simply as an act of violence, but as an act of 'violence against women who were set in a special relationship to him'. Accordingly, it needs to be removed from the category of 'rural violence' and placed in the context of family violence. To that end, she links

---

65 Foucault, 1982a, pp 10 and 24–30.
66 Foucault, 1982a, pp 16, 92 and 96–7.
67 Foucault, 1982a, pp 89, 14, 21 and 24–5.

Pierre to family-killers in late twentieth-century Australia. Writing in 1989, Marcus referred to contemporary cases of custody battles resulting in men murdering their wives and children, and to research indicating the disproportionate numbers of women killed in Australia by men in so-called 'domestic murders'. Like Pierre, these Australian family-killers were asserting power 'once and for all over their wives and children'. They were not giving voice to 'a truth that could otherwise not be spoken', nor were they resorting to violence simply because it was 'an historically violent time'.[68] Rather, violence was 'inherent in everyday life' and 'real physical violence against real bodies' is the way in which, 'in the end, and no matter how inefficiently, existing power relations will be upheld'. Moreover:

> It is the logic of violence in conjunction with the logic of a hierarchical and obsessively unrestrained masculinity that leads some men to assert themselves through a murderous demonstration of practical power relations. The family killer may be frustrated by discursive contradictions, but they are those that result from a hierarchy of genders, not from a lack of class or status equality.[69]

Foucault, Marcus suggests, was misled by his micro-vision of power to develop a form of analysis that actually obscured the 'most immediate relations of power' – those within the family. A wider study of men who kill 'their' families might have subverted the gender-blind 'patriarchal' perspective which prevented him achieving the very thing he sought to achieve – 'an understanding of discourse and power'.[70] Of course, Foucault was also committed to reclaiming subjugated knowledges, yet gender-blindness prevented him from seeing how Pierre's highly partisan and self-serving regime of truth effaced the subjugated knowledges of his silenced victims.

Marcus's analysis highlights just how unfaithful Foucault was to his own rules for studying power. Certainly, he did identify some of the key techniques of power that operated in nineteenth century French rural courts, notably the increasing medicalisation of offenders. But he appears to have forgotten that he saw 'the level of the family' as an example of a properly 'local' study of power, telling us to identify the 'real agents' of power – for example, parents – and not to 'lump them under the formula of a generalised bourgeoisie'. What was needed, he said, was an historical analysis that began at the 'lowest level', specifically 'at the effective level of the family, of the immediate environment'.[71] Yet what else does he do here but lump the

68 Foucault, 1982a, pp 73 and 76–9.
69 Marcus, 1989, p 81.
70 Marcus, 1989, pp 81–2.
71 Foucault, 1980c, p 100.

power relations within the family under a generalised peasant class, thereby overlooking gendered power relations within that class and failing to identify 'the real agents' of power? He missed the 'micro-mechanisms of power' that he tells us operate in daily life to subject bodies and govern gestures. He forgot to ask how things work at the level of on-going subjugation. He overlooked the subjugated, violated bodies of the two peasant women and a child annihilated by a violent, angry peasant rebel. So much for claiming that 'power relations can materially penetrate the body in depth' and for proclaiming the value of an analysis that focuses on 'our bodies, our lives, our day-to-day existences' in order to highlight the power relations that exist between 'every point of a social body', such as 'between a man and a woman'.[72] Such is the power of what Marcus, writing in 1989, called 'patriarchy' – or of what I prefer to call the power of hegemonic masculinist discourse to pass as truth – that it derailed the theorist dedicated to exploring the local, leading him to forgo his own methodological rules for studying the problem of domination and subjugation at the most immediate and intimate levels of existence.[73]

Foucault's hands-off approach where, 'owing to a sort of reverence' for the killer's tale, he refused to interpret it is clearly untenable. A neutral, purportedly 'objective' interpretation of 'family' violence is simply not possible inasmuch as all interpreters of violence speak from a social location; all have a standpoint. From an anti-feminist and misogynist perspective, Madame Rivière deserved to die because she was 'shrewish' and disrespectful of her husband's authority. Foucault's interpretation – the one he thought he did not make – is more 'moderate'. He may have declined to comment on the killer's homicidal rationalisations, but he did have an opinion, and a transparently masculinist one at that. For it is only from that partisan viewpoint that one could describe the Memoir as beautiful or speak of 'reverence' for a text justifying a man's lethal violence against women and her children.[74]

Conclusion – *for* Foucault, still

It may be that Gramsci would have been better placed than Foucault to grasp the really crucial power relations at the heart of the Rivière family. As Renate Holub notes, both theorists saw power as ubiquitous, but it was Gramsci who emphasised 'the equally ubiquitous uneven relations of power'

---

72 Foucault, 1980b, pp 186–7.
73 While Marcus speaks about 'patriarchy and 'gender' in a way that is reminiscent of modes of speech typical of the era when the sex/gender distinction ruled ok, she certainly does not lose sight of the fact that 'the representation and control of women's *bodies*' were crucially at stake in the Rivière case: Gatens, 1996, p 17, original emphasis.
74 Foucault, 1982a, p iii.

– while power was everywhere, it was not everywhere in the same form or to the same degree.[75] Moreover, while Foucault focused on the 'how' of power – on how power operates at the local level – Gramsci was far more interested in exploring why power exists and for whom.[76] In Holub's view, this makes him a better candidate for feminist appropriation than Foucault. Be that as it may, it is clear that had Foucault not bracketed the question of *who* holds power, he might have noticed that the driving force behind Rivière's homicidal violence was the view that his mother, and women in general, had taken too much power from men. He might even have noticed that Victoire Rivière paid for that transgression with her life. But Gramsci might not have noticed that either. For it seems to take a feminist sensibility to register not only the 'real deaths of real women' silenced by their killers, but also the interpretative process by which they are then discursively obliterated – 'turned into objects so that the killer can be a subject'[77] – in non-feminist scholarship.

Finally, it seems that only a feminist analyst can make links between historical and contemporary cases of men's violence against women. Sadly, non-feminists appear incapable of registering the rationalisations of men's violence against women and children that are as alive and well today as they were when Foucault reflected on the sheer beauty of a memoir explaining why a man hacked to death his mother, sister and brother. While this is not to say that these rationalisations take the same form across time and space, it is nevertheless instructive that Rivière believed that the courts favoured women over men. Railing against a social order in which he believed women had too much power, he determined to die for his father and then tell the judges that while 'in former times' women were locked in power struggles with men – 'Charlotte Cordays against Marats' – now men must 'employ this mania'. For 'it is the women who are in command now in this fine age which calls itself the age of enlightenment, this nation which seems to be so avid for liberty and glory obeys women'. He had planned to tell the judges, too, that it was not right that he 'should let a woman live who is disturbing my father's peace and happiness'. And 'in time', after his execution, he believed his ideas about women's proper place would eventually be vindicated.[78] Such beliefs, as Marcus shows, still have resonances today in the views of men who rail against family courts decisions, kill children or family court judges when they lose custody battles or, more commonly, kill their wives for real or imagined slights and then plead provocation.

It *is* staggering that Foucault, who devised a methodology specifically for studying power at the local level, at its extremities, overlooked the local

75 Holub, 1992, p 29.
76 Holub, 1992, p 200.
77 Cameron, 1994, p 112.
78 Foucault, 1982a, pp 107–8.

power relationships within the Rivière family. It is remarkable too that a theorist who set such stock on analysing the interweaving of effects of power and knowledge and on revealing the discursive production of truth could not see the gendered power relationships at the heart of the homicidal violence; and moreover, that he could miss all this while elevating men's viewpoints and values. He may be a saint, even a 'fucking saint' to Foucauldians like David Halperin, but to a feminist student like the one who penned 'Ode to Foucault', he was most definitely not. It did not take her long at all to work out that:

> he wasn't a saint, he wasn't that good with women
> In fact when it came to feminism he was in the deep end barely swimming.[79]

Still, Foucault can be forgiven his lapses for he has bequeathed to us such valuable methodological advice about how to study power and how to unravel discursive constructions of 'reality' and 'truth'. He has also, of course, enlightened us, albeit in ways that escaped him, about the close relationship between men's violence against women and discourses about that violence. As we shall see later, feminist scholars have deployed Foucauldian discourse analysis in a variety of ways to illuminate questions of sex, violence and crime. They are not deployments Foucault envisaged, but he, surely, would have been the first to applaud the drive to utilise his methodological insights in ways he could never have imagined, even against him. For that, as he said himself, was the only valid tribute to thought.

79 Halperin, 1995, p 6. Alexia Peniguel, 'Ode to Foucault', 1998, cited with permission.

Chapter 4

'Critical' criminology, postmodernism and the 'Man' question

In Chapter 2 we saw that mainstream criminologists have overlooked several decades of feminist critique of conventional accounts of men's violent acts against women that confuse the issues of who is doing what to whom. Oblivious to this work, they continue to churn out ostensibly gender-neutral explanations of 'intersexual' violence that feature provoked 'males' being upset by irritating, non-compliant 'females', and 'females' being equally or more violent than men. We saw too that feminist queries about the 'sex' of sex crimes have had a negligible impact on mainstream criminology. Then, in Chapter 3, we saw that Foucault, a renowned anti-criminologist, also slipped up when faced with regimes of truth about men's violence against women. Foucault, however, was by no means the only critical thinker to do so. Several varieties of so-called 'new' or 'critical' criminology that followed in the wake of his ground-breaking work, *Discipline and Punish*, also stumble over the 'Man' question.

In its earliest manifestations nearly four decades ago, critical criminology was a force to be reckoned with. Most crucially, it provided a formidable challenge to positivistic criminology's classificatory and etiological obsessions with individual offenders and the factors driving them to commit crime. Critical criminology has a number of founding fathers, perhaps none more influential than David Matza who, in his now classic book, *Delinquency and Drift*, argued that young offenders are not so much driven to crime by predisposing background factors, but rather drift into, and out of, delinquency. Crime, he and others started to suggest in the 1960s, was less an identity than a label imposed by law enforcement agents.[1] Since that time, many criminologists have taken what has been called the 'constructivist turn' – a turn away from positivism's correctionalist bias and essentialising 'deviant'-versus-'normal' categories and towards the state's power to criminalise. With etiological questions off the agenda, at least as far as asking about how individuals become deviants and criminals, critical criminologists

1 Matza, 1964.

set about demolishing the unitary notion of crime and other positivistic assumptions about crime's 'reality' as a distinctive, measurable phenomenon. The emphasis shifted to criminalisation processes that impacted disproportionately on subordinated and marginalised social groups and that detracted attention away from the enormous social harms done by powerful social groups and institutions. The key question became: how is crime socially constructed?

Since the publication in 1973 of Taylor, Walton and Young's, *The New Criminology*, another key foundational critical text, critical criminology has proliferated into several sometimes competing branches, including left realist, conflict, Marxist, feminist, abolitionist, postmodern and 'cultural' criminologies. This development has transformed the criminological enterprise, although it should be said that the most rigorous debates within the discipline have been between critical criminologists, rather than between mainstream and critical ones. Perhaps the most notable debates have been those between left realism – spawned as a result of a perceived 'etiological crisis' brought on by anxiety about abandoning causal analysis – and its many feminist and abolitionist critics. What follows, however, is not an overview of these internal differences of opinion, much less a critical assessment of the various contributions to an understanding of crime and punishment made by various brands of critical criminologists. This chapter focuses instead on some strange moments in masculinist versions of critical criminology. This is not to say that feminist criminology has not had its strange moments. As Beverley Brown observed 20 years ago, something very odd indeed happened on the way to developing a feminist criminology. Not only were its early proponents themselves the first to express doubts about whether such a project was feasible; they also completely misread what the positivistic fathers of criminology had to say about the 'female criminal'.[2]

The extraordinarily complex conundrums besetting the 'Woman' question in criminology that Brown so carefully delineates need not detain us.[3] Our concern is with the 'Man' question which I have formulated as the querying of the place occupied or vacated by men in accounts of men's violence against women. This chapter asks, first, what happens to men, discursively speaking, when critical criminologists put sex, violence and crime into discourse? Second, given this book's investment in placing sex,

2 According to Brown, feminists were so preoccupied in establishing their own 'foundation-by-denunciation' that they assumed that their 'misogyny-and-biological critiques' could take aim at theories of female criminality that did not in fact toe the line of biological determinism: Brown, 1985, pp 356–60 and 385–6.
3 Brown also has a 'Man' question which she formulates as the 'endless re-discovery of the link between "normal" and criminal conduct': Brown, 1985, p 401. For other versions, see Ferguson, 1993 and Naffine, 2003.

violence and crime in a postmodern frame, how do critical criminologists frame postmodern theory? Third, what happens when critical criminologists extol the virtues of focusing on emotion or 'foreground' factors in order to understand crime's putatively seductive quality? And finally, what happens when they place masculinity – or, increasingly frequent, masculinities – in the foreground of their criminological work?

At the risk of giving away too much about the depths to which critique can sink when critical criminologists address men's violence, I will foreshadow some of the strange and decidedly uncritical things that have happened. Carried away perhaps with the excitement of being up close and personal with the sensual thrill of it all, some critical criminologists resort to outmoded conceptualisations of 'gender' reminiscent of the old-order criminology they claim to have supplanted. Others revert to the time-honoured etiological focus on inadequate working-class mothers and their much-put-upon sensitive sons who grow up to be violent men. And while some appear to be beset by a knowing defensive cringe, a sort of masculinist *mea culpa* angst in the face of the massive numerical imbalance of lethal and non-lethal attacks committed by men against women, still others are completely oblivious to the fact that the question of men is a question at all when it comes to thinking about violent crime. Perhaps strangest of all, the anti-feminism of much of this putatively 'critical' criminology has slipped under the radar of most feminist criminologists.

We begin with Stan Cohen's rabidly anti-postmodern *States of Denial*, then move on to consider a self-identifying 'postmodern criminology' that emerged in North America in the last decade of the twentieth century. Postmodern criminology has attracted surprisingly little attention, and certainly far less than left realism. Here it is well to recall Carol Smart's assessment of left realism as hopelessly 'modernist'. Modernism, she points out, is an 'intellectual mode of modern thought' identified by numerous critics as synonymous with racism, sexism and Eurocentrism.[4] We shall see whether postmodern criminology supplies any reason to reassess Smart's damning indictment of the whole criminological enterprise, from its modernist through to its supposedly critical manifestations. Next, we examine a branch of crime and masculinities studies that cavorts under the name of 'social psychology'. Finally, we return briefly to the question of serial killers to see how their homicidal violence is framed in social constructivist and poststructuralist-inflected analyses. Readers should not expect a substantive critique of any of this work. Our focus remains firmly on what happens to men, discursively speaking, when critical criminologists put sexed violence into discourse.

4 Smart, 1990a, p 75.

Critical criminology meets postmodern theory – nervous encounters

Critical criminologists have had wildly divergent responses to postmodern theories. While some endorse them cautiously, others embrace them, putting them to work on criminology-related projects. At the other end of the spectrum of opinion, some critical criminologists have penned wholesale condemnations, holding postmodernism responsible for the demise of critical thinking and, worse, for denying 'reality'. Rather than getting embroiled in such skirmishes, let us turn instead to a book review that, in a most helpful way, prises open the door for a critique of critical criminology's encounter with postmodern theory and of its discursive constitution of sexed violence. The reviewer is Ngaire Naffine and the book is *The Futures of Criminology*, an edited collection which has as a key theme the impact of postmodernism on the criminology discipline. But as we shall see, some contributors not only confound the idea of what postmodern theory *is*; they make nervous judgments about what it *does*.

The editor, David Nelken, is a case in point. Nelken is very ambivalent about postmodernism. On the one hand, he rejects the idea that postmodern methodologies such as Derrida's deconstruction lead to nihilism. On the other hand, he is nervous about postmodernity's challenge to modernist certainties, declaring it to be 'more important to find means to check the reality of our representations rather than put in doubt representationism itself'.[5] Postmodernism is worrying because it seems to unsettle 'our' efforts to represent the world. This claim prompts Naffine to ask some probing questions about 'the reality' against which 'our representations' are to be checked. Who, she asks, is in charge of representations of 'reality' and how do they reach agreement about 'reality'? Could it be that agreement is reached through the suppression of those with different opinions? Most pertinently to our inquiry here, Naffine suggests that the family might seem to be real, and 'a fine, solid human institution' at that, when women lacked a voice to reveal the violence which often occurs within in it. If women are silent about men's violence in the home, they may provide 'much greater social certainty' for those, like Nelken, who worry about postmodern challenges to representational practices – the social world might look 'more inviolate, more real' when discordant voices are suppressed.[6]

Relatedly, Naffine notes a tension in the volume that is particularly evident in Nelken's introduction. On the one hand, Nelken recognises that concepts of crime are culturally variable and that comparative criminology can help criminologists to see the partiality of their own perspectives. On the

5 Nelken, 1994, p 17. This and the following section expand on an earlier critique: see Howe, 2000b.
6 Naffine, 1995, pp 198–9.

other, he is very wary of looking too closely at his frame of reference, leading Naffine to remark on his disinclination to 'entertain more than a modest amount of critical self-reflection'.[7] Certainly, there is much to evidence this disinclination on Nelken's part. He is nervous about the prospect of going 'too far' in the direction of reflexivity and deconstruction; he worries about the effects of some forms of postmodern writing on 'the normal proprieties of intellectual debate'; he puts considerable emphasis on 'the limits to our ability to take into account the influence of our identity, interests and cultural values in the way we formulate our questions', and he rails against going too far with 'open declarations of partiality, bias and relativism'.[8] But who, exactly, are the ones with such a limited ability to take account of their own identity? Are they the same ones who determine the 'normal proprieties' of debate? Privileged, white, middle-class, heterosexual, 'benchmark' men are the usual suspects.[9] Does Nelken speak for them when he suggests that criminologists interested in 'sexual, racial and ethnic difference' may assist in finding 'new ways to incorporate "outsider" voices'?[10] Is he implying that the incorporation of outsider voices is not a job for those at the centre, but rather those on the periphery who do work on the question of difference? Does he simply assume that those unencumbered by the mark of difference are too busy speaking for everyone to acknowledge their own privileged difference and partiality?

And what has become of the key constructivist insight that 'reality' is discursively constituted? Nelken resists its implications, refusing to let go of the idea of a world existing beyond representation, and also holding fast to a belief in 'the impartial, the unbiased and the objective – of that against which we can match our cultural constructions to see if we have got them right'. But, Naffine asks, 'where is this place?'.[11] Her response bears quoting in full because it restates so lucidly the much-misunderstood postmodernist take on the relationship between 'reality' and representation. Nelken, she says, 'stops short of examining the limits and the means of representation, which is of course always effected through language'. She continues:

> His implied allusions to the real, the undistorted, seems to suggest that there is a point at which we can stop navel gazing and free ourselves from our own devices for making sense of the world, when we can check our linguistic representations against some reality unsullied by interpretation. But what he seems reluctant to concede is that we are always stuck with and within representation – that there is no unrepresented or

7 Naffine, 1995, p 199.
8 Nelken, 1994, pp 18, 21 and 24.
9 The phrase 'benchmark men' is borrowed from Thornton, 1996, p 2.
10 Nelken, 1994, p 23.
11 Naffine, 1995, p 200.

uninterpreted reality with which to compare our representations, for as soon as we endeavour to approach that notional uninterpreted reality, we find that we can only ever do so with yet more representations.[12]

Furthermore, to insist that it is not possible to get outside of representation or to have direct, unmediated access to the real is not to say that nothing is real, or that nothing meaningful can be said about it. On the contrary, paying attention to our speaking positions and 'rules of our language games' is not an act of denial. To examine 'the means by which we represent reality', whoever 'we' are, is to 'engage in a positive task of critical reflection on how we make sense to each other'.[13] In Naffine's view then – and mine – post-modernism is far from being a destructive or nihilistic force as anti-postmodernists like eminent critical criminologist Stan Cohen assume.

Cohen's state of denial

We met Cohen in the Introduction, where we left him deploring post-modernism as a sign of intellectual failure and moral turpitude. Cohen's dismissal of postmodernism as 'mindless relativism' in *States of Denial* turns out to be the latest in a series of denunciations. In his chapter in Nelken's *Futures of Criminology*, for example, Cohen does his best to ensure that postmodernists do not have a future in criminology, accusing them of pro-posing that crime and fear of crime can be 'deconstructed away'.[14] Once again, Naffine does her best to counter this allegation, pointing out that deconstruction, Derrida's method, far from eliminating the ability to com-municate, makes us 'more attentive to the way meaning works'. Moreover, postmodern methods such as deconstruction or discourse analysis help us appreciate the limits to our own frames of references and 'the value of listening to others'.[15] Taking leave of Naffine and her valiant efforts to explain postmodern theory to its uninformed opponents, let us turn now to explore what happens to the problem of men's violence in a virulently anti-postmodern critical criminology text like Cohen's *States of Denial*.

Given the sheer scale of reports and statistical analyses recording the prevalence of 'domestic' and other forms of men's violence against women across the globe, one might have expected to find suffering on such a scale to occupy a prominent place in *States of Denial*. It is barely mentioned. An attack on a woman, Kitty Genovese, in a New York street in 1964 is men-tioned several times, but we are never told by whom she was assaulted, and

12 Naffine, 1995, p 200.
13 Naffine, 1995, pp 201–2.
14 Cohen, 1994, p 85.
15 Naffine, 1995, pp 202–5.

there are no references at all to the tens of thousands of women attacked in the street by men during the four decades that elapsed between that attack and the publication of Cohen's book. Moreover, Cohen configures the Genovese case as one of bystander passivity, not of men's violence, just as child sexual assault is a case of a mother not knowing, or denying, that her husband is assaulting her daughter. While he acknowledges that states of denial divert attention away from the violence and sexual abuse committed in the family, he writes about violence committed by ungendered and unnamed 'family members' who cause 'family suffering' to unspecified individuals in the private realm. We learn that the assailant is a man in one case only because the denier is a woman telling herself that her husband could not have done that to their daughter.[16] With the focus kept firmly on the problem of the denier, the violence of the perpetrator is left unaddressed.

How does a book about suffering and states of denial manage to avoid discussing the huge number of documented cases of women and children suffering at the hands of men in the private and public spheres? First, it re-assembles the private/public distinction carefully dismantled by feminist and other critical scholars over the last three decades. This enables forms of private suffering such as 'domestic violence against women' to be trivialised. For while it is acknowledged that a great deal of 'human suffering' takes place in private, such 'private' or 'everyday' human suffering is simply a precursor to the main event in *States of Denial*: 'the worlds of mass suffering and public atrocities'.[17] This in itself is a palpable form of denial and, interestingly, most of the fleeting references to domestic violence in the book appear in the chapter on 'denial at work'. Domestic violence, we are informed, used to be denied. It was 'normalised, contained and covered up' before feminist movements exposed it, leading to the instigation of support services for victims. So now it is much harder for offenders to offer excuses such as the old standby: 'she-asked-for-it'. The countries where this has happened are never specified. We are told only that domestic violence has not been exposed in some 'contemporary societies' where 'cultural interpretations and neutralisations' encourage 'a dulled, passive acceptance of violence', exemplified by the notion that 'this is what men are like' – men finally making their one and only appearance in the discussion of domestic violence. Significantly, however, the contemporary societies that Cohen has in mind do not appear to be Western ones inasmuch as the only example he provides is that of Palestine where women are 'trapped in a culture' that blames them for their husbands' violence.[18]

For over 30 years now, critical scholars have launched scathing attacks on

16 Cohen, 2001, pp 3–7.
17 Cohen, 2001, pp 15 and 51.
18 Cohen, 2001, pp 51–2.

precisely this kind of orientalist framing of an enlightened, progressive West and a backward and uncivilised 'non-West' that is invariably represented by a Muslim country. Feminist scholars, for example, have exposed how Western attitudes to women and to men's violence against women are informed by exculpatory and frequently misogynist cultural scripts. 'We', too, have a culture and cultural interpretations of violence against women that are re-inscribed in Western criminal laws, notably in the provocation defences resorted to by men who kill their current or former women partners. Copious feminist research on the way in which provocation operates as a cultural defence in Western jurisdictions has not impacted on Cohen's telling of the story of 'domestic violence'.[19] As I pointed out earlier, the emphatic distinction made between private ('domestic') suffering and public suffering and atrocities that take place in 'political settings' serves to valorise the latter as 'real' suffering, while demoting gender-specific states of injury experienced by women.[20] This, in turn, effectively depoliticises men's violence against women, whether it occurs in private or public 'settings'. In short, three decades of feminist efforts to politicise men's violence against women are barely recognised in *States of Denial*.

Just as paradoxical for a book about suffering and states of denial is the handling of the complex issue of adults dealing with repressed memories of child sexual abuse. The Recovered Memory Movement is condemned – oddly, in decidedly postmodern terms – for holding the 'essentialist' view that there is 'only one truth' that is there 'just waiting to be uncovered'. Such is Cohen's disdain for meddling therapists and for personal accounts of suffering as opposed to 'histories of known atrocities' that he is prepared to adopt a postmodern perspective on the construction of 'truth'.[21] Only when he moves on to the world of public, and therefore 'political' suffering, does he recover his composure, returning to the fray to berate 'postmodern forgetting' – a dastardly form of forgetting that supplements older states of denial of political atrocities with a 'mindless relativism' that insists on 'the stupid idea that there must always be another point of view'.[22] So, in one context – the private one of child sexual assault – it is stupid to believe there is only one truth; in others – the public world of real suffering – it is stupid to believe in multiple perspectives. In what a poststructuralist might describe as a stunning 'act of conceptual mastery', Cohen simply assumes the right to decide when truth claims are stupid or not.[23] Clearly, he has no interest in reflecting on how his privileged speaking position is imbricated in a field of power. Leave that to the postmodernists who might be moved to point out

19 See, e.g. Bandalli, 1995, Volpp, 1996, Howe, 2004b.
20 Cohen, 2001, pp 75–6.
21 Cohen, 2001, pp 124–5.
22 Cohen, 2001, p 244.
23 Butler, 1992, pp 6–7.

that one of the most deleterious effects of Cohen's preoccupation with the alleged sins of postmodernism in *States of Denial* is a profound state of denial about men's violence against women.

In sum, women's suffering at the hands of men is completely effaced in Cohen's account of suffering and denial, disappearing under an onslaught of anti-postmodern *animus*. Does that suffering attract more serious attention in texts produced by critical criminologists who are *for* postmodern theories? Let us see how the 'Man' question is handled in a brand of critical criminology that calls itself postmodern criminology.

'Postmodern criminology'

The dubious distinction of fathering postmodern criminology belongs to Henry and Milovanovic, advocates of a form of 'affirmative postmodernism' that they call 'constitutive criminology'. It might be helpful to begin by outlining the main premises of constitutive criminology, but this is no easy task. As Naffine has observed, postmodern criminologists have a tendency to misread the various theories that are clustered under this sign as meaning 'that anything goes', leading them to write 'nonsense'. She cites, by way of pertinent example, a passage from one of Henry and Milovanovic's elaborations of constitutive criminology – in their chapter in Nelken's *Futures of Criminology*. The passage Naffine cites certainly supports her claim that convoluted prose renders their argument virtually incomprehensible.[24] One also searches in vain for a clear, non-vacuous exposition of their theory in their book, *Constitutive Criminology: Beyond Postmodernism*, which, judging by the title, is not so much promoting postmodern as post-postmodern criminology. Here they repeat the familiar charge that some versions of postmodern theory are 'nihilistic', while insisting that their 'affirmative postmodernism' is to be distinguished from sceptical and nihilistic varieties because it recognises 'the potential of infinitely revisable recovering subjects in conjunction with a dynamic, fluid and emergent structure' – whatever that means.[25] For the most part, affirmative postmodernism reads like an eclectic mishmash, or affirmation, of everything criminology has ever offered. Nothing is to be dispensed with, much less criticised. The trick seems to be to stay positive about the redemptive powers of every idea the discipline has ever had to offer. Even biologically-based personality theories that represent humans as subject to criminogenic predispositions, are included in the list of criminological perspectives that add 'insight to our knowledge about crime'.[26]

---

24 Naffine, 1995, p 204 citing Henry and Milovanovic, 1994, p 114.
25 Henry and Milovanovic, 1996, p 241.
26 Henry and Milovanovic, 1996, pp 1–2.

Our affirmative postmodern criminologists appear to have forgotten that such theories are precisely the kind that critical criminologists attacked when they set about making an epistemological and political break with positivistic criminological paradigms. It seems unlikely, however, that theirs could be characterised as a 'postmodern forgetting' – the kind that Cohen despises – for they share Cohen's concerns about postmodernism, or at least, its earlier, apparently nihilistic forms. Affirmative postmodernists are not to be confused with those 'sceptical postmodernists' whom Cohen decries as being preoccupied with 'deconstructive critique'.[27] These sceptics, they agree, are altogether too negative, relativistic and fatalistic, even apparently, prone to denying that there are 'concrete victims'.[28] By contrast, affirmative postmodernists aim at reconstruction. Theirs is 'a paradigm not only for deconstructing oppressive forms, but also for affirmatively reconstructing the new order'.[29]

While it is not easy to decipher exactly what affirmative postmodernism entails, three strategies stand out. First, be inclusive. Throw everything into the pot – modernist positivistic theories, anti-positivist postmodern theories, at least the 'affirmative' variety, and even feminist theories, at least, the less 'extreme' versions – and stir it into a 'replacement discourse' that 'goes beyond' the nihilism of the sceptics.[30] Second, state that you are abandoning 'the futile search for causes of crime'; then modify your position, reclaim causation as an important criminological concern, and take 'an alternative postmodernist position on causality'. This position provides 'an alternative mapping of "causal" chains where the very notion of "cause" becomes problematic'.[31] That is to say, causes might be problematic but they should not be abandoned as they are by 'extreme' or sceptical postmodernists who think that traditional, mainstream criminology is 'hopelessly' modernist and 'devoid of *any* utility'.[32] Third, acclaim Jack Katz's book, *Seductions of Crime*, as a 'vibrant criminology' that is well on the way to developing a theory of causality 'consistent with postmodern analysis'.[33]

Henry and Milovanovic go to great lengths to show that they do not wish to reject 'all components of modern thought' as they believe the sceptics do.[34] They want to be reconstructive. Even when it comes to the fraught issue of causation, they strive to be rehabilitative. To that end, they give Katz

---

27 Henry and Milovanovic, 1996, p 5.
28 Cohen, 2001, p 111.
29 Milovanovic, 1996, p 567.
30 Henry and Milovanovic, 1994, p 130.
31 Henry and Milovanovic, 1994, pp 120 and 150–2.
32 MacLean and Milovanovic, 1997, p 76, original emphasis, citing Howe, 1997a. My work is said to exemplify the 'nihilistic form of postmodern analysis' in Milovanovic, 2000, p 213.
33 Henry and Milovanovic, 1994, p 158.
34 Henry and Milovanovic, 1996, p 76.

pride of place in a newly-devised lineage of a 'postmodern' explanatory model that they trace back to David Matza's concepts of 'drift' and 'the invitational edge' and forward to constitutive criminology. Katz's approach might be rooted in a 'modernist' paradigm, but it foregrounds subjective factors that are 'Nietzschean in character'.[35] Importantly, his notions of humiliation, righteousness, rage and transcendence can be linked together with Stephen Lyng's concept of 'edgework' or voluntary risk taking. In this synthesis, Katz's work on the seductions of crime is read as a 'phenomenology of pleasure', as 'a general account of the attractions of exciting and transcending activity, focused down to explain particular types of crime'. So, while there might appear to be major differences between voluntary risk takers and 'criminals driven by rage', Henry and Milovanovic subscribe to the view that synthesising Lyng and Katz's ideas can show how criminals and 'legitimate edgeworkers' all act on strong sensations to 'sweep aside the rational constraints of modern Western culture in order to achieve emotional transcendence'.[36] For affirmative postmodernists, it is this 'Katz-Lyng synthesis' which provides the basis for a 'more postmodern-orientated model' for explaining crime. This model helps to explain why a person who feels degraded and humiliated might translate these emotions into 'an aggressive display' or even a violent attack culminating in 'righteous slaughter' – that being one of Katz's much-admired case studies of transcendental achievement. In brief, they believe that the postmodern explanatory model is very useful for understanding 'escalating hostilities in various interpersonal situations'.[37]

Dense and confusing though readers might find affirmative postmodernism, two questions may spring to mind. First, how can positivistic theories be forged together with postmodern theories when, from any postmodern perspective, positivism has so many well-documented conceptual inadequacies? Second, does the affirmative postmodernist explanatory model not look a lot like the positivistic paradigm that searches for factors driving individuals to commit crime – the very same paradigm that Matza explicitly rejected? Leaving these puzzles aside for the moment, let us turn to Katz's book to see why it has struck such a 'responsive chord' with critical criminologists who have acclaimed it as an exciting new post-positivistic approach to criminality.

The seductions of crime

While Katz never claimed to be a postmodern criminologist himself, *Seductions of Crime* does commence with an ostensibly strong anti-positivistic

35 Henry and Milovanovic, 1996, p 156. See Matza, 1964 and 1969.
36 O'Malley and Mugford, 1994, pp 194–6 and 209.
37 Milovanovic, 1996, pp 590–2.

stance, presenting itself as a challenge to the traditional criminological focus on background causes of criminal behaviour. The problem with positivistic criminology, according to Katz, is that it has failed to explain crime. On the one hand, many folk in the 'supposedly causal categories' do not commit crime. On the other, many who do not fit the categories do commit crime. Furthermore, many who do commit crimes do not do so all the time. To really understand crime we need to shift the focus from 'background forces' such as 'defects' in the psychological backgrounds or social environments of offenders to 'foreground' factors – the 'positive, often wonderful attractions within the lived experience of criminality', the 'seductive qualities' of crime no less. In short, we need to discover the 'magic in motivation'. Yet for all the acclaim Katz has received for providing a 'novel' approach to understanding crime, he remains committed to causal analysis. Not only does he argue that 'something causally essential happens in the very moments in which a crime is committed', he also names 'emotional processes that seduce people to deviance' as a 'causal condition' of crime.[38] Moreover, while staking his claim to fame by extolling 'the lived mysticism and magic in the foreground of criminal experience', he does not give up on background factors, instead calling for a 'systematic empirical theory' that can explain 'the causal process of committing a crime' at the individual and aggregate levels.[39]

But Katz's positivistic commitment to extending causal analysis is not the only troubling aspect of *Seductions of Crime*. Worryingly, the key to unlocking crime's 'seductive appeal' lies in tracing 'the emergence of distinctive sensual dynamics' and in grasping the 'magic in the criminal's sensuality' and the 'sensual attractions of doing evil'. Take, for example, the 'sensual magic' of turning 'initially lighthearted thrusts and parries' during sex into 'the real thing without warning'. Identifying such sensual attractions requires an 'aesthetic finesse in recognising and elaborating on the sensual possibilities' of 'criminal projects' such as hot and cold-blooded murder, property crime and commercial robbery. More specifically, it requires an ethical sensibility, one attuned to 'moral emotions' such as 'humiliation, righteousness, arrogance, ridicule, cynicism, defilement and vengeance'. Crucially, the most compelling and often fatal attraction of crime lies in 'overcoming a personal challenge to moral – not to material – existence'. This is the spark that sets off the potential impassioned killer to strive to embody 'through the practice of "righteous" slaughter, some eternal, universal form of the Good'. The ultimate aim is to show that 'a theory of moral self-transcendence can make comprehensible the minutia of experiential details in the phenomenal foreground, as well as explain the general

---

38 Katz, 1988, pp 3–4 and 321.
39 Katz, 1988, pp 311–12.

conditions that are most commonly found in the social backgrounds' of different forms of criminality.[40] Moral transcendence – the taking and holding of a 'moral' position and refusing to be driven from it – is the key to understanding the causal essence of crime.[41]

The very first type of case considered in *Seductions of Crime* is described as 'a typical homicide', an impassioned killing where people kill 'in a moralistic rage'. Katz calls this 'righteous slaughter'. His examples include an irate husband who kills his wife's lover; a woman who kills her husband after years of domestic violence; a man who kills his wife because she wants to leave him, and a man who kills his wife because she allegedly called out her boyfriend's name during sex. Given his celebration of a generic magic of violent acts, it comes as no surprise to find Katz equating a man's killing of a woman because of sexual jealousy with a woman's killing of her husband in self-defence after suffering years of abuse at his hands. For him these are indistinguishable cases of 'righteous slaughter'.[42] Committed as he is to a generalised notion of 'typical' homicide, Katz needs to render these 'righteously inspired' killings as equivalent cases of moral transcendence. To fit the category of righteous slaughter in which the killer makes 'an impassioned attempt to perform a sacrifice to embody one or another version' of 'a primordial Good', the woman could not be acting simply in self-defence, despite enduring years of violent assaults. Her actions must be reinterpreted as 'righteously inspired' by the American dream of bettering oneself through education. Her homicidal violence is 'a last stand in defence of respectability', not a defence of her life. She is upholding a universally understood and 'eternally recognised Good', just as the 'virile male' does when he kills a woman to avenge his slighted manhood. Just as the male killers strive to transcend the humiliation 'which always embodies an awareness of impotence' and a 'stand in defence of respectability', battered women who kill their husbands are also striving to transcend humiliation.[43] Numerous studies have documented the extraordinary violence experienced by battered women killers at the hands of their partners, but Katz converts their last acts of self-defence against their violent male partners into a 'last moral stand' in defence of 'traditional versions of the female identity'.[44]

How could this pass as critical, let alone 'vibrant' criminology? When a reviewer describes Katz's text as 'a wonderful book that induces the reader to think like him', and finds his explanations of certain types of crime 'totally convincing',[45] a feminist reader can only wonder if she is reading the

---

40 Katz, 1988, pp 4–10.
41 For a rare challenge to Jack Katz's anti-positivistic credentials, see the review by Steven Katz, 1989.
42 Katz, 1988, pp 13–15.
43 Katz, 1988, pp 15–20.
44 Katz, 1988, pp 48–9.
45 Newman, 1990, p 179.

same book. She is unlikely to find a man's account of his homicidal fury against his wife 'emotionally compelling'. Nor is she likely to be seduced by the idea of recovering 'the lived mysticism and magic in the foreground of criminal experience' or feel 'compelled to acknowledge the power' of 'the sensualities of defilement, spiritual chaos and the apprehension of vengeance'.[46] As for the idea of turning 'the light-hearted thrusts and parries' of a sexual encounter into 'the real thing without warning', a feminist would most likely identify this as a common rape fantasy. She might also reach for some of the vast literature on 'domestic' homicide revealing that while women almost always kill their male partners in self-defence after enduring years of physical, sexual, economic and emotional violence, men do not kill women in such circumstances. As countless murder and manslaughter cases show, men kill their women partners because of sexual slights, unfaithfulness, real or imagined, and for leaving them or attempting to leave. Moreover, in most Western jurisdictions, women are at far greater risk of being killed by their male partner than men are of being killed by their female partner. Australian homicide statistics, for example, show that approximately one in four homicides are 'domestic' and that approximately 75 per cent of spouse killers are men.[47] In the UK, the killing of two women a week by a male partner has become a widely-publicised statistic, thanks to feminist investigative and campaign work. These statistics cannot be wished away, notwithstanding the best efforts of criminological positivists to render 'male on female' and 'female on male' killings commensurable. Nor can they be disappeared by 'vibrant' criminologists like Katz dismissing what he calls 'the minor measure of the predominance of men in family homicides'. Generalising from the atypical situation in the United States where women kill men in domestic homicides at a much higher rate than women kill men in other jurisdictions, Katz claims that in domestic homicide cases in 'the modern West', the rates for men and women are fairly even.[48] Elsewhere in the 'modern West', however, men continue to kill far greater numbers of women in domestic homicides.

Furthermore, there is now a considerable body of feminist research on battered women killers and the difficulty they have accessing self-defence laws that are structured around men's actions. Their accounts of the violence they endured at the hands of their partners are dismissed in *Seductions of Crime* as 'systematically biased'. Speaking of bias, Katz has no hesitation in speculating that the battered women killers who recounted sadistic sexual practices by their violent male partners may have received an 'erotic reward' when they killed them. He is happy too to attribute to these women a

46 Katz, 1988, pp 310–12.
47 Howe, 2002.
48 Katz, 1988, pp 47–9.

'superior refinement and moral sensibility'. Leaving these utterly unfounded comments aside, it is notable the first woman killer in Katz's list of righteous slaughters fits exactly the feminist profile of a battered woman killer. She kills her violent male partner when he is asleep and then fails in her self-defence plea.[49] It is yet another case highlighting the singularity and gender-specific nature of the circumstances in which women kill male partners. As such it does nothing to bolster Katz's notion of a typical un-gendered righteous slaughter. As for the archaic reference to 'the seductress' as provocateur in one of his cases of virility-challenged male killers,[50] it is a mystery how any critical criminologist could have let this pass without comment. Feminist criticism of the way the provocation defence operates as deeply sexed excuse for murder has been available for long enough for 'vibrant' scholars like Katz to have educated themselves out of hegemonic discursive constructions of badly-behaved women who provoke men to kill.[51] Given what we now know about spousal killings in all Western jurisdictions, an un-gendered concept of 'righteous slaughter' cannot be allowed to conceal the hard material realities of homicidal violence. The hardest reality of all for non-feminists to grasp is the vastly different situations in which women and men kill each other. While men kill women on the slightest provocation – her desire to leave him will do, or the whiff, imagined or not, of an interest in another man – women rarely kill men for these reasons. In almost all cases, women kill men in situations of abject violence and terror. Yet within the Katzian analytical framework, much vaunted by critical criminologists, alleged challenges to a man's virility are regarded as the moral equivalent to threats to a woman's life.

While Katz's case studies of 'badass' ghetto tough guys, muggers, robbers and cold-blooded killers fall outside the parameters of this study, the omission of sexual assaults and sex killings from his list of criminal projects is noteworthy. Their inclusion would have exposed the discrepancy in the numbers of men and women experiencing the sensual pleasures of violent crime. A theory about the universality of the 'sensual magic' and 'lived sensuality' of sexual violence would have collapsed very quickly in the face of the massive imbalance in the number of male and female rapists. Moreover, if Katz had included rape, sexual assault and so-called 'lust' killings in his list of sensually attractive crimes, it might have become difficult for critical criminologists to overlook the profoundly sexed constitution of the sensual attraction of violent crime.

49 Katz, 1988, pp 48–9.
50 Katz, 1988, p 13.
51 See, e.g. Howe, 2002 for a discussion of the extensive feminist literature.

Excitable transcendent criminologists – desexing sexed violence

Seductions of Crime has been acclaimed as 'a fine book, a rewarding book, and yes, at times, a dazzling book', one that will 'enrich the field' by bringing back the 'sting of excitement and high-level theorising that has been missing'.[52] Interestingly, it is prominent critical criminologists who have led the hallelujah chorus, declaring it to be one of 'the most original criminology texts in recent years' – it is 'constantly fascinating, insightful and thought-provoking'.[53] For them, the book inspires hope that 'here might be the foundations for a novel paradigm', one 'compatible with currently popular postmodern, anti-materialist theorising'. Moreover, by focusing on the 'seduction of emotionality' linking opportunity and meaning, Katz is said to have bridged 'the gap between agency and structure'.[54] *Seductions of Crime* has been frequently described as a seminal book, one that puts a 'correct emphasis' on neglected foreground factors and earning its author pride of place in a new 'criminology of transgression' with the by-line 'Merton with energy, Katz with structure'.[55] Katz, it is pointed out, was one of the first to 'make good the neglect of human emotions within criminological theorising'.[56] In doing so, he has provided critical criminologists with a new methodological understanding of the need to situate themselves inside the criminal moment in order to apprehend 'the terrors and pleasures of criminality'.[57] More, in recognising the 'existential sensuality of crime', Katz plays a key role in deciphering 'the emotions of postmodernism'.[58] And if he does seem to be 'overly concerned with the criminal's point of view' – at least in the view of right-wing critics, and preoccupied with the notion of 'some latent human evil', in the view of the left – his thesis is 'likely to remain influential' because of its insistence that 'all of us' readily engage in conduct that has been labelled criminal.[59]

Critical criminologists have continued to build uncritically on Katz's thesis, without so much as an inkling that it provides an untenable foundation for any avowedly 'critical' criminological project. Moreover, while from a feminist perspective – *any* feminist perspective – the limitations of Katz's theory are blatantly obvious, one has to look hard to find a feminist critique of *Seductions of Crime*. A rare feminist article that questions the 'we' of Katz's universalising perspective can be found tucked away in an Australian

---

52 Goode, 1990, pp 6 and 11.
53 Jefferson, 1997a, pp 552–3.
54 O'Malley and Mugford, 1994, pp 189 and 210.
55 Young, 2003, pp 391 and 408.
56 de Haan and Loader, 2002, pp 243–4.
57 Ferrell, 1997, p 11.
58 Morrison, 1995, pp 359 and 464.
59 Muncie *et al*, 1996, p 65.

cultural history journal where his normalisation of 'the bliss of brutality' is read as 'an apology for fraternity'. When Katz speaks of transcendent violence as the sacred resort of the sovereign individual who holds fast against chaos, 'he could be talking about anyone'. But 'he isn't. *He is talking about men*'.[60] And so he is. At first, Katz's criminal actor is coded interchangeably as a male and as an ungendered human person, but he soon emerges as always already male. It is the humiliated individual 'himself' who is compelled to act 'by forces beyond his control'. Katz might not be surprised that 'homicide among mates' frequently springs from complaints about sexual performance inasmuch as humiliation 'always embodies an awareness of impotence'. But it is clear that the homicidal 'mates' he has in mind are men in heterosexual relationships, as he would be hard pressed to find cases of women who kill men because the man had complained about the woman's sexual performance. It is most definitely a 'he' that Katz has in mind when he speaks of the humiliated person being 'overcome with an intolerable discomfort', forcing 'him to feel himself as soul'.[61] Furthermore, he dresses up the emotions of rage and humiliation, which for him are inextricably linked with a felt sense of impotence, in hopelessly sexed and sexist terms. While rage is inscribed as a 'penis threatening to ejaculate' or, alternatively, as 'the screaming red-faced birth of a self', the experience of humiliation is 'metaphorically the perfect opposite: a return to the womb'.[62] So: while men are virile or dangerously impotent and on the verge of exploding in rage, women are 'seductresses' and custodians of those troublesome wombs. Interestingly, Katz himself expresses doubts at one stage about the universality of his theory, most notably when he acknowledges that 'the phallic metaphor embodied in the way of the badass makes compelling sense to relatively few men and to virtually no women'.[63] Still, the transcendent purpose that moves all righteous killers is revealed, in the end, to be 'the transcendent purpose of violent men'.[64]

Intriguingly however, few feminist criminologists appear to have noticed how deeply problematic Katz's theory of the seduction of crime is. Certainly some have noted that risk-theory, including Lyng's notion of edgework or thrill-seeking, seen by some critical criminologists as forming a supposedly dazzling 'synthesis' with Katz's theory, is rooted in male experiences.[65] They

---

60 Davies and Rhodes-Little, 1993, pp 23–4, original emphasis.
61 Katz, 1988, pp 24–5.
62 Katz, 1988, p 29.
63 Katz, 1988, p 238.
64 Perhaps it is this 'purpose' that prevents a feminist reader from catching the 'piercing reflection' that disturbs Katz as he glances at all those 'evil men': Katz, 1988, p 324–5.
65 e.g. Sandra Walklate notes how Lyng's analysis reinforces traditional cultural images of men and women, with men having a positive and women a negative relationship to edgework: Walklate, 1997, pp 40–1.

have also pointed out that risk-assessment is a highly gendered activity, 'risk' for women entailing risk avoidance more often than risk-taking. As Betsy Stanko observes, risk for women is not so much about 'modernity and the ontological insecurity people experience', as about 'misogyny and the continued perpetration of women's oppression through fear of crime and blame for their situation'.[66] Yet even when feminists take risk theorists to task for failing to understand how risk is 'part of the way in which women's subjectivities are produced', Katz's notion of exciting criminal projects escapes censure.[67]

It is only when reviewing one of Katz's later books, *How Emotions Work*, that Stanko notices that Katz's construction of social relations is just as problematic as Lyng's. Katz, she observes, uses examples of violent behaviour from people who differ in age, race, gender and nationality. But in doing so, he 'attempts a form of theorising that transcends and at the same time merges the social with the emotional', thereby ignoring the way in which the emotional is mediated by hierarchical social relations.[68] Katz's response to this rare feminist criticism of his work is instructive. Returning to his argument in *Seductions of Crime*, he explains that he had tried to demonstrate that 'if we start by establishing the contingencies of distinctive social experience, we can then study relations to various background conditions such as power, gender, social class, ethnicity etc'.[69] Missing here is any understanding of the key insight developed in many fields of social inquiry, that gender, class, race and ethnicity cannot be conceptualised as mere etcetera background conditions to be tacked on to foreground experiences. They are themselves lived experiences. More to the point of our inquiry, it is little wonder that the specificities of men and of men's violence against women are lost in *Seductions of Crime*. They have disappeared under the weight of an unreconstructed framework untouched by critiques of universalising analytical paradigms that ignore the myriad ways in which human relationships are gendered and sexed.

What's postmodern about postmodern criminology?

Returning to the question of the postmodernism of postmodern criminology, we might begin by reiterating that Katz's book is a very strange choice as a foundational text for postmodern criminology, or indeed for any brand of critical criminology. Recall that the new or critical criminologies of the

---

66 Stanko, 1997, p 492.
67 Chan and Rigakos, 2002, pp 756–7. Walklate describes his theory as 'interestingly different': 1995, p 183.
68 Stanko, 2002, pp 368–9.
69 Katz, 2002, 376.

1970s attempted to make an epistemological break with positivism's individualism, with its assumption of a unitary category of crime and, most crucially, with its all-embracing causal explanations of criminal behaviour. Focusing on what causes individuals to commit crime is, as Carol Smart observes, the 'defining characteristic' of positivistic criminology. Yet despite his rejection of the 'positivistic explanatory perspective' that looks for the background causes of crime, Katz's project remains firmly positivistic. He focuses unashamedly on the causally crucial 'foreground' factors propelling individuals into crime and he is committed to the development of a 'systematic' general explanation of crime that combines a foreground factor approach with a search for crime's supposed 'correlations with biographical and ecological background factors'.[70] Furthermore, *Seductions of Crime* displays all of the damning traits of 'modernism' that Carol Smart attributes to positivistic criminology. Totalising 'master' narratives that hold out the promise that they can reveal 'the truth about human behaviour' are, she claims, sexist, white, racist and Eurocentric, and the reduction of cultural and sexual differences to one dominant set of values renders these narratives 'antediluvian' and 'politically suspect'.[71]

Katz's incorrigibly masculinist theory of the seduction of crime that masquerades as a general, non-gendered theory of crime is a perfect example of just such a totalising modernist narrative. It is all very well for our affirmative postmodernists to acknowledge feminist critiques of Foucault's profoundly masculinist work, and to proclaim that postmodern criminology must take account of feminist perspectives, including poststructuralist feminist critiques of criminology and penology.[72] But how then, in the same breath, can affirmative postmodernists serve such lavish praise on Katz's *Seductions of Crime* where the purportedly genderless person who is seduced into violent crime is transparently male and gender-neutral language is constantly betrayed by lapses into a masculine subjectivity? After all, it is 'the individual himself' in all 'his subjectivity' who is transported by an *'authentic'* compulsion and 'the authentic efficacy of passion'.[73] In reading this uncritically, affirmative postmodernists not only overlook feminist critiques of male subjectivity masquerading as an un-gendered and un-sexed human subjectivity; they also appear to have forgotten that poststructuralists reject the modernist conception of an 'authentic' liberal human subject in favour of an understanding of the subject as discursively constructed. The many poststructuralist warnings against misrecognising the self – let alone 'the individual himself' – as the guarantor or 'authorial source of meaning', have

---

70 Katz, 1988, p 312.
71 Smart, 1990a, pp 71–5.
72 Henry and Milovanovic, 1996, pp 202–3, citing Howe, 1994, p 114.
73 Katz, 1988, pp 7–8, original emphasis.

evidently not been heeded by these critical criminologists.[74] As for the 'very strong criticisms of the subject as an instrument of Western imperialist hegemony' made by theorists of postcoloniality, they may have registered with white poststructuralist feminists such as Judith Butler,[75] but they are not even specks on the horizon of the all-white and supposedly 'postmodern' criminological worldview.

Indeed, Katz's supposedly vibrant criminology represents its subjects in racialised and racist ways. Speaking from an unexamined white, male perspective, he claims that his theory applies to everyone. All of us, men and women, white, black and minority ethnic subjects get seduced by the thrill of crime. For example, the agents of righteous slaughter are specified as white, black and Mexican-American to buttress his argument that everybody subscribes to 'an eternally recognised Good' – that we are all vulnerable to emotions that might lead us to succumb to the exciting prospect of criminal violence.[76] This universalising strategy that effaces the specificities of minority ethnic experiences is matched by more blatant othering strategies when it comes to analysing offences committed by African-American and Hispanic youth. His wariness that he might be reinforcing racist stereotypes in his study of the relationship between robbery and race does not prevent Katz from suggesting that the 'bad-nigger' identity is a 'transcendent response to the racial humiliation of ghetto blacks by ghetto blacks'.[77] That minority ethnic young men might object to this expropriation of their lived experiences by a white commentator does not cross his mind. Nor does it worry his affirmative postmodernist admirers. Moreover, they are untroubled that the critical criminologists who developed the 'Katz-Lyng synthesis' describe 'non-Anglo' street gangs as emerging from a 'humbled background', a 'culture humbled at the prospect of entering modern, rationalised society'. Nor are affirmative postmodernists fazed by a description of 'urban racial ghettoes' as appearing to be 'less civilised than rich, white suburbs' and their inhabitants as valuing 'expressivity and spontaneity' over rationality.[78] Ascribing 'nonrationality' to 'non-white' people and depicting African-Americans as expressive and emotionally spontaneous – as 'full of emotion' – are much-criticised racist practices, but this too has escaped their notice.[79] Dressing up the subculture of violence thesis as a case study of 'moral transcendence' cannot save Katz and his followers from the charges of racism that have been levelled against that thesis. The resort by

74 Weedon, 1987, p 113.
75 Butler, 1992, p 14.
76 Katz, 1988, pp 15–16.
77 Katz, 1988, pp 238 and 247.
78 O'Malley and Mugford, 1994, pp 190 and 200.
79 Razack, 1994, p 42; Spelman, 1989, p 264.

supposedly 'critical' analysts to a white imperialist construction of a racialised minority group as socialised into criminality in humble, culturally backward, pre-modern ghettoes marks Katzian-inflected critical criminology as an irredeemably racist modernist discourse.

There are so many un-postmodern moments in Katz's text that one can only wonder how it could ever have been acclaimed as a dazzling forerunner to postmodern criminology. Incredibly, 'deviance' is never problematised, notwithstanding the fact that 'deviance' had been thoroughly deconstructed by the time Katz sat down to write *Seductions of Crime*. Critical criminologists might have spent the previous twenty years debunking untheorised assumptions about the existence of constitutional deviants and criminals, but they parade as triumphantly across the pages of Katz's book as they ever did in unreconstructed positivism. Men and women are universalised, essentialised and chalked up as 'males' and 'females' without a passing thought for constructivist, let alone performative, theories of gendered and sexed identities. And they are all spoken for, whatever their ethnic, racial or class background. Yet none of this unreconstructed biological essentialism has deterred affirmative postmodernists and other critical criminologists from proclaiming *Seductions of Crime* as a precursor to postmodern criminology. Postmodern feminist interrogations of the 'contingent foundations' of subject positions, feminist and masculinist alike, have simply not registered with Katz or his followers.[80] Postmodernists in other fields might rail against modernist generalities and universalising strategies, but postmodern criminology embraces a quintessentially modernist 'eternally recognised Good' and an equally archaic un-gendered theory of the transcendent postmodern subject, all the while disavowing that they are making 'a *general* statement concerning crime'.[81]

And how can the unreconstructed emotionality/rationality binary that pervades *Seductions of Crime* possibly rate as a postmodern methodology? Certainly, it is in no danger of being misrecognised as Derridean, Derrida having trashed such limited binary thinking so thoroughly. The Katzians – as we might refer to Katz's following – believe that Katz has come up with a convincing 'general account of the attractions of exciting and transcending activity' such as crime. But he and Lyng have erred in assuming that the process of transcendence is trans-historical, when in fact it is 'peculiarly modern'. It is, specifically, the 'modern, rationalised age' that prevents 'spontaneous expression of emotional extremes', thereby creating the conditions of emergence for 'postmodern emotions' such as 'moral self-transcendence'.[82] In this schema, modernity is coded as rational and

---

80 Butler, 1992.
81 Milovanovic, 1996, p 586, original emphasis.
82 O'Malley and Mugford 1994, pp 195–6 and 199.

post-modernity as emotional, while supposedly trans-historical human subjects try to negotiate the problems of modern life. In the words of two Katzians:

> As the crisis of self is accelerated by the process of commercialising human emotional labour and the real increasingly subverted by the hyperreal, a possible transcendent route for the individual lies in adopting pursuits that, by their excess and danger, stir powerful emotions that recreate and reassure oneself of oneself.[83]

This is, of course, precisely the sort of stunningly silly claim that gives postmodernism a bad name. Yet Milovanovic applauds this passage as pointing to 'a legitimate and fruitful focus of criminological inquiry', before adding his own equally vacuous suggestion that postmodern criminologists can enhance understanding of crime by exploring how (un-gendered) subjects, feeling the increasing effects of 'postmodern society', reclaim their subjectivity in a 'confrontation with the invitational edge' that tempts us all into illegalities.[84]

Such assertions cry out for poststructuralist feminist interrogation. First, how could our affirmative postmodernist criminologists have forgotten that postmodernists understand the subject to be discursively constituted in various, sometimes fragmentary but certainly never transcendental ways? Second, and more specifically, how could the question of the gendered subject – one of the most densely theorised questions of 'our' time – be omitted from any bid to specify the historical context of the transition from modernity to postmodernity? Feminist and non-feminist postmodern contributions to late-twentieth century theories of subjectivity have exposed major flaws in the Enlightenment concept of a universal subject – a 'transcendental, unified, rational subject'.[85] Consider, for example, Cameron and Frazer's analysis of the sexual murderer as 'the quintessential modern hero' and sexual murder as 'masculine transcendence', as a search for freedom and pleasure in transgression against a repressive society. Tracing the historical origins of the idea of 'man-as-transcendence' back through European Enlightenment literature, their book provides a critique of Enlightenment and post-Enlightenment philosophy's conflation of 'the Subject with the masculine subject' and its 'endless preoccupation with freedom, transcendence and transgression' which should have given pause for thought, if not put a rest to Katz's thoroughly modern and masculinist project.[86]

---

83 O'Malley and Mugford, 1994, p 203.
84 Milovanovic, 1996, pp 586–7.
85 Moore, 1994a, pp 140–1.
86 Cameron and Frazer, 1987, pp 58 and 166–9, acknowledging Genevieve Lloyd's (1984) now classic critique of the 'man of reason'.

Third, poststructuralists across a range of fields of social inquiry have deconstructed modernism's emotion/rationality duality and, in the process, exploded the idea that emotions are universal. Emotions, it is now clear, are gendered – they occupy 'an important place in Western gender ideologies'.[87] To take a pertinent example, postmodern feminist glosses on 'dumb' and 'cognitivist' theories of anger leave Katz's universalising account of righteous rage in tatters. As Elizabeth Spelman notes, rage differs from anger which, according to cognitivist theories, involves a judgment about when and how to express anger. When anger is given a history, it becomes very clear that it is dominant subjects who have felt entitled to be angry. It follows that when dominant groups deploy the 'systematic denial of anger' as 'a mechanism of subordination', the expression of anger becomes an act of insubordination.[88] Such a politicisation of the expression of anger by subordinated groups is a far cry from the de-politicised notion of engaging in moral transcendence, or taking a 'transcendent route', as conceptualised by Katz and his followers. A familiarity with feminist theories of emotion might have saved critical criminologists from an uncritical appraisal of Katz's theory of crime as one addressing those supposedly universal passions that drive us to respond to deeply felt injuries to personal honour, status or authority that 'we' all experience.

Finally, Katzian critical criminologists believe they have accounted for any possible feminist criticism by responding to Eleanor Miller's marxist feminist critique of Lyng's theory of edgework. It is, she says, 'inattentive' to class, race, ethnicity and gender. But rather than rejecting it on these grounds, her solution is to buttress the edgework thesis by adding African-American sex workers to Lyng's list of white, middle-class male edgeworkers.[89] Miller's incorporatist ethos is readily embraced not only by Lyng himself, but also by Katzian criminologists.[90] They think it shows that their account of emotionality can be 'a general account for all people', notwithstanding the small matters of 'double standards and the extra jeopardy that women face in sexual relations' (read: sexual violence) – everyone can engage equally in edgework, apparently, especially now that 'gender roles' are becoming androgynous under the impact of consumerism.[91] How might we respond to this utterly inadequate rejoinder to a feminist query about the purported universality of transcendental subjects engaging in edgework? One might begin by noting that if consumerism has had androgynous effects on social mores, there is nothing remotely androgynous about crime statistics or convictions for murder, manslaughter or sexual assault. As for the

87 Lutz, 1988, p 54.
88 Spelman, 1989, pp 270–1.
89 Miller, 1991.
90 Lyng, 1991.
91 O'Malley and Mugford, 1994, pp 206–8.

unreflective reference to 'gender roles', this betrays a spectacular ignorance of three decades of critical work on sex/gender questions that have left gender role theory in tatters.[92] And if the throwaway line – 'the extra jeopardy that women face in sexual relations' – is meant to be an allusion to the risk of violence women face in sexual encounters with men, 'extra jeopardy' surely rates as a classic in the genre of discursive manoeuvres that conceal who is doing what to whom when it comes to sexual assault, domestic violence and domestic homicide.

Let us conclude this discussion of *Seductions of Crime* and the putatively postmodern criminology it gave rise to by noting that some feminist scholars have argued that representations of violence are themselves violent. They are also intrinsically gendered inasmuch as their meaning is dependent on the gender of the violated object depicted. It follows that violence is always already 'engendered in representation'.[93] Witness the numerous celebrations of a book about the seductions of crime that discursively erases the butchered victims of contentedly seduced violent men seeking moral transcendence. Getting transported inside the immediacy of crime, losing oneself in the seductive moment of violence and in other allegedly 'postmodern emotions' implies, for the Katzians, 'a certain emotional empathy', but it is empathy reserved for the male perpetrators, not the victims. For these criminologists, it is the 'adrenaline rushes and outlaw emotions' experienced by violent men, and not empathetic identifications with their victims, that enhance 'our understanding' of crime.[94] As Katz makes so clear, it is the humiliation of a man – typically, the cuckold – that triggers the search for transcendence:

> Humiliation forces him to feel himself as soul ... Humiliation takes over the soul by invading the whole body. The humiliated body is unbearable alive; one's very being is humiliated.[95]

No wonder men kill women. That murdered women have experienced pain, suffering and humiliation at the hands of unbearably alive perpetrators is of no consequence whatsoever. All that matters is appreciating that the guys were adopting pursuits in search of transcendent routes. Still, by producing a version of postmodern theory that would be unrecognisable to postmodern theorists in other fields of critical inquiry, this branch of critical criminology has served one useful purpose – it has provided a sharp contrast to the feminist-inflected Foucauldian postmodern approach to sexed

92 See Chapter 1.
93 de Lauretis, 1987, pp 32–3.
94 Ferrell, 1997, p 13.
95 Katz, 1988, p 25.

violence advocated in this book, an approach that refuses totalising and universalising master narratives that purport to explain the emotions driving 'us' all to violence.

Crime and masculinities – in defence of anxious men

If critical criminologists like Cohen are too bent on trashing postmodern theory to notice the suffering caused by men's violence against women, and affirmative postmodernists too engrossed by the seductive qualities of crime to register the deeply sexed constitution of that seduction, what have other critical criminologists had to say about violent men? Let us turn to consider the work of critical criminologists who are well aware that the question of men – or rather 'masculinities' – needs to be addressed. Research on the relationship between men, masculinities and crime is now, as Richard Collier notes, a 'well-established feature of the criminological landscape', with a 'visible presence' in mainstream criminology textbooks and journals, especially, we might add, in critical criminology texts. Unlike constitutive criminology, masculinity studies have attracted considerable critical attention, not least from Collier who has challenged its 'core assumption' that there is an analytic gain to be made by taking masculinity seriously and trying to connect it to crime.[96] He develops his argument with reference to the work of prominent British critical criminologist Tony Jefferson. As Collier explains, Jefferson has developed a so-called 'third stage' in thinking about masculinities in order to 'correct' earlier masculinity studies that have wrongly assumed that the experience of being masculine is premised on the domination of women and children. The ostensible aim of this third stage – the 'psychosocial approach' – is to shift thinking about the relationship between masculinity and crime to 'a different level'. Criminologists should focus on the psychodynamic dimensions of masculine experience, the complex interaction between the social realm and the individual psyche that motivated particular men to commit violent crimes. The picture that will then emerge is that of a violent man who, far from being an empowered masculine subject, often experiences emotional ambivalence and contradictory feelings of empowerment and powerlessness. He is a 'defended' subject, defensive about his place in the world and locked in a battle with unconscious anxieties that originate in a troubled childhood.[97]

Collier offers a range of criticisms of this theory although he puts them, as he says, as 'mildly' as he can. He suggests that Jefferson's 'third stage' thinking 'betrays a profoundly positivistic notion of progression (from first, to second, to third stage) in depicting what is, ultimately, a "grand theory" of

96 Collier, 2004, p 285.
97 Collier, 2004, pp 293–5.

the crimes of men'. As such it smacks of that totalising discourse that has been dismissed as problematically modernist. Collier also notes growing criticism of the concept of 'masculinity' which has led to a reappraisal of what it means to depict men's gender 'as something which "floats free" from what men *do*'. Such an approach effaces men's responsibility for their actions. This leads Collier to query the purpose of criminology's 'masculinity turn'. In his view, it remains suspect in that it masks issues of power.[98]

But what exactly are these masked issues of power? Collier does not spell them out. Nor does he discuss the supposedly inadequate earlier stages in thinking about the relationship between masculinity and crime. Turning to Jefferson's ubiquitous writings on crime and masculinities, we discover that he relegates to the 'first stage' the radical feminist bid to theorise the 'maleness' of violent crime, especially rape, in the 1970s. The cardinal error of the radical feminists was to implicate '*all* men' with their infamous slogan, 'all men are potential rapists'.[99] Radical feminists might have inspired subsequent anti-violence feminist work, but in Jefferson's view, their concept of masculinity was too totalising, reductive and deterministic.[100] The second 'stage', Messerschmidt's attempt in *Masculinities and Crime* to move away from such reductive essentialism, focuses on the idea of masculinities as performance. This stage is a 'significant advance on early radical feminist explanations', although it too over-emphasises the constraints masculinity places on men. Also, Messerschmidt failed to explain why particular young men resort to violence to accomplish their masculinity and to ask about the 'subjective gratifications' of, say, gang rape. Jefferson's third stage – his own work – fills these gaps by picking up on the missing social and psychic dimensions of subjectivity that are implicated in men's violent actions.[101] A 'better sense of the complexities of men's experiences' could only be achieved with a 'socially literate' and 'psychoanalytically complex' approach that enables an understanding of violent men as experiencing a 'fragile and conflicted masculinity'. Take the case of the 'Yorkshire Ripper', 'painfully torn' between the tough masculinity of his father and 'the quiet, gentle femininity of his beloved, long-suffering mother, with whom he strongly identified'. Given the 'multiple ambivalences that this contradiction produced' and his failure to 'live up to the social expectations of manliness', it is little wonder that this serial killer came to 'blame the feminine in himself, to hate part of himself, and then externalise that hatred and destroy women'. The psychosocial approach renders his life 'comprehensible'.[102]

98 Collier, 2004, pp 296–9, original emphasis.
99 Jefferson, 1997a, p 541, original emphasis.
100 Jefferson, 1996a, pp 338–9.
101 Jefferson, 1996a, pp 340–1.
102 Jefferson, 1997a, pp 544–6.

Focusing on the individual violent offender, the psychosocial approach checks for 'an emotionally impoverished and rejecting background' in order to understand the man's attempts to 'build up a more powerful sense of masculine identity'.[103] Take the case of the convicted rapist, Mike Tyson. He emerges in Jefferson's account as a confused man, one who has suffered 'chronic poverty, an absent father, a mother who could not cope, who drank and fought with her boyfriend', as well as constant moves into deprived neighbourhoods, a big head and body and a soft voice that made him vulnerable to bullying. His life was 'constantly trouble-strewn', starting with the absence of a 'coping mother' and ending with allegations of sexual assault made by 'angry women', a stormy marriage, deaths of significant others and a 'sensational rape trial' leading to a six-year sentence.[104] To find the 'deeper, emotional truth' about Tyson's rape trial, it becomes necessary to once again indict the 'feminist orthodoxy' – embalmed in the slogan 'all men are potential rapists' – that has prevented more advanced thinking about the complexity of dating and raping. If one lets go of 'victim feminism' and strives for an empathetic understanding of the rapist, one learns of Tyson's vulnerable side which he split off and projected onto others, notably his victim. This is the 'emotional truth' of the rape. Tyson was unconsciously attempting to ward off the anxiety produced by his desire for intimacy. Ambivalent about his sexuality and about women, he had a 'suppressed desire for intimacy' that was displaced onto 'desires for sexual gratification'. This reveals Tyson's similarity to many men, a point which Jefferson concedes accords with the much-maligned radical feminist idea of 'a continuum of male sexuality'. Leaving this small slip aside – the radical feminist continuum is one of 'male violence', not male sexuality – it is noteworthy that Jefferson finds it difficult to identify with Desiree Washington, Tyson's victim. Lacking a 'reservoir of similar experiences' from which he might have attempted 'an empathetic account' of her 'discursive choices' or a knowledge of what it would be like to be 'young, black and female in small-town Mid-America', he could only speculate about her subject position vis-à-vis her rapist. Of course, no such reservations prevented this white male criminologist from empathising with her black male rapist.[105]

Masculinities, social literacy and a few good men

Jefferson's call for a focus on the troubled psyches of violent men has a number of disturbing effects. By depicting violent men as much-put-upon sensitive and ambivalent souls beset by traumatic childhoods, non-coping

103 Jefferson, 1997a, p 547.
104 Jefferson, 1996b, pp 155–66.
105 Jefferson, 1997a, pp 281 and 292–6.

mothers and a bewildering array of conflicting feelings, Jefferson is just a step away from providing rapists and killers with the 'understandable' motives gifted to violent men by positivistic criminologists. His aim, after all, is to make the lives of such violent men *comprehensible* – his word, my emphasis – by showing how they have experienced emotionally impoverished and rejecting backgrounds. Furthermore, his 'third stage' sounds like old-fashioned positivism with its list of background factors such as childhood experiences and inadequate parenting, and a long-suffering working class mum. Left unexplained is why it is simply assumed that the killer's mum represents his despised 'feminine' part which must be annihilated. Surely the social and psychic dimensions of deep-seated misogyny in Western culture need to be examined closely in socially literate accounts of rapists and woman killers.

An extraordinary anti-feminist *animus* informs the psychosocial theory of masculinity and crime. Feminist work in the field is rejected as simplistic, theoretically-naïve and not as 'advanced' as it should be. The least advanced of all are the radical feminists – the folk who put men's violence on the criminological and political agenda all those years ago. Relegated to the lowest ranks on the hierarchy of scholarly achievement in the field, they are berated for continuing to dominate 'the rape debate' with their outdated notions of 'male power'.[106] To make this claim it is necessary to drop into a footnote Carol Smart's enormously influential poststructuralist feminist book, *Feminism and the Power of Law*, published in 1989, which challenged the very terms of that debate. It also entails ignoring the impressive body of feminist poststructuralist scholarship on rape and rape law reforms that has challenged radical feminist hegemony in the field for over two decades.[107] With all this work relegated to the sidelines, the path is open to celebrate the most 'advanced' theorists – the ones who frame the problem of men's violence and masculinity in 'socially literate' psychoanalytic terms, thereby learning to appreciate the ambivalent feelings, the anxieties and defensive projections of, say, a rapist or a serial killer. Focusing on the social and psychic dimensions of criminal violence shows that the radical feminists were wrong. Men's violence is not about male power – the picture of the rapist or paedophile that emerges in psychosocial profiles is that of a weak and inadequate man. At the same time, reminding us that girls can be murderously violent serves as a warning against 'pinning everything on gender difference', as feminists tend to do, apparently.[108]

Had Jefferson read post-1970s feminist work on violence closely, he may well have found it to be very advanced indeed, and none more so than

106 Jefferson, 1997a, p 546.
107 See Chapter 5.
108 Jefferson, 1997a, p 548.

feminist critiques of representational practices that are themselves violent. One pertinent example is Elisabeth Bronfen's searching analysis of a series of drawings of a woman dying of cancer. Querying precisely what it is that constitutes violence – her death or its representation – she concludes that the drawings themselves are violent inasmuch as they stage 'the absence of violence', thereby permitting 'a blindness toward the real'.[109] Just such a blindness towards the real – the reality of the violence men inflict on women and of the pervasiveness of that violence – characterises crime and masculinity studies. If Bronfen seems to be taking us too far astray from the question of masculinity and violent crime, Henrietta Moore's analysis of the problem of explaining violence in the social sciences brings us back to that very question. Moore suggests a link between what she calls 'the thwarting of investments in various subject positions based on gender' and interpersonal violence. The thwarted individual is unable to 'sustain or properly take up a gendered subject position, resulting in a crisis, real or imagined, of self-representation and/or social evaluation'. A thwarted individual who fails to receive the expected rewards from taking up a particular gendered subject position might, she suggests, resort to violence. That violence, crucially, is the result of a crisis of representation, for example that of 'a providing husband/father' who beats his wife for imagined infidelities.[110]

Moore's work on the psychic investments of thwarted individuals has parallels with Jefferson's studies of violent men. Ignoring Foucauldian problematisations of 'truth', Jefferson offers his own truth in response to Cameron and Frazer's critique of serial murder as masculine transcendence – 'the truth', he says, 'is that most men's transcendent strivings get thwarted *en route*'. The masculine subject is not the powerful figure feminists seem to assume. He feels insecure, vulnerable and anxious.[111] The crucial difference between Jefferson's and Moore's analysis of thwarted subjects is that Moore manages to theorise the engendered subjectivities of thwarted violent men without losing sight of the violence they inflict on women. This is the crux of the problem. In the final analysis, it is lack of empathy with or even sympathy for the victims that so troubles feminists. As Deborah Cameron explains:

> The egregious discourse of the Ripperologists is erected (apt word) on the real deaths of real women whose real names we know, but the voices and lives of those women are utterly silenced by the discourse, reduced to those clinically degrading images of their final agony. Then and now, they must be turned into objects so that the killer can be a subject.[112]

109 Bronfen, 1992, p 50.
110 Moore, 1994a, pp 151–3.
111 Jefferson, 1994, pp 11–13.
112 Cameron, 1994, pp 152–3.

What then, would Cameron make of the spectacle of the critical criminologist who is bent on opening up 'life-histories' for convicted rapists and serial killers while completely ignoring the suffering of their victims?[113] Would she see it, as I do, as no less execrable than that of the lumpen positivist questing after Jack the Ripper?

It is worth reiterating here that critical criminologists claim to provide a fundamentally different, critical approach to crime that would rock the foundations of the criminology discipline. According to Pat Carlen, for example, critical criminology 'must try not only to think the unthinkable about crime, but also to speak the unspeakable about the conditions *in which* and *by which* it is known'. For her, a truly critical criminology should be constantly questioning, even denying the conditions of its own existence and not 'pulling its punches' in order to conform to 'contemporary academic fashions'.[114] Ironically, Carlen expresses this opinion in her contribution to a critical criminology text that not only extols the virtues of Jefferson's psychosocial approach, but provides him with yet another platform to wax lyrical about the tortured subjectivity of a convicted rapist. It doesn't take much to name the conditions in which and by which Jefferson speaks – a hegemonic masculinity so powerful that everyone, self-identified feminist criminologists included, succumb to the seduction of his 'highly original', 'riveting' and 'welcome' approach.[115] Their uncritical stance leaves Jefferson free to condemn what he calls the 'unfortunate theoretical consequences' of feminism's political commitment to women victims of male violence – its 'tendency' to take women's 'apparently higher fear' of crime seriously and to tar 'all men with the brush of patriarchal commitment to power over and control of women'.[116]

For over a decade now, Jefferson has espoused this virulently anti-feminist polemic, tiresomely attributing to 'feminism' a viewpoint that has rarely been voiced since the 1970s, and even earning feminist praise for 'courageously' offering 'ways to conceptualise men's psychic and social complexities'.[117] He might claim to have no wish to 'downplay the horror of male violence against women', but what else does searching for the 'authentic inner world' of violent men do?[118] With feminist criminologists in thrall to the psychosocial approach, it has been left to scholars such as Bob Connell to point out that if batterers and rapists feel remorseful and ashamed, they also have 'feelings of entitlement, justifications and the intention to establish control'. He notes too that the use of threat of force is still widely accepted

---

113 Jefferson, 1994, p 30.
114 Carlen, 2002, p 249, original emphasis.
115 Carrington and Hogg, 2002, p 8 and Carrington 2002, p 121.
116 Jefferson, 2002a, p 149.
117 Newburn and Stanko, 1994, p 5.
118 Jefferson, 2002b, pp 70–3.

in Anglophone communities as 'part of men's repertoire in dealing with women and children'.[119] To take another example, Jeff Hearn has shown that 'masculinity' has taken the place of 'sex roles' in diverting attention away from what men do. How masculinity relates to 'what men do, to men's material practices' – that is usually overlooked in masculinity studies.[120] How ironic that it has been left to male scholars to refocus attention on 'the crimes of men *as men*', and to note how '*the actions of men* are routinely effaced' in critical and non-critical criminologies alike.[121] Even more ironically, it has been left to a leading critical masculinity scholar to point out that criminology has 'its own male-dominated history of men behaving badly within in it', as 'traditional patriarchal men' and as 'younger aggressive "radical" men'. In his view, it is unlikely that his 'critical' male colleagues will be able to develop a 'pro-feminist' criminology unless 'they themselves change to become pro-feminist, not only in written word but also in deed'.[122]

Serial sex killers in a 'critical' frame

Finally, what, if anything, have critical criminologists contributed to an understanding of serial sex murder? Beyond Jefferson's sympathetic account of the Yorkshire Ripper's vulnerabilities and anxieties, they have given this problem very little attention, with the exception of a predictable attempt to shift the focus from the long roll call of male serial killers to that of 'female serial killers'. In *Using Murder: The Social Construction of Serial Homicide*, Philip Jenkins provides a social constructionist account of serial homicide that acknowledges the radical origins of this approach, and the influential work of Stuart Hall in particular. Jenkins, however, deploys this method in a decidedly reactionary way – by exploring the uses made of the serial killer phenomenon by radical groups, especially 'feminists'. A whole chapter is devoted to debunking radical feminist constructions of serial murder as 'femicide'.[123] Appalled by the suggestion that all men are potential rapists or

---

119 Connell, 2002, pp 93–4. Connell takes the opportunity here to point out that there is 'no such thing as "*the* hegemonic masculinity thesis" '. It is a concept that may function in a number of ways in analyses of violence, e.g. it may help to explain 'the cultural embedding and specific shape of violence in communities where physical aggression is expected or admired among men'. It can also help to explain the knee-jerk reaction of critical criminologists to feminist work on men's violence.

120 Hearn, 1996, pp 207–8.

121 Collier, 1997, p 193, original emphasis.

122 Hearn, 2003, p 13.

123 Another chapter debunks the view, attributed to African-American commentators, that serial murder is racial persecution by predominantly white men. Minority ethnic serial killers, he insists, 'undoubtedly exist': Jenkins, 1994, p 45. It soon becomes apparent why he wants them to exist – he believes that taking account of 'the black component' of serial homicide counters the feminist argument that this is a hate crime: Jenkins, 1998, pp 17–20.

sex killers, Jenkins condemns 'the feminist' interpretation of pathological violence as the logical end point of 'otherwise harmless behaviour' such as pornography or sexual harassment. Such a view not only denigrates men; it leads, he believes, to 'extreme or militant action' such as vigilantism and censorship of sexually explicit material. Feminists, he says, have used serial killers to advance their anti-male political agenda by propagating an expansive view of sexual violence as a generalised and systematic assault on women and girls, as 'gender terrorism' no less. Some have even used the Yorkshire Ripper case to 'indict the whole structure of government and media in a patriarchal society', while others have rejected non-feminist women-blaming explanations of serial killers as 'at best a form of collective male denial'.[124]

In Jenkins' view, the best way to respond to all this feminist finger-pointing at men is to challenge the stereotype of the serial killer as male. Women, he insists, have been serial killers too, and in much bigger numbers than previously realised. Pointing to 'the undoubted existence of numerous women through history who have murdered repeatedly', he guesses that 'perhaps 10 to 15 per cent of known American serial killers are women'.[125] The source for this 'undoubted' truth turns out to be Hickey's study of North American serial killers from 1800 to the 1980s. What Jenkins fails to mention is that the study identifies only 34 women killers, 17 per cent of the total number of 203. Moreover, 15 of the 34 women – nearly half – had male accomplices, reducing the number of lone women killers to 19 over a 180-year period, and none fit the bill of a ripper killer. Indeed, according to Hickey, since 1975, women killers have been 'much more likely to kill in response to abuse of various forms' than they used to be, an undisclosed number of the cases in his study having reported violence 'at the hands of husbands, lovers, friends, and other family members'.[126] In other words, Hickey's list of 'female serial killers' includes women who killed men in self-defence. Completely ignoring this important observation, Jenkins declares that Hickey's estimate that women comprise 'at least 15 percent of the whole' number of serial killers represents only the '*known* cases'.[127] Taking a leaf out of Hickey's book – which draws on Pollack's well-known misogynist argument that criminal statistics hide the true extent of women's crime because of 'their innate ability to deceive'[128] – Jenkins surmises that women serial killers are 'likely to be seriously underestimated in any list of offenders'. After all, poisoning, their weapon of choice in the nineteenth

124 Jenkins, 1994, pp 139–45.
125 Jenkins, 1994, p 151. This figure is updated to 'at least fifteen per cent' in Jenkins, 1998, p 18.
126 Hickey, 1991, pp 107–11.
127 Jenkins, 1994, p 45, original emphasis.
128 Hickey, 1991, p 121.

century, was difficult to detect before the development of modern forensic science.[129] So, all in all, feminist claims that serial murder is predominantly committed by men and is attributable to 'a violent male sexual culture' can be dismissed as an ideological rant lacking in 'scholarly merit'.[130]

Intriguingly, this line of argument has been picked up by Mark Seltzer, a scholar boasting such an impressive critical pedigree that he was asked to write a book about violence, sex and addiction by a leading North American feminist. The book, *Serial Killers: Death and Life in America's Wound Culture*, a densely-theorised critique of the 'relentless banality' of the cliché-ridden serial killing literature is strikingly non-feminist, dismissing in a footnote feminist texts that foreground the maleness of serial murder. It would be easy to deride this tactic, to joke that it's good to know the masculinist footnote fetish is alive and well when it comes to receiving feminist work, and leave it at that. But it pays to take a closer look at Seltzer's analysis because it shows so clearly how non-feminists dismiss feminist work by eliding significant differences between various feminist perspectives, making it easier to lump them all indiscriminately into 'the' feminist viewpoint and drum them quickly out of the critical canon.

The feminist texts dropped ceremoniously into the footnote are said to be 'programmatic'. This term is never defined, but is clearly meant to be derogatory, imputing a kind of banal constructivism to feminists who motivate 'motiveless violence' as expressions of 'male power' and invoke a social determinism to account for actions – the killer is 'a product of his social order'.[131] We might note in passing that Jenkins' constructivist but virulently anti-feminist account of serial murder escapes criticism. In fact, in an earlier essay, Seltzer praises Jenkins for his 'astute and generally reliable reassessment' of conventional constructions of serial murder as an almost exclusive white male business, accepting his 'evidence' against this popular 'misconception' without question.[132] Returning to the putatively far less reliable feminist texts discussed in Seltzer's book, we find that they include texts we first encountered in Chapter 2. Cameron and Frazer's *Lust to Kill* is said to be 'somewhat programmatic'. It depicts male violence as an expression of 'male power' and overplays the constructionist card, depicting serial killers as over-socialised men with under-specified 'socially constructed'

---

129 Jenkins, 1994, p 45. If the murders committed by Harold Shipman, the UK's leading serial killer, were added to the list, they might help to challenge the essentialist idea of women's innate ability to deceive. Shipman's murders were undetected when Jenkins wrote his book.

130 Jenkins, 1994, p 156.

131 Seltzer, 1998, p 83.

132 Seltzer dutifully regurgitates Jenkins' report of Hickey's finding that 10 per cent–15 per cent of known female killers are women: 1995, pp 126–9.

desires.[133] Seltzer does not bother explaining why he finds Caputi's *Age of Sex Crime* 'utterly programmatic', but it is not hard to guess the reason: it is vintage radical feminism, condemning rape-murders and other sex crimes as 'crimes of political, patriarchal domination', as logical steps in 'the procession of patriarchal roles', as simply the 'latest expression' in a misogynist tradition of 'gynocide'.[134] Universalising trans-historical and cross-cultural assumptions about men's 'roles' rampage through *Age of Sex Crime* as if there were no tomorrow. In fact, there is no tomorrow for unmodified radical feminists. There is only 'the same old horribleness' of men against women – a '2000 year Reich of endless violence always ever repeated'.[135] As we shall soon see, feminists have launched searching criticisms of this viewpoint over the last four decades. But before turning to that work, it is worth pausing to consider Caputi and Seltzer's very different responses to an early expert speculation about Jack the Ripper, for they go to the heart of what is problematic about both radical feminist and non-feminist framings of sexed violence.

In his pioneering late-nineteenth century study of sexual murder, *Psychopathia Sexualis*, Richard von Krafft-Ebing famously suggested that the Ripper 'does not seem to have had sexual intercourse with his victims, *but very likely the murderous act and subsequent mutilation of the corpse were equivalents for the sex act*'.[136] To Caputi, this diagnosis of the fusion of sex and violence misses the mark inasmuch as the merger is represented as a 'bizarre aberration', when in her view it is 'very much the norm in the patriarchal world'. When a 'male supremacist culture' reigns supreme, sex '*is* violence' and it is used to subjugate women. In the 'Age of Sex Crime', which she dates from the late nineteenth-century ripper killings, the 'sex' in sexual murder is 'patriarchal/pornographic, fundamentally political, sex'. While the 'pure equation of sex and violence is endemic to patriarchal culture', what distinguished the Age of Sex Crime was 'the new mode for such sexual expression' – mutilation sex killing. Moreover, this paradigmatic sex crime coincided with, and arose in opposition to, the emergence of Western feminism.[137] Caputi's collapse of 'patriarchal' sex into violence typifies the radical feminist perspective critiqued in Chapter 1. But at least she registers that there is something ghastly about Krafft-Ebing's speculation that murders and mutilation of corpses are equivalents for

133 Seltzer, 1998, p 83.
134 Caputi, 1987, p 3.
135 I am indebted to Beverley Brown for this précis of the radical feminist perspective in email correspondence.
136 Quoted in Caputi, 1987, p 11 (original emphasis) and in Seltzer 1998, p 149 (without any emphasis).
137 Caputi, 1987, pp 11–12, original emphasis.

sexual acts. By contrast, all that Seltzer has to say about it is that it 'logs' a 'logic of equivalence, or substitution-mania', an equivalence that is simply 'inexplicable'.[138]

The plot thickens slightly here. It is precisely this logic of equivalence that Deborah Cameron queries in her withering critique, quoted earlier in this chapter and in Chapter 2, of 'Ripperology' – the enduring fascination of non-feminists with Jack the Ripper. Yet rather than taking her critique on board, Seltzer places it on his list of annoying 'programmatic' feminisms. In his view, Cameron falters when she depicts serial killers as 'a pathological symptom of a certain kind of masculinity' located 'at the extreme end of a continuum of sexual violence whose less extreme manifestations are normalised by a culture structured around systematic gender inequality'. Seltzer has no time for such 'bottom-line gender explanations' that posit a continuum between 'normal and pathological males'.[139] But had he read on, he would have found Cameron pointing out something important about early expert interpretations of addictive violence that he completely overlooks. As she shows, Krafft-Ebing – unlike today's experts – recognised that what distinguished the homicidal violence of men like Jack the Ripper was 'precisely, the *fusion* of sexual desire and the desire to punish and obliterate its object'. This 'conflation of lust and loathing', Cameron says, 'ought to be impossible to overlook when it is pushed to the limit of murder'.[140] Yet not only is it overlooked in late twentieth century non-feminist accounts of serial murder – anyone raising their head to say so runs the risk of being dismissed as 'programmatic'.

Such is Seltzer's disdain for what he sees as feminism's 'levelling conviction' that sadistic violence is 'a permanent and transhistorical component of the male psyche' that he overlooks a very significant development – the challenge to that very conviction mounted by feminists themselves. First, he drops Maria Tatar's *Lustmord: Sexual Murder in Weimar Germany* into a footnote without bothering to indicate that Tatar contests the representation of male violence as universally sadistic.[141] In her historical account of male violence in the context of artistic production in Weimar Germany, violence is the expression of a sexual politics of a very specific cultural moment, and *not* 'a transhistorical phenomenon wholly resistant to change'.[142] Second, and even more telling, Elizabeth Frazer, dismissed as a 'programmatic' feminist, is on record as expressing discomfort with Caputi's depiction of 'men's torture of women as a constant, manifesting itself in a variety of ways in

138 Seltzer, 1998, p 149.
139 Seltzer, 1998, pp 83, 127 and 142–3 quoting Cameron, 1994, p 151.
140 Cameron, 1994, pp 152–3, original emphasis.
141 Seltzer, 1998, p 143.
142 Tatar, 1995, pp 39–40.

every epoch'. On the contrary, Frazer believes that sex killing is a 'highly specific cultural phenomenon that cannot easily be assimilated into an age-old tradition'.[143] That many feminist scholars have dissented from radical feminist constructions of men's violence as eternally constant is of no consequence to Seltzer, who shares the standard non-feminist penchant for painting all feminist views as equally 'extreme' and 'anti-male'.

Once again, then, Collier's 'crimes of men *as men*' are obscured, this time in Seltzer's self-consciously critical psychoanalytically-inflected account of addictive violence in 'the pathological public sphere' of Western societies. Psychoanalytical insights that 'in our unconscious we are all killers', in 'the real of our desires we are all murderers' and 'we are all killers in the unconscious of our desires' – reassert the universal 'we' challenged in feminist work on violence. With the 'Man' question effectively bracketed, the path is open for Seltzer's account of a 'wound culture' in which we all participate in a 'pathological cultural sphere'.[144] And so, in the final analysis, this interpretation of serial violence turns out to be no more socially literate than Jefferson's psychosocial or Jenkins' social constructivist offerings. It is surely past time to turn to the feminist work on men's violence that is continually ignored, misrepresented and traduced by not so critical 'critical' commentators inside and outside the criminology discipline.

143 Frazer, 1989, p 232.
144 Seltzer, 1998, pp 142, 256 and 266.

Chapter 5

'Men's violence' on the agenda – proliferating feminisms

Confining feminist perspectives to two chapters as originally planned has proven to be impossible. Feminist interjections have peppered this book from the start; such is our determination to legislate the 'proper' handling of the fraught social problem of men's violence. We are, it could even be said, constitutionally incapable of remaining silent whenever non-feminist commentators say something spectacularly silly, as they so often do, in defence of violent men. But who, exactly, are 'we' and what do we think is the best way to tackle the 'Man' question? Four decades of proliferating feminisms has ensured that there is no single feminist viewpoint on this or any other sex/gender issue, and the movement's conceptualisations of sex, violence and crime are all the more enriched for it. There has even been a hearty discussion, in various feminist camps, about whether 'women' exist. As for the thorny question of how to tackle men's violence against women, such is the depth and diversity of feminist theoretical and political work in that field that whenever I hear or see a reference to '*the*' feminist view, I reach for my revolver.[1]

This chapter addresses the quandaries faced by feminists when they put men's violence – the crimes of men *as men*, no less, against women – on the political agenda. It is centrally concerned with exploring some of the political and theoretical interventions that have made it impossible to refer to '*the* feminist perspective', or even 'feminists', without displaying a rank ignorance of the richly diverse body of work that calls itself 'feminist'. Speaking of rank ignorance, none are more wilful than the non-feminist analyses that brought Chapter 4 to a close. Why then, begin this chapter with yet another execrable non-feminist misrepresentation of a feminist text – one, as it happens, that helped bring Chapter 2 to a close? There are two good reasons for doing so. First, it serves as a final salutary reminder that this book's 'main

---

1 Fellow Foucauldian David Halperin reaches for his revolver whenever he hears anyone who does not share Foucault's political vision invoke 'truth': Halperin, 1995, p 185. I reach for mine then, too.

enemy' is not radical feminism, but rather anti-feminists who deny that men's violence is a problem and launch ill-conceived attacks on feminists who say that it is. Second, reclaiming this particular feminist text from yet another untoward anti-feminist attack helps to pinpoint a significant and previously unheralded moment in the transformation of feminist thought, a moment, in the late 1980s, when some feminist scholars began to take the postmodern or discursive turn, shifting to poststructuralist-inflected articulations of sexed violence. Such moments are, of course, profoundly significant for anyone intent as I am on distinguishing radical feminist from poststructuralist articulations of the 'Man' question.[2]

On the cusp of post-radical feminism

In Chapter 4, we saw that Seltzer praised Jenkins' supposedly 'reliable reassessment' of the serial killer literature. Let us test Jenkins' reliability by considering how he handles Wendy Hollway's analysis of the 1981 Yorkshire Ripper trial, published in *Feminist Review* that year. According to Jenkins, this piece typifies the execrable radical feminist representation of serial murder as 'femicide'. To make his case, he quotes the following passages:

> Sutcliffe's trial demonstrated men's collaboration with other men in the oppression of women . . . the trial refused to recognise the way in which Sutcliffe's acts were an expression – albeit an extreme one – of the construction of an aggressive masculine sexuality and of women as its objects. This 'cover-up' exonerates men in general even when one man is found guilty.[3]

Ignoring her evidence-based argument in its entirety, Jenkins then proceeds straight to her final salvo:

> . . . the voice Sutcliffe obeyed was not the voice of God or delusion, but of the hoardings on the streets, of newspaper stands, of porn displays and of films. It is the voice which addresses every man in our society and to that extent, as the feminist slogan claims, all men are potential rapists.[4]

---

2 Characterising feminism as being divided into more and less developed forms is, of course, problematic. I do so in the same spirit as Beverley Brown – in the hope that mine, like hers, provides 'topoi for reflection and formulation not prescriptions': Brown, 1990, p 154. I discuss the trap of constructing a binary opposition between 'low' liberal feminism manifested as lumpen legal feminism and 'high' poststructuralist and postcolonial feminisms in Howe, 1995, pp 64–9.

3 Quoted in Jenkins, 1994, p 14.

4 Quoted in Jenkins, 1994, p 22.

Naturally, such sweeping generalisations, which abounded in radical feminist texts at the time, upset non-feminist men.[5] But what is interesting is that Jenkins misquotes Hollway in two telling ways. First, he omits her inverted commas around the words 'cover up' – a sure sign that she is intent on problematising the notion of a male conspiracy. Then he omits two crucial sentences, the very ones in which Hollway stands the entire conspiracy theory on its head:

> It is *not* necessary to argue that the men whose accounts I cite were doing this consciously or intentionally. The power of a discourse resides in its hegemony, in the way it passes as truth, in the way its premises and logic are taken for granted.[6]

Two points are salient here. First, Jenkins' assessment, far from being reliable, misrepresents Hollway's argument, and thus misses what is so significant about it. Second, there *is* something new and important in the way in which Hollway frames the problem. Certainly, there is a tension in her argument. On the one hand, she seems to join in the radical feminist refrain that all men collaborate to oppress women. But on the other, she makes an important move towards an understanding of the power of dominant discourses to determine what counts as 'truth'. These discourses, she suggests, 'have the effect of distorting systematically (though not necessarily intentionally) the understanding of men's masculinity and its expression through their sexuality'.[7] In Foucauldian discourse analysis, of course, discursive effects are everything; there is nothing remotely systematic or intentional about them. Still, Hollway's analysis is an important early intervention that stands on the cusp of a new post-radical feminist approach to sexed violence.

As alluded to in Chapter 2, another text standing on the cusp of a new approach is Cameron and Frazer's *Lust to Kill*. Notice, first of all, how their radical feminist perspective is placed in the past tense in their preface:

> Our interest in the subject of murder came out of our involvement in political work on pornography and rape. Alongside our sisters in various groups we had developed a radical feminist analysis of male violence, but we were still mystified by the brutal and irrational desires underlying it.[8]

---

5 Interestingly, while Jefferson praises some feminist analyses of the Yorkshire Riper case, he does not mention Hollway's, although he does draw on her later work exploring the investments individuals make in contradictory subject positions to help him formulate his 'socially literate' view of violent men: Jefferson, 1997a, p 546.

6 Hollway, 1981, p 33, emphasis added.

7 Hollway, 1981, p 33.

8 Cameron and Frazer, 1987, p ix.

Tellingly, their demystifying method of choice is Foucauldian discourse analysis, a method enabling them to query the assumption of researchers on the subject of 'sex murder' that 'somewhere there is a kernel of truth about why it occurs'. Challenging the idea that interviewing sex murderers will reveal that truth, Cameron and Frazer argue that the accounts the killers give of themselves, and the accounts of psychiatrists and other experts are nothing but 'constructed texts'. As such, 'they depend, like biographies and news reports, on the codes of the culture to give them meaning'. The killer is not telling us 'the truth' about his crime when he says 'I really loved her' or 'I was just cleaning up the streets' – he is resorting to a learnt formula, a cultural code, such that the 'discourse by which sex-killing is made intelligible to us, whether it comes from the killer, a psychiatrist or *The Sun*, is not parasitic on some higher truth: it is the heart of the matter'.[9] Interestingly, of all the examples they could have chosen to illustrate the close relationship between murder and discourse about murder, they pick the 'celebrated' Pierre Rivière case, the one Foucault used to demonstrate the indissoluble links between desire, text and action, and that I used against him in Chapter 3. While Cameron and Frazer do not suggest that the available discourses '*caused* Rivière to kill', they insist that 'human culture crucially involves processes of representation, and the representations available to Riviere shaped the form of his killing and the way he understood it'.[10]

Here we see the beginning of a very different kind of feminist analysis, one that not only recognises that dominant discourses are implicated in violence, but also asks Foucauldian questions about the power of discourse to construct truth. For students learning to appreciate that discourse is the heart of the matter when it comes to understanding sex, violence and crime, *Lust to Kill* serves as a useful foundational text, unlike Selter's book in which men disappear completely under his anti-constructivist onslaught – a staggering accomplishment in a book about serial killers. In sum, Cameron and Frazer's pioneering feminist analysis of the lust to kill is noteworthy for its attempt to break out of the radical feminist mould. For all its constructivist faults, it paved the way for postmodern feminist framings of the 'Man' question to which we now turn – framings that ostensibly 'critical' non-feminist studies consign to footnotes or the ether so as not to contaminate their constructions of 'the' feminist perspective on men's violence. So let us turn our backs at last on anti-feminist critiques masquerading as reliable and

9 Cameron and Frazer, 1987, pp xi–xii.
10 Cameron and Frazer, 1987, pp xii–xiii, original emphasis. That Cameron and Frazer do not give any indication – in a book about the maleness of the lust to kill – that they find Foucault's 'heroic' interpretation of this male killer problematic is a particularly poignant example of the blinding power of this the dominant view of the case.

objective agenda-free assessments of early feminist theoretical encounters with 'sex crime'. It is surely past time to turn to feminist political and theoretical interventions that have fundamentally transformed 'the' feminist response to the problem of men's violence against women.

Proliferating feminisms – upping the anti

There are many ways of telling the story of the proliferation of widely divergent feminisms in the late twentieth century. All are fraught with dangers of commission and omission. As postcolonial critics have noted, an inherent problem with narration and representation is that something always gets left out, requiring us to ask: what is 'covered over', what kind of 'reading is being privileged', 'what is not there?'.[11] What then will be left out of my story? Let it be said from the start, a great deal. Extensive debates within legal feminism about rape and pornography are barely alluded to; French feminist theory and psychoanalytic theory not at all. There is very little either on non-Foucauldian poststructuralist feminist interventions. My story, informed by feminist appropriations of Foucault and by the black, minority and Third World feminist writings that informed my teaching in the 1990s, is a necessarily selective account. It draws on some of the key texts, now canonical in my courses, which helped to transform feminist framings of the 'Man' question. Paying tribute to these texts is a small contribution to the larger project of de-subjugating feminist knowledges buried and silenced by non-feminists.

In the last third of the twentieth century, Western feminism underwent some spectacular transformations. Most crucially, as early as the 1970s, the speaking positions of feminists making globalising claims on behalf of women came under close scrutiny *within* the women's movement. The first significant challenge, led by black and minority ethnic women, and by postcolonial and Third World women activists and theorists, took the form of a wholesale attack on dominant or 'imperial' feminism – that is, any denomination of white feminism that presumes to speak for all women. Another important intervention was that of feminists influenced by poststructuralist theories. To be clear: while they had different starting points, these were not completely separate developments – some black and minority women favoured poststructuralist theories, others rejected them; white feminists joined anti-racism movements; many were adamantly opposed to postmodern theory. But together, they helped bring about an explosion of vibrant feminisms that confronted class, heterosexist and ethnocentric biases within dominant feminist thought by focusing attention on the

11 Gunew, 1990, p 61.

significant social, economic, sexual and racial differences that divided women.[12]

While 'difference' was to become a constant feminist preoccupation in the 1980s and 1990s, especially in poststructuralist feminist circles, it should be emphasised that it was black women, women of colour, minority ethnic women and Third World women who placed the very different agendas of differently located women on the feminist table.[13] Well before white post-structuralists philosophers started questioning the 'we' of the feminist movement, black, Third World and postcolonial feminists forged powerful critiques of white Western feminism's tendency to universalise the experi-ence of white Western women across cultural and national boundaries and its presumption to speak for others. Black and other 'minority' critiques came first; poststructuralist feminist interrogations of the 'highly ethno-centric biases' of any strategies that resort to a universal 'we', a poor second. Blessed though we may have been with postmodern-inflected theoretical tools for dismantling authoritative voices, white feminist theorists did not usually set off interrogating our own ruses of power until well after minority women had interrupted the self-authorising move through which white fem-inists assumed a right to speak for all women.[14] White poststructuralist feminist critiques of the old analytical standbys of second wave feminism – its commitment to a global feminism, its presumption of a universal category of women – provided no more than a supportive background chorus to the voices of feminist women marked by dominant groups as racially 'other'. Cumulatively though, all these challenges to the dominant liberal and radical feminisms of the 1970s helped to ensure that the vital questions facing the feminist movement in the 1980s and 1990s were internal ones – questions related to heterosexism, to unacknowledged com-plicities with imperialism, to state violence and to what Third World scholar Chandra Mohanty called the 'institutionalisation of difference *within* femi-nist discourses'.[15] Drawing on decolonisation movements, movements for racial equality and gay and lesbian movements as well as Marxist, psycho-analytic and poststructuralist methodologies, feminist theorists and activists set about problematising white radical feminist assumptions about the uni-

12 Robyn Wiegman addresses these issues when narrating 'the imperative towards difference among women' in the United States: Wiegman, 2001, pp 359–60.
13 Key texts include Trinh, 1989 and hooks, 1990.
14 Butler, 1992, pp 6–7. Chandra Mohanty puts it this way (in a footnote): the feminist turn to postmodernism in the 1980s helped to fragment 'unitary assumptions about gender' and facilitated a 'more differentiated analysis of inequality' between women, but this critique was 'prefigured in the earlier political analysis of Third World feminists': Mohanty, 1989–90, p 181, n 4.
15 Mohanty 1992, pp 74–5, original emphasis.

versality of 'male oppression'. In the process, they ushered in new ways of formulating feminist agendas.

Much of the story of this political and intellectual ferment falls outside the scope of this book. The in-fights and stand-offs over postmodernism, the dastardly othering of other feminisms as inferior, the close interrogations of our own and others' speaking positions, these have all been documented elsewhere.[16] Nor is there space to explore complex analyses of the incapacity of any social group, even marginalised ones, to escape entanglement with power and domination.[17] What is noteworthy, however, is that by the close of the twentieth century, feminist theory and practice had moved light years from 1970s and 1980s-style radical feminism. In particular, by 1990, the universalising and essentialising all-men-are-potential-rapists viewpoint that so many non-feminists still today like to portray as *the* feminist view had been well and truly debunked by a host of proliferating and often conflicting feminisms.

One of the most difficult conceptual issues to be addressed was that of how to reframe 'male violence' so that it could deal with the fact that specific incidents of that violence are experienced differently – and represented differently – by women living in diverse social locations. For even when the analysis is confined to Western countries, many women do not name their experiences of sexed violence as violence, and many do not feel solidarity with other women victimised by men. What follows is not a definitive list of early challenges to hegemonic feminist theory and practice in this field, but rather some representative samples of so-called 'minority' feminist critiques of dominant white feminism featured in reading materials for my course. As we shall see, these critiques did not usually prioritise the issue of men's violence, but nevertheless, they were to radically alter its discursive and political framing.

Against imperial feminism – who speaks for whom about what?

Minority feminist criticism of dominant white feminist claims to speak for all women came from many quarters. Several early texts have now achieved canonical status, perhaps none more so than *This Bridge Called My Back*, an anthology of writing by self-defined radical women of colour living in the United States – Black, Asian, Latina and Native Americans – first published in 1981. Their stated aim was to tell women, especially white middle-class women, about experiences which divided them as feminists, and to examine 'intolerance, prejudice and denial of difference within the feminist

16 Howe, 1995.
17 Bar On, 1993.

movement'.[18] For Cherríe Moraga, one of the book's editors, ranking oppressions and failing to specify oppressions or question how we internalise our own oppression were dangerous practices. Taking this challenge further, she suggested that even the word 'oppression' had 'lost its power'. New words were needed to 'describe women's fear of and resistance to one another'.[19] In the meantime, fundamental class and race differences between women had to be addressed by privileged white women. As contributor Audre Lorde put it, difference was a 'fund of necessary polarities between which our creativity can spark like a dialectic'. Recognising differences between women and making them strengths was the most powerful force for change – and the best chance, as she famously put it, of dismantling 'the master's house'.[20]

Because the contributors were so clearly focused on the failure of white feminists to adequately address the question of differences between women, violence within the master's house barely figured in *This Bridge Called My Back*. It is mentioned only in passing, for example, when Nellie Wong said she had 'questions and more questions about violence against women, against children, against ethnic minorities, against gays'.[21] Even when a contributor queried whether there was 'any oppression that women experience that is that total', meaning that it 'literally affects their physical well-being on a day to day basis', the first response of another contributor was to 'make a joke' by nominating heterosexuality. Her second choice was 'battering' – she felt that was 'maybe something, but not necessarily, only in extreme incidences'.[22] It seems the contributors to *Bridge* were too involved in the broader struggle against what the Combahee River Collective called 'racial, sexual, heterosexual and class oppression' to single out violence against women as a concern, although the collective did set up a refuge for battered women.[23]

A similarly framed struggle was taking place in Britain where, in the early 1980s, Valerie Amos and Pratibha Parmar contested the claims of white feminism to speak for all women in their widely acclaimed article, 'Challenging Imperial Feminism'. In their view, the British women's movement, rooted as it was in an imperial history, was 'oppressive' to black and Asian women and profoundly ignorant of the ways in which white women's gains 'have been and still are' made at their expense. The time had come to move away from celebrating universality in order to work through the implications of differences among women's experiences, particularly in the

---

18 Moraga and Anzaldúa, 1983, p xxiii.
19 Moraga, 1983, pp 29–30.
20 Lorde, 1983, p 99.
21 Wong, 1983, p 179.
22 Smith and Smith, 1983, p 115.
23 Combahee River Collective, 1983, p 210.

family.[24] White feminists tended to pathologise minority families, creating images of passive Asian women subjected to oppressive family practices or black women subjected to particularly virulent 'sexism' in Afro-Caribbean communities. As for the 'hysteria in the Western women's movement' over issues such as arranged marriages, purdah and female-headed households, this was beyond 'the Black woman's comprehension', tied as it was to imperial feminism's notions of good and bad practice.[25]

A key way in which this black British feminist challenge to white feminism differed from that in *Bridge* was the specific critical attention given to feminist campaigns around sexual violence. For Amos and Parmar, these campaigns had failed to problematise how violence against women is always already raced violence. Historically, highlighting white women's vulnerability to sexual violence in order to bring in legislation justifying an extension of state power had oppressive implications for men and women living in colonial countries. There were double standards for white men who were rarely penalised for sexually assaulting black women, while black and immigrant men were still, in contemporary Britain, racially denigrated as the main perpetrators of violence against women. It followed that Amos and Parmar agreed with white feminist Vron Ware who insisted that 'any talk of male violence that does not emphatically reject the idea that race or colour is relevant automatically reinforces these racist images'. It was then, not the family that was 'the main source of oppression' for black and especially Asian women – 'the British state through its immigration legislation' had destroyed Asian families, separating husbands and wives, parents from children, and demanding proof that arranged marriages were 'genuine'. Black and Asian feminists therefore demanded the right to 'struggle around the issue of family oppression ourselves' without political interference from judgmental white imperial feminists.[26]

In the 1980s, these demands came to the centre of Western feminist forums. In Australia, for example, several hundred women protested at the handling of black and migrant women's issues at the 1984 Women and Labour Conference. Sri Lankan immigrant Suvendi Perera, who attended the conference, put it this way: white feminists were a long way off from 'getting it right'. They needed to learn to 'let minority women define their own experience in its specificity', to be more responsive to different women's priorities and most importantly, they needed to think about these issues more carefully 'so that they have more to offer than good intentions and a haphazard willingness to accommodate minorities within their already

24 Amos and Parmar, 1984, pp 3–7.
25 Amos and Parmar, 1984, pp 8–11.
26 Amos and Parmar, 1984, pp 11–15.

defined frameworks'.[27] That was a hard lesson for white Australian feminists to learn, as the so-called 'Bell debate' – a classic case of white settler women speaking for and appropriating the voice of a racialised minority – was to demonstrate.

The 'Bell' debate was sparked in 1989 when white anthropologist Diane Bell published 'Speaking about Rape is Everyone's Business', her account of sexual assault within Aboriginal communities in Central Australia. The article itself was controversial enough. First, it was tantamount to a declaration that white feminists had a right to speak on behalf of Aboriginal women experiencing violence from Aboriginal men. Second, she used an Aboriginal woman, Topsy Napurrula Nelson, as informant and 'co-author'. Making matters worse, the editors of the journal that published her article refused to publish a letter of protest written by Jackie Huggins and 11 other Aboriginal women expressing their objections to the idea that rape is 'everybody's business'. That was nothing more than 'white imperialism of others' cultures which are theirs to appropriate, criticise and castigate':

> One might see rape as being everyone's business from a privileged, white middle-class perspective, however, when you are black and powerless it is a different story.

Furthermore, white settler women needed to question their complicity in violence:

> ... just because you are women doesn't mean you are necessarily innocent. You were, and still are, part of that colonising force. Our country was colonised on both a racially and sexually imperialistic basis. In many cases our women considered white women worse than men in their treatment of Aboriginal women, particularly in the domestic service field.[28]

The 'Huggins-Bell debate', as Aboriginal writer Eileen Moreton-Robinson referred to it, raised central issues within feminism about 'irreducible differences, incommensurabilites and white race privilege'. It gave Aboriginal women a public space in which to rebuke white feminists for appropriating

27 Perera, 1985, p 123.
28 Huggins *et al*, 1991, p 506. Huggins circulated the protest letter and the editor's letter of rejection at a Women and Anthropology Conference in Adelaide in 1990, where she urged the white feminist audience to question the complicity of settler white women in racism and colonial violence. My response was to undertake to ask the editors to reconsider their decision to refuse to publish the letter of Huggins *et al*. They flatly refused to do so. The letter was not published until 1991 after a great deal of pressure from feminist groups. The editors denied that they had refused to publish the letter: Editorial, 1991, p 505.

their experience and to contest the assumption that there is 'a universal feminist voice which can speak on behalf of all women'[29] – even, or perhaps especially, about men's violence.

Of course, questions about dubious representational practices such as the appropriation of 'other' voices are not just questions for feminists – they trouble all social movements seeking to mobilise political support. Addressing these issues in the context of post-colonial, anti-imperial and multi-cultural politics, postcolonial critic Gayatri Spivak, speaking with Sneja Gunew in 1986, suggested that the question of 'Who should speak' is less important than the question of 'Who will listen?'. Consider, she asks, what happens when white 'hegemonic people' take up a position of 'cardcarrying listeners' who listen to 'someone "speaking as" something or other':

> When *they* want to hear an Indian speaking as an Indian, a Third World woman speaking as a Third World woman, they cover over the fact of the ignorance that they are allowed to possess, into a kind of homogenisation.[30]

Even to state 'this is a white position' is, Spivak argues, to homogenise. As for the self-effacing response of the privileged, 'politically correct' white man (or woman) who declares that they cannot speak for others precisely because of their privilege, she responds wryly: 'Why not develop a certain degree of rage against the history that has written such an abject script for you that you are silenced?'. On the other hand:

> It is not a solution, the idea of the disenfranchised speaking for them-selves, or the radical critics speaking for them; this question of represen-tation, self-representation, representing others is a problem . . . there has to be a persistent critique of what one is up to, so that it doesn't get all bogged down in this homogenisation.

It was just such 'a very problematic field', but as long as this was recognised, there was some hope.[31]

As we have seen in previous chapters, non-feminists are frequently oblivi-ous to the fact that representational and self-representational practices are problematic fields. But by the 1990s, the problem of speaking for others was

---

29 Moreton-Robinson, 2003, pp 71–2. Moreton-Robinson's recollections of the audience's response to Huggins at the Adelaide conference do not accord with mine. In her discussion of the dispute, Anna Yeatman questions Nelson's co-authorship and outlines her own inter-vention in the debate at a conference in Melbourne at which she asked her 'sister white audience' to think about our complicity in racism: Yeatman, 1993, pp 239–44.

30 Spivak, 1990, pp 59–60, original emphasis.

31 Spivak, 1990, pp 62–3.

firmly on Western feminist agendas. Sneja Gunew's question – 'who speaks for whom about what?' – posed in Australia in 1991, compressed layers of internal political challenges made to white feminism over the previous two decades. So-called 'minority' women – indigenous women, black and migrant women – were 'tired of being spoken for and repeatedly represented as victims who were incapable of taking responsibility for their own liberation'. In fact, they were tired of being called 'minorities' and especially tired of having their life stories 'used as grist to the mill of victimage' – as stories of total domination by patriarchal husbands. They objected strenuously to being cast in a narrative as 'authentic' sufferers weighed down by 'unrelieved oppression' and seeking enlightenment which supposedly would come from mainstream feminism.[32]

Dominant feminism's homogenising narratives of 'victimage' are also targeted in Chandra Mohanty's now classic 'Under Western Eyes: Feminist Scholarship and Colonial Discourses'. First published in 1986 and since republished several times, this article was one of the most influential late twentieth-century interventions against white feminist narrations of global women's oppression. In question was not only the notion of a hastily derived notion of 'universal sisterhood' that assumed a commonality of gender experience across race and national lines. More specifically, Mohanty provides a scathing critique of dominant feminism's uncritical deployment of analytical categories that coded Third World women as 'other'. As she explains:

> An analysis of 'sexual difference' in the form of a cross-culturally singular, monolithic notion of patriarchy or male dominance leads to the construction of a similarly reductive and homogenous notion of . . . 'Third-World difference' – that stable, ahistorical something that apparently oppresses most if not all the women in these countries.[33]

Bluntly, there is no universal patriarchy and 'no international male conspiracy or a monolithic, transhistorical power structure'. Accordingly, a model which pits all women against male domination and invokes a global sisterhood of first and Third World women must be rejected as 'ethnocentric universalism'. So too must a binary analytical framework in which Western feminists constitute themselves as political subjects and Third World women as a homogenous, undifferentiated group leading 'essentially truncated' and victimised lives[34] – 'crushed by the combined weight of "their" traditions, cultures and beliefs, and "our" (Eurocentric) history'. These were all

32 Gunew, 1991, pp 32–3.
33 Mohanty, 1988, p 63.
34 Mohanty, 1988, pp 63–5.

unacceptable analytical frameworks. Western feminists needed to stop deploying an ahistorical category of 'women' that implies that women are globally oppressed by men, regardless of their location. They had to stop ignoring the impact of imperialism. And finally, they had to cease producing Western women as the only legitimate subjects of struggle while representing Third World women 'as fragmented, inarticulate voices in (and from) the dark'.[35]

Interestingly, Mohanty chooses 'women as victims of male violence' as her first illustration of the problematic way in which Western feminist discourses construct 'Third World women' as 'a homogenous "powerless" group often located as implicit *victims* of particular cultural and socio-economic systems'. Discourses that define women systematically as 'the *victims* of male control', as 'archetypal victims' no less, have unfortunate effects. Most problematically, such definitions freeze women into 'objects-who-defend-themselves', men into 'subjects-who-perpetrate-violence', and (every) society into a simple opposition between the powerless (read: women) and the powerful (read: men) groups of people. On the contrary, 'male violence' – and Mohanty questions whether that is 'the appropriate label' – must be theorised and interpreted 'within specific societies'.[36] Interestingly too, she draws on Foucault to critique the understanding of the functioning of power implicit in Western feminist discourses that homogenise Third World women's experiences of men's violence. Such discourses provide a 'false sense of the commonality of oppressions, interests and struggles between and among women globally. Beyond sisterhood, there is still racism, colonialism and imperialism!'. But more than that, the setting up of a 'commonality of Third-World women's struggles across classes and cultures against a general notion of oppression (primarily the group in power – i.e. men)', also assumes 'something like what Michel Foucault calls the 'juridico-discursive' model of power in which power is exercised within a binary system by one homogenous group against another. This model presupposes '*originary* power divisions' and understands power relations to be 'structured in terms of a unilateral and undifferentiated source of power and a cumulative reaction to power'.[37] Men, it is assumed, possess an original or eternal oppressive power; women form a powerless, unified oppressed group that reacts against men's power. As Mohanty reminds us, Foucault rejected this binary model for an understanding of power as exercised by everyone, not by one group over another. It followed that resistance should not be defined as 'cumulatively reactive' to a generalised oppression, but as rather 'inherent in the operation of power'. Pitting a

35 Mohanty, 1989–90, pp 180–1.
36 Mohanty, 1988, pp 66–7, original emphasis.
37 Mohanty, 1988, pp 77–9, original emphasis.

homogenous group of oppressed and victimised women against an equally homogeneous group of oppressive and violent men will simply not do.[38]

Here we see the beginnings of an analysis that would force imperial feminism, or sections of it, to fundamentally rethink itself. By the early 1990s, minority feminists had made significant inroads into dismantling dominant feminism's most problematic discursive practices – speaking for others, appropriating the experiences of marginalised women and mistranslating their concerns. Some had even begun to explore their own complicity in white imperialism and neo-colonialism. As for men's violence, that was rarely named as a pressing issue. Mohanty was not even sure that 'male violence' was an 'appropriate label'. What mattered were specific issues in specific locations. Over the next decade, black, minority ethnic, immigrant women and Third World women would continue to contest white Western feminism's assumptions and presumptions about men, women and violence in their increasingly complex theorisations of the local and the global. We shall explore some of them in Chapter 6. For now, I want to conclude this section by suggesting that Mohanty's analysis in 'Under Western Eyes' perhaps best illustrates how, as Teresa de Lauretis puts it, Foucault's understanding of the social as a diversified field of power relations was 'brought home in the early 1980s when women of colour constituted themselves as feminist critics of feminism.' Certainly, their practice of 'speaking out *within* and *against* feminism' was thoroughly Foucauldian – whether named as such or not – in its focus on local power relations between dominant and marginalised women.[39] Indeed, by the late 1980s, Foucauldian feminism had become a force to reckon with in academic feminism.

Foucauldian feminisms – an introductory note

By now I hope to have disabused readers of any notion that the movement of minority feminists against dominant white feminism and the new theoretical interventions made under the sign of postmodernism that contributed so decisively to the intellectual ferment of 1980s feminism were entirely separate developments. Many black, Third World and minority ethnic feminists utilised postmodern theories, including the influential African-American feminist writer bell hooks, to take a prominent example. In 'Postmodern Blackness', her defence of postmodern theory, hooks explores its possibilities for African-Americans committed to 'reformulating outmoded notions of identity'. The critique of the notion of a universalised, 'static

---

38 Mohanty, 1988, pp 79–81.
39 de Lauretis, 1990, pp 31–3, original emphasis. But see the critique of the institutionalisation of 'a particular brand of postmodern theorising in the U.S. academy' in Alexander and Mohanty, 1997, pp xvii–xviii.

over-determined identity' was, she felt, especially useful for dismantling outmoded essentialist notions of blackness and identity, and for opening up new possibilities for political agency.[40] In 'Choosing the Margin as a Space of Radical Openness', another of her pivotally important contributions to the development of what she called 'counter-hegemonic cultural practice', hooks pinpoints language as a 'place of struggle', a place in which to articulate her own 'multiple voices'. In the lived experience of marginality, resistance to the 'coloniser's tongue' came about through the production of a counter-hegemonic discourse or 'counter-language'. And crucially, this counter-language facilitated resistance to the construction by 'those who name themselves radical critical thinkers, feminist thinkers' of that highly problematic 'discourse about the "Other"'. bell hooks was fed up with dominant groups, feminists included, talking about difference. She wanted them all to stop talking about the 'Other', to 'stop even describing how important it is to be able to speak about difference', and to recognise that 'it is not just important what we speak about, but how and why we speak'.[41]

To take another enlightening example: it was Linda Alcoff, calling herself 'a Panamanian-American, and a person of mixed ethnicity and race: half white/Angla and half Panamanian mestiza', who penned what I regard as the definitive Foucauldian account of 'the problem of speaking for others'. Drawing on Foucault, she called for an analysis of 'rituals of speaking' to identify discursive practices of speaking and writing that demonstrated how the location of the speaker 'turns out to be as important for meaning and truth as what is said'. Understanding that rituals of speaking are 'politically constituted by power relations of domination, exploitation and subordination' helps to reveal how certain privileged locations are 'discursively dangerous'. In particular, the practice of privileged individuals and groups speaking for less privileged groups has resulted in 'increasing or reinforcing the oppression of the groups spoken for'. No wonder that practice was being rejected in some communities.[42] For her part, Alcoff rejected a general retreat from speaking for others, but not before she had thoroughly canvassed arguments, including Foucault's, for and against this controversial political strategy.

In privileging language as a key site of resistance in marginalised local spaces and closely analysing rituals of speaking, hooks and Alcoff gave the lie to the neo-colonialist notion, said to be fashionable within some sections of feminist cultural studies in the 1980s, that black and other minority women were too busy telling the story of their 'minority experience' to play

---

40 hooks, 1990, p 28.
41 hooks, 1990, pp 145–51.
42 Alcoff, 1990–1, pp 6–12.

'postmodern games with language'.[43] While Alcoff engaged with Foucault's work, hooks' yearning for a counter-language could be described as implicitly Foucauldian. Let us turn now to other feminist analysts who – writing explicitly under the sign of postmodernism – made important contributions to the process of rethinking the sex-violence problematic. As we saw in Chapter 1, feminist critics of radical feminism took issue with its near monopoly of the feminist anti-violence agenda from the start. Universaling categories of oppressive, rapist men and oppressed, rapable women, denials of women's sexual agency, assumptions of an essential, cross-cultural women's 'experience' – all of these have been contested by feminists. They have also dissented strenuously from radical *and* liberal feminism's construction of 'a monolithic adversary' of 'male violence'. Recall that, according to Judith Vega, liberal feminists disagreed with radical feminism's wholesale condemnation of heterosex, believing it to be 'natural for women to consent to sex with men'.[44] But both schools of thought saw sexual coercion as 'a social and political fact, invariable in its meaning and context'. Both had a global, static image of 'male violence', a concept evocative of 'a natural masculinity, a postulated male aggression' in opposition to a non-violent femininity. To this, Vega objected that it was 'precisely this thinking in opposites, this tendency to formulate a static problem of violence as diametrically opposed to freedom, that characterises and paralyses feminist thought about sexual violence'.[45] The goal of radical feminism's feminist opponents was to unfreeze that disabling thought process.

In focusing mainly on Foucauldian feminisms, or more broadly, on those informed by a Foucauldian sensibility that may or may not be made explicit, I do not mean to suggest that other poststructuralist feminisms, for example, derridean and psychoanalytical ones, are not worthy of attention. Nor, on the other hand, do I wish to suggest that Foucauldians have won the day in the feminist theory wars. The 'chant of anti-postmodernism', as Judith Butler called it, with its tirelessly repeated chorus line that 'if everything is discourse, then there is no reality to bodies' could be heard loud and strong in countless feminist texts in the 1990s, and still today.[46] Many feminists opposed postmodern thought and Foucault's in particular because they could not see how feminist thought could proceed 'without presuming the materiality of women's bodies, the materiality of sex'. But as Butler explains, this was to miss the point that there is no pre-discursive materiality, no pre-discursive sex – 'sex does not *describe* a prior materiality, but produces and regulates the *intelligibility* of the *materiality* of bodies',

---

43 Gunew 1991, p 33.
44 Vega, 1988, pp 76 and 86.
45 Vega, 1988, p 84.
46 Butler, 1992, p 17. See, e.g. some of the contributions to Ramazanoglu, 1993.

imposing a duality and uniformity on them 'in order to maintain repro-ductive sexuality as a compulsory order'. Moreover, this discursive ordering and production of bodies is itself a 'material violence', one, crucially, that had important implications for understanding representations of violence against women. A case in point is the manner in which law regulates what counts and does not count as rape. As Butler suggests, there is already in this regulation a foreclosure, or 'a violence at work', a marking off in advance of what will or will not qualify as 'rape' in the eyes of the law.[47]

Already this is getting very dense. To simplify: for poststructuralist femin-ists, representational practices need to be carefully scrutinised, and not only those of non-feminists. Feminist discourses are also material practices that can have exclusionary and violent effects in the 'real' world, for example, when they posit a universalising category of women that is actually founded on white women's experience as an analytical and political starting point. As we shall see now, the charting of problematic feminist representational practices was to become a key strategy in the disaggregating of that ugly global monolith, 'male violence'.

Foucauldian feminisms – against radical feminism; rethinking sex, violence and power

While liberal feminists shared with radical feminists the view that male power is omnipotent and male violence an inescapable global phenomenon, critical attention has tended to focus on radical feminism's absolutist stance on sex and violence, and on Catherine MacKinnon's in particular. A case in point is Carol Smart's intervention in the debate over whether rape is about violence or about sex that raged in the 1980s. As we saw in Chapter 1, Smart agreed with MacKinnon that taking the sex out of rape by calling it a crime of violence, as the liberal feminists did, overlooked what was problematic about heterosexuality. But Smart was careful to distinguish her own notion of phallocentric sex from MacKinnon's thesis that all 'heterosex' is coercive. No wonder that a non-feminist 'critical' criminologist felt the need, as we saw in Chapter 4, to drop Smart's very influential Foucauldian feminist book *Feminism and the Power of Law* unceremoniously into a footnote where it could not interrupt his fantasy tale about a radical feminist monop-oly of 'the rape debate'. Retrieving the book from the footnote, we find Smart dissenting from MacKinnon's radical feminist framework in its entirety.

Consider, for example, her view of how feminists should tackle porn-ography. Given the difficulty of identifying clear distinctions between femi-nist approaches in this fraught field, Smart begins by stating her preference

47 Butler, 1992, pp 17–18, original emphasis.

for Beverley Brown's elucidation of the differences of opinion as between 'pornography-as-violence' feminists, who see pornography as violence and demand legal intervention, and 'pornography-as-representation' feminists, who see it as a specific mode of representing the real that demands textual analysis. Placing themselves in the latter camp, Brown and Smart distance themselves from pornography-as-violence feminists like MacKinnon who, as we have seen, thinks that victims' reports of rape not only look a lot like women's reports of heterosexual sex, they also look very similar to what pornography says is sex. In Brown's characterisation of the pornography-as-violence position, pornography reflects and reinforces 'the reality of male power at its most coercive – force and the threat of force. Pornography is the theory; rape is the practice'.[48] But if heterosex is a form of coercion, as MacKinnon maintains, it follows that for her '*any* representation of explicit heterosexuality is a representation of coercion' and so must be banned. Such an all-encompassing definition of pornography leads to a position indistinguishable from the moral right in its reliance on legal censorship – hardly a position that feminists should find comfortable.[49] By contrast, pornography-as-representation feminists like Smart define pornography not in terms of explicitness of images, but as a 'way of seeing'. It is a 'regime of representation' or 'pornographic genre' which encodes women's bodies with a pornographic meaning and pervades cultural forms, from advertising to romantic novels and soap operas. It follows that legal regulation of such pervasive images is not a viable feminist strategy.[50]

MacKinnon's investment in the legal regulation of pornography is not all that bothers Smart. She also finds her broad conceptualisation of women's experience of sexual subordination as a lever to generate law reform to be highly problematic. After all, the idea of a generalised women's experience had been much-criticised within feminism, with the 'most crucial criticism' coming from black women who were 'tired of being included in the sweep of white women's experience'.[51] In Smart's view, a more fruitful line of inquiry than that of postulating a 'women's experience' that no longer had the power to claim a universal validity is to examine precisely how law and other dominant discourses disqualified and silenced women. Take the rape trial. The process of the rape trial is a 'specific mode of sexualisation of a woman's body – a body which has already been sexualised within the codes of a phallocentric culture' – one that is 'structured to meet the needs of the masculine imperative'. In the rape trial, the victim's body becomes literally

48 Brown, 1990, pp 136–7.
49 Smart, 1989, pp 121–2, original emphasis.
50 Smart suggests that feminists need to invent new strategies, perhaps along the lines of a campaign around the 'reform of forms of feminine visibility' suggested by Brown. Smart, 1989, pp 124–8; Brown; 1981, p 15.
51 Smart, 1990b, p 200.

saturated with sex. Moreover, every rape trial tells the same story – a story of a humiliating, degrading ordeal. Now if this sounds similar to the radical feminist understanding of rape, the crucial point of difference is that rather than accepting this story as eternal and unchangeable, Smart asks how it came to be the dominant account. To answer this question, she draws on Foucault's identification of the body and sexuality as 'sites for the deployment of power in the emerging disciplinary societies of the eighteenth and nineteenth centuries'. The construction of sex and sexual desires as central to identity or 'the ultimate truth of a person' was, he argued, a pivotal mechanism of power. The saturation with sex of the woman's body in the rape trial exemplifies this process. But the point is that it *is* a process, a cultural process – and a challengeable one at that. Sex is not 'something which occupies a space outside culture' positioning women as eternally sexed as victims, thus providing no hope for the possibility of 'desexuating' women's bodies. Understanding how women are discursively constituted as raped and rapable within dominant discourses allows for the possibility of telling a different, counter-hegemonic story about rape – a story of resistance rather than victimisation.[52]

Women as men's eternal victims, condemned by their sex and by sex itself to be forever subordinated to men, is what really irked radical feminism's many feminist critics. Why, they asked, would a feminist want to see 'forcible violation of women' as 'the essence of sex'?[53] What investment could they have in wanting to find political origins in 'an originary penetrative sexual violence'? Is this not the quintessential patriarchal fantasy – 'the phallus as origin of all value, signifier of signifiers'? Why, they asked of MacKinnon, 'concede to the penis the power to push us around, destroy our integrity'; what is 'the desire at work' that collapses the distinction between victims' reports of rape and women's reports of sex.[54] MacKinnon's view that heterosexuality is 'the cause of women's oppression *tout court*' was simply far too reductive an explanation of the operations of power around sex. Foucault's theory about the discursive production of sexuality was more convincing to many feminists who saw that his work led to a recognition that feminist work is 'not just a critique of the ways in which sexuality is spoken about' – but also is 'itself a part of the discourse on sexuality'. As such, his work too had to attract critical scrutiny. One needed to ask of any feminist intervention: does it 'continue or subvert ways of speaking about sexuality'; does it correspond to non-feminist ways of talking about sex or do they undermine them?[55] The verdict was in early on radical feminism –

52 Smart, 1990b, pp 205–7.
53 MacKinnon, 1989, p 329.
54 Gatens, 1996, pp 87–8 quoting MacKinnon, 1989, p 336.
55 Bell, 1993, pp 24–6.

see sexual violation as the essence of sex, concede ultimate power over women to the supposedly violating penis? Never.

But Foucauldian feminists did not rest there. They took aim at Foucault, too. His failure to consider 'the *gendering* aspects of sexuality', to consider how the strategies of sexuality that he uncovered 'affect the relationship *between* men and women as gendered individuals', that, as Vicki Bell observed in her study of feminism, Foucault and the problem of incest, was the 'real stumbling block' to a Foucauldian feminism. On reflection, she suspected that the real problem was that Foucault's concept of power seemed to preclude a model in which power is held over one group by another.[56] Certainly, disputes between feminists about the utility of Foucault's theory of power did, indeed, keep feminists busy in the 1980s and 1990s. Keeping our focus firmly on how those disputes played out around the sex-violence problematic, we find the sticking point was Foucault's claim that violence and power are inherently different and separable. Where 'the determining factors saturate the whole', he said at one point, 'there is no relationship of power'.[57] But, his feminist detractors asked in an apparent reprise of radical feminism, what of women's experience of rape, battery and psychological abuse?

> To define male power as an inherently separable phenomenon from male force and domination, as Foucault would have us do, is to disregard the ways in which this power is frequently transformed into violence. A woman living in an abusive relationship feels the continuum of her partner's anger and force, sees that the day-to-day exercise of power is the stuff out of which explosions of abuse and violence are made.[58]

It was all very well for Foucauldian feminists to want to see victims of rape and other forms of men's violence as resisters, emboldened by Foucault's claim that power was everywhere, but what they were forgetting was how women actually experienced violence – namely, as domination. This forgetting was attributed to their Master's injunction that local, variable power relationships, the kind that can 'operate between individuals, in the bosom of the family' for example, had to be distinguished from 'states of domination', in which relations of power, instead of being variable, are 'firmly set and congealed'.[59] In the eyes of Foucault's feminist critics, this distinction between power and domination was inadequate for an understanding of the peculiarities of women's oppression. Sometimes power relations are reversible, sometimes not; they are '*constricted*' rather than congealed.[60]

56 Bell, 1993, p 27, original emphasis.
57 Foucault, 1982b, p 221.
58 Deveaux, 1996, p 225.
59 Foucault, 1988d, p 3.
60 Allen, 1996, pp 277–8, original emphasis.

Well, Foucault's feminist defenders reply, he came to that very same understanding, albeit belatedly. As he explained in a late interview:

> In many cases the relations of power are fixed in such a way that they are perpetually asymmetrical and the margin of liberty is extremely limited. To take an example, very paradigmatic to be sure; in the traditional conjugal relation in the society of the eighteenth and nineteenth centuries, we cannot say that there was only male power; the woman herself could do a lot of things: be unfaithful to him, extract money from him, refuse him sexually. She was, however, subject to a state of domination, in the measure where all that was finally no more than a certain number of tricks which never brought about a reversal of the situation.[61]

Thus, domination, defined here as a state of 'perpetually asymmetrical' power relations, is still based on the operations of power. For Vicki Bell, it follows that a Foucauldian feminist, recognising contradictions within domination, can be optimistic because 'if power is exercised not possessed, contingent rather than static, feminist opposition to the various operations of power may expect to identify more gaps and weaknesses in power's operations'.[62] Male power was neither total nor eternal – it was eminently challengeable.

Not that Foucauldian feminists did not have issues with Foucault's formulation of the sex-violence problematic. Take his infamous dismissal of child sexual abuse as a 'bit of theatre' and his controversial view that adult-child sex should never be subjected to legislative proscription.[63] His call for its decriminalisation was crossing a bridge too far, even in the eyes of his feminist supporters. The first difficulty was that feminist analyses of incestuous abuse, postmodern ones included, emphasise asymmetrical power relations – the sort that he seemed to concede with his belated recognition of 'states of domination'. Foucault on the other hand, being fixated in his earlier work on *how* power is exercised rather than on *who* is exercising it, had not yet factored 'domination' into his analysis of adult-child sex.[64] The second difficulty was that it was feminists who had put adult-child sex onto the political and law reform agenda by naming it as child sexual abuse, and there were not many feminists around who would disagree that this was a necessary endeavour.[65] Then, when he waded into the rape debate with French feminists in the late 1970s, Foucault was getting in deeper than his understanding of power could carry him. In arguing that sexuality – even violent

---

61 Foucault, 1988d, p 12.
62 Bell, 1993, p 41.
63 Foucault, 1988c, pp 271–85.
64 Bell, 1993, pp 71–2.
65 See, e.g. Smart, 1989 and 1999.

sexuality – should never be subjected to law, he was arguing in effect for a 'desexualisation' of rape in which it was treated as a violent assault, not a sexual crime. This position was similar to that of feminists who argued during the violence-versus-sex debate that raged through the 1980s that rape was an act of violence and was not about sex. But that debate, as Vicki Bell argues, ran into deep 'conceptual muddles' because the participants used the term 'sex' differently and also because there were actually '*three* terms at stake: sex, power and violence'. How the debaters mapped their perspectives onto 'this triangle of terms' is what differentiated them.[66]

By 2000, feminist theorisations of sexual violence had proceeded at such a pace that one feminist analyst felt able to dispense with the entire sex-versus-violence debate in a footnote.[67] However, there is one analytical development that emerged from the disputes that deserves attention – namely, the decisive shift away from radical feminism's preoccupation with the 'terrifying facticity' of rape to explorations of the '*gendered grammar*' of what came to be called the 'rape script'.[68]

New strategies – beyond the 'terrifying facticity' of 'male violence'?

When Sharon Marcus set about drawing up a politics of rape prevention, she began by trying to disabuse feminists antithetical to postmodernism of the idea that poststructuralist theorisations of the discursive constitution of reality were incompatible with feminist political action against rape. One of feminism's most powerful contentions about rape, she reminded them, is that rape is 'a question of language, interpretation and subjectivity'. Feminists have insisted on 'the importance of *naming* rape as violence', and of '*recounting* rape', thus suggesting that experiences of rape 'cannot be said to exist in politically real and useful ways until they are perceptible and representable'. Extending this point, Marcus argues that an effective feminist strategy needed to understand rape 'as a language' and to use that insight 'to imagine women as neither already raped nor inherently rapable'. In this way, she positioned herself directly against the old radical feminist belief in 'the political efficacy of seeing rape as the fixed reality of women's lives', and against 'an identity politics which defines women by our violability'. In brief, her aim was 'a shift of scene from rape and its aftermath to rape situations themselves and to rape *prevention*'.[69]

Crucially, Marcus's explicitly poststructuralist strategy was founded on a recognition of the limitations of law reform for a politics of rape prevention

66 Bell, 1993, pp 161–3 and 170, original emphasis. See further Bell, 1991.
67 Hengehold, 2000, p 204, n 15.
68 Marcus, 1992, pp 387 and 392, original emphasis.
69 Marcus, 1992, p 387, original emphasis.

and more particularly on 'the notorious racism and sexism of the United States police and legal systems' that compromise feminist goals in particular. As Carol Smart and others had argued, attempting to stop rape through legal deterrence is a limited *post facto* kind of strategy – the rape had already occurred, the woman was already raped and, if she decided to take the matter to court, she would have to endure the degrading, humiliating experience of the rape trial. Marcus wanted to start the fight against rape much earlier. Rape should be seen 'not as a fact to be accepted or opposed, tried or avenged, but as a process to be analysed and undermined as it occurs'. Refusing to view rape as 'an inevitable material fact of life', as 'the real fact in our lives', she suggested treating it 'as a *linguistic* fact' – we need to ask 'how the violence of rape is enabled by narratives, complexes and institutions which derive their strength not from outright, immutable, unbeatable force but rather from their power to structure our lives as imposing cultural scripts'.[70]

What does it mean to say rape is a 'linguistic fact'? Several things. It can be taken as referring to the cultural productions and images of rape which transmit assumptions such as women are rapable, women deserve or provoke rape or, on the other hand, lie about rape. It also refers to speech during rape. Another important way to analyse rape as a linguistic fact is to understand that rape is 'structured like a language, a language which shapes both the verbal *and* physical interactions of a woman and her would-be assailant'. Moreover, the language of rape can be outlined along 'raced' as well as gendered axes. In the United States, for example, it had induced white women to fear non-white men as potential rapists, while legitimising 'white men's sexual violence against all women and retributive violence against non-white men in the name of protecting or avenging white women'. More generally, the language of rape solicits women to see themselves as violable, while inviting men to position themselves as 'legitimately violent and entitled to women's sexual services'. It 'structures physical actions and responses as well as words' – for example, 'the would-be rapist's feelings of powerfulness and our commonplace sense of paralysis when threatened with rape'.[71] Rape is a 'scripted interaction which takes place in language' and can be 'understood in terms of conventional masculinity and femininity'. To speak of a rape script – understood as 'a framework, a grid of comprehensibility which we might feel impelled to use' to organise and interpret events – implies a '*narrative* of rape'. Importantly, this narrative can be interrupted and, Marcus argues, stopped by a rewriting of the script:

> Rape does not happen to pre-constituted victims; it momentarily makes victims. The rapist does not simply *have* the power to rape; the social

70 Marcus, 1992, pp 387–9, original emphasis.
71 Marcus, 1992, pp 389–90.

script and the extent to which that script succeeds in soliciting its target's participation help to create the rapists' power. The rape script pre-exists instances of rape but neither the script nor the rape act results from or creates immutable identities of rapist and raped.

Elaborating, Marcus explains that the rape script takes its form from 'a *gendered grammar of violence*, where grammar means the rules and structures which assign people to positions within a script'. For example, white men are positioned as 'legitimate subjects of violence between all men and as subjects of legitimate sexual violence against all women', while men of colour are portrayed as 'ever-threatening subjects of illegitimate violence against white men and illegitimate sexual violence against white women'. Within an intra-racial context, however, the grammar of rape 'generically predicates men as legitimate perpetrators of sexual violence against women'.[72]

What follows from this analysis? What follows for Marcus is that a feminist strategy against rape has to focus on displacing what the rape script promotes – male violence against women – and put into place what has been excluded, namely 'women's will, agency and capacity for violence'. Her argument builds on an earlier feminist study, one of the few on rape prevention, that had argued against the belief that resisting rape would only anger the would-be rapist and lead to further violence. That study showed that many women had successfully resisted rape, sometimes with assertive remarks or loud screams. Translating this finding into the terms of her analytical framework, Marcus suggests that the grammar of violence defines rape as an act committed against a subject of fear and not against a subject who fights back. So to prevent rape, women must counter the rapist's attempt to place women in 'a sexualised, gendered position of passivity' by 'positioning ourselves as if we were in a fight'. What we need to do, in short, is to revise the gendered grammar of violence and represent women 'in militant new ways'.[73]

Fighting words and very influential ones at that. Several feminist analysts have taken the postmodern or linguistic turn, pursuing its radical shift in focus from the terrifying fact of rape to the cultural scripts which legitimated rape and other forms of violence against women. Some have found Marcus's paradigm of a 'rape *syntax*' – the idea that 'it is not the *fact* of our bodies', but rather the gendered script of violence that 'inexorably inserts us into a circuit of violence' – compelling. Not that they all think the paradigm is beyond criticism. Nina Puren, for example, argues that Marcus's paradigm can only account 'for the female body that is legible as raped' – the body of

72   Marcus, 1992, pp 390–2, original emphasis.
73   Marcus, 1992, pp 395–400.

the all too rare 'enfranchised female subject'. Much more frequently, the victim's account of violation is overpowered in the courtroom by the defendant's narrative of a consensual, romantic encounter.[74] By contrast, Susan Hirsch, one of the first to answer the call to fight rape by treating it as a linguistic fact, compares US and Kenyan media accounts of a 'night of madness' at a Kenyan boarding school in which many young women were raped and several killed by their male schoolmates. She found that these cross-cultural media images of rape and rape identities presented a particularly useful site for contesting rape scripts by revealing the ways in which they are culturally constructed. The 'event', as narrated in the Kenyan press, absolved the boys from blame. It was just a 'tragedy', devoid of acting subjects and embodied victims – 'Besides the 19 who lost their lives, more than 100 were injured. Somehow, in the melee after the boys broke in, 71 were also raped'. Explanations ranged from a decline in school discipline to strained gender relations in Kenya. In sharp contrast, US media accounts blamed traditional African culture and, in tension with that explanation, the 'sexism that plagues women across all cultures'.[75] Kenyan women were collapsed into the category of 'oppressed women', much along the lines of the Western depiction of the subordinate 'Third World Woman' critiqued by Chandra Mohanty. Hirsch concludes that drawing on cross-cultural examples reveals how 'power/knowledge relations configure rape through language and other representational practices', but she warns against constituting 'new global grammars that embrace essentialising assumptions' about rape victims' experiences without adequate interpretations of cultural 'difference'. Multiple mediations of 'the incident', she contends, challenge '*our* understandings of the feminist project against sexual violence'.[76]

While Hirsch does not name her own speaking position, she does raise the critical issue of the central role played by culture and context in legal translations of violence. This brings us to Sherene Razack's analysis of judicial cultural bias in the context of sexual violence against Aboriginal women in Canada; in my view, the definitive study of the 'controversy over culture' in the courts. Identifying herself as a member of a 'non-dominant' group – and more specifically as a woman of colour who does not experience the same degree of marginalisation as do Aboriginal women – Razack argues that in racist societies, any discussion of culture and violence within Aboriginal and immigrant communities can be dangerous. It is especially dangerous for 'racialised' women – women who are 'raced' by their ethnicity, skin colour, accent, religion and 'other visible markers' in the eyes

74 Puren, 1995, pp 17–18, original emphasis.
75 Hirsch, 1994, pp 1032 and 1044–5.
76 Hirsch, 1994, pp 1031 and 1055–6, emphasis added.

of dominant white groups. The violence can be perceived as 'a cultural attribute', a sign of 'backwardness', rather than 'a product of male domination'. Indeed, 'in the face of racism, it has sometimes not made sense for feminists working in the context of violence against women' in these communities to talk about culture at all. The risks are especially acute when it is 'the dominant group who controls the interpretation of what it means to take culture into account'.[77] In her study of Canadian courts, Razack found that white judges accept 'culture' as a defence in sexual assault cases when the accused is an Aboriginal man, handing down lenient sentences on the basis of so-called 'cultural sensitivity'. White male concepts of 'culture, community and colonisation' are used by the courts to 'prevail over gender-based harm', thereby sustaining gendered power difference within groups and at the same time reinforcing the idea that sexual violence within these communities is a cultural attribute, rather than an abuse of power. In the courts' judgments, concepts of culture and community remain unexamined and ungendered, while 'the subtext of colonialism (never named as racism and thus a legacy of the past and not part of the present) informs white judicial cultural sensitivities'.[78]

While Razack's study is unmarked by poststructuralist references, she too subscribes to the poststructuralist idea that rape is 'scripted' in the courtroom. Extending critiques of problematic constructions of deserving and undeserving victims in rape trials, she notes that racialised women are treated as 'inherently less innocent than white women, and the classic rape in legal discourse is the rape of a white woman'. Consequently, the rape script is 'inevitably raced whether it involves intraracial or interracial rape'.[79] Sexual assault emerges once more as a scripted interaction in Alcoff and Gray's superlative analysis of 'survivor discourse', the discourse of survivors of rape, incest and sexual assault. Describing themselves as survivors who have been active in the anti-violence movement and as working 'within (and sometimes against) postmodern theories', Alcoff and Gray subject survivor speech to Foucauldian discourse analysis. They begin with a paradox. Foucault argued that speech is an important site of struggle in which domination and resistance are played out. This suggests that 'speaking out in and of itself' can transform power relations and subjectivities. But he also claimed – as we saw in Chapter 1 – that confessional speech, far from being liberating, is an instrument of domination. Bringing things into 'the realm of discourse' works to 'inscribe them into hegemonic structures and to produce docile, self-monitoring bodies who willing submit themselves' to the authority of experts. Far from attempting to resolve this paradox, Alcoff and Gray

---

77 Razack, 1994, pp 895–7.
78 Razack, 1994, pp 907–8.
79 Razack, 1994, p 899.

draw on 'the contradictory space' of these two claims to initiate a discussion and evaluation of survivor discourse as a political tactic.[80]

What they find especially useful about Foucauldian discourse analysis is that it helps to explain why feminist naming of sexual violence meets with such resistance from dominant discourses. According to Foucault, discourses set out not what is true or false, but what is 'statable' – that is, they 'structure what it is possible to say' through rules of exclusion such as the prohibition of certain words. The term 'rapist father' is an example of prohibited survivor speech. Rendered inconceivable by dominant discourses, it meets near insurmountable obstacles on its way to becoming statable.[81] Alcoff and Gray do believe that survivor speech has been transgressive in challenging conventional speaking arrangements and in presuming 'objects antithetical to the dominant discourse'. For example, the term 'husband rapist' calls into question 'rules of the dominant discourse for forming statements about whether a rape occurred and how to distinguish rape from sex'. But they warn that dominant discourses tend to silence such speech or failing that, try to channel it into 'non-threatening outlets', recuperating their hegemonic position by subsuming survivor discourse 'within the framework of the discourse in such a way that it is disempowered and no longer disruptive'. Examples of such 'strategies of recuperation' include categorising survivor speech as mad or hysterical. Another version of recuperation occurs when survivors incited to speak about or confess stories of childhood sexual abuse, have their stories mediated and interpreted by experts for public consumption on television shows. The dangers of the confessional mode, as Foucault warned, are many – survivor speech becomes a media commodity; it focuses attention on the victim, thereby deflecting attention from the perpetrator; it invites mediation, thus depriving the survivor of her agency and reinstating a binary opposition between 'raw experience' dismissed as 'subjective' and 'objective' knowledge. Most worryingly, breaking the silence about violence when used as a political tactic can become 'a coercive imperative' for survivors to recount their assaults, give details and do so publicly.[82]

How then can survivors overcome the dangers of confessional speech? How can they speak subversively about sexual assault? How else, according to Alcoff and Gray, but by following bell hooks's advice to strive to create discursive spaces in which survivors are enabled to tell theoretically-informed stories about their experiences of abuse and to dispense with expert mediators that soften the impact of their challenges to dominant discourse. So Foucault was right to suggest that discourse is a critical site of

---

80 Alcoff and Gray, 1993, pp 260–3.
81 Alcoff and Gray, 1993, pp 265–7.
82 Alcoff and Gray, 1993, pp 268–79.

conflict. But rather than retreat from bringing sexual violence into discourse – as he might suggest we do – survivors and their feminist supporters must continue to search for new discursive forms. What we need, they conclude, is 'not to confess, but to witness' – to bear witness to the truth of pervasive sexual violence against women and children 'in ways that cannot be contained, recuperated or ignored'.[83] In short, discourse is still the power to be seized, this time by survivors of sexual violence.

Let us conclude this survey of the analytical move from the 'facticity' of sexual assault to its discursive constitution with Carol Smart's historical study of the fight to construct child sexual abuse as abuse in English law. In Smart's telling of the story, this was a classic discursive struggle pitting the medical and legal establishments against child protectionists, women doctors and early feminist campaigners striving to form a counter-discourse in which to name child sexual abuse as a harm. Of all the tactics deployed by twentieth-century apologists for men having sex with children, one stands out. She calls it the 'discursive trick' – the trick of renaming victims of sexual abuse as hysterics or liars. It was this trick, conjured up by male doctors and defence lawyers, which was the most serious hindrance to feminist campaigners trying to redefine sexual abuse as a crime against children. Having unearthed evidence of the legal fraternity's historical and ongoing opposition to the naming of adult-child sex as a harm, Smart believes she had demonstrated the extent to which the criminal justice system and legal practice are perhaps 'the most problematic sites for radical redefinitions to take root'. Crucially, however – and this is a point to which we shall return in Chapter 6 – Smart remained convinced that law, 'understood in its widest meaning, is still one of the most important sites of engagement and counter-discourse'.[84]

Disaggregating 'male violence' – proliferating too far?

While legal feminists have continued to work towards law reforms that will assist victims of sexual assault, feminist analysts opting to take the linguistic turn have opened up the floodgates to a variety of proliferating and sometimes conflicting perspectives. Most importantly, they have opened up spaces in which to engage with what the anthropologist Henrietta Moore calls 'issues of positionality and representativity'.[85] Questioning the universality of women's experience, checking practices of self-representation, refusing to assert the primacy of sexual difference to the exclusion of other forms of difference – all of these made significant conceptual advances for

83 Alcoff and Gray, 1993, pp 280–6.
84 Smart, 1999, pp 404–7 and 392.
85 Moore, 1994b, p 79.

the feminist project. If only they could have been heard outside feminist forums, postmodern feminisms would also have made impossible that facile and reductive non-feminist gesture of referring to *the* feminist approach to the 'Man' question. Eschewing the radical feminist binary analytic dividing always already oppressive, sexually predatory men from oppressed, rapable women, postmodern feminists radically shifted feminist attention to cultural scripts, notably she-asked-for-it provocation scripts and more broadly to the cultural formation that they named as the pornographic genre. In the process, they started to dismantle that creaky lumpen construct, 'male violence'.

As we have seen, questions about white Western feminism's all-encompassing rubric of 'male violence' were first raised by black, immigrant and Third World feminists who objected to the construction of a cross-cultural 'male violence', even questioning the pertinence of that term. State violence and the discursive violence of imperial feminism were more pressing issues to them. Recall that in my telling of the story of proliferating late twentieth-century feminisms, it was minority feminists who forced questions of social location and representation onto the feminist agenda, well before white postmodern feminists started checking – often somewhat perfunctorily it has to be said – for the ethnocentric biases and exclusionary effects of universalising political strategies. It was their interventions that laid the foundations for later studies revealing that throughout history 'sex/gender difference' has been profoundly racialised; that the intersection of race and sex/gender ideologies had even produced 'the ideal of femininity' as white thus serving to 'police racial as well as sexual boundaries'; that 'the process of heterosexualisation went hand-in-hand with that of colonisation' and that, as a result, 'in contemporary Western settings sexual othering is inextricably entangled with racial othering'.[86]

A strong case can therefore be made for suggesting that these critiques of white Western feminism's assumption that 'male domination' is universal did more than poststructuralism to dislodge gender as feminism's most basic category of analysis. Certainly, some white feminists have wrestled with the problem of developing a language that could 'express the links between race and gender without prioritising'.[87] But while some white feminist poststructuralists have demonstrated 'a deep ethical commitment to race, in particular, as a factor which mediates the experience of being sexually marked', it is race 'that always *mediates* sex' in their texts and sex that is posited as 'the superior term of a sex/race opposition'.[88] Even when it is recognised that a

---

86 Helliwell, 2000, p 812. See also Stoler, 1995 and Markowitz, 2001.

87 Ware, 1992, p xiv.

88 Sandland, 1998, p 322, original emphasis, referring to the work of Drucilla Cornell. In the view of historian Catherine Hall, 'the most sustained critique of essentialism' was first developed by black women such as hooks, Amos and Parmar, whereas 'poststructuralism has given little actual thought to ethnicity beyond the ritual invocations': Hall, 1991, pp 209–10.

racial 'shared consciousness' might have prior claims to gender, they still tend to insist that the analysis of the female subject must start with gender, thus overlooking the frequently reiterated statement of minority feminists that 'there are other relations to be accounted for' – that something 'more than an account of gender' is required.[89] Still, whichever way one chooses to narrate the story of proliferating feminisms, whichever particular framework one privileges in its telling, it is indisputable that the once bold claims about women's universal violability sank under the weight of their cumulative challenges.

While many feminist analysts have rejoiced at its demise, others worry that the institutionalisation of difference and the dismantling of the universal category of 'woman' in feminist thought had gone too far. Already by the 1990s, the analytical possibilities of a postmodern feminist approach were being questioned by those arguing that 'the proliferation of axes of analysis obviates effective critique'.[90] Indeed, postmodernism itself came under fire, at least to the extent that it claimed to be 'the privileged site of (good) politics', the one most attuned to the 'play of difference', while everything else was reductive and essentialist. As Linda Alcoff pointed out, it is all very well to use postmodern methods, but to attempt to 'colonise the entire discursive field of the political' made her feel uncomfortable. After all, to argue for the universal applicability of postmodern feminism is to forget its founding strictures against such acts of self-privileging conceptual mastery. Rather than 'championing postmodernism as uniquely theoretically correct and trying to win for it discursive hegemony', Alcoff advocated the deployment of postmodern ideas in 'a guerrilla war, where every gun used is a stolen one'.[91] Alcoff, the very same analyst who deployed Foucauldian discourse analysis so effectively against the silencing and recuperative tactics of dominant discourses, also came to believe that to theorise rape adequately, one had to have 'recourse to embodied experience, and not merely the various possible and actual discursive interpretations of that experience'. Studying the established meanings of rape within existing discourses was, she said, 'insufficient'.[92]

Here Alcoff highlights one of the central dilemmas raised by all this critical work – how to link violence to its cultural representation. The paradox of violence, as Sally Merry argues in her account of domestic violence cases in nineteenth- and twentieth-century Hawaiian courts, is that it is 'both outside representation and always represented'.[93] Violence, this suggests, is 'at the boundary of the socially constructed world' – it is 'real' in that it is a

89 Alarcón, 1990, p 364, referring to de Lauretis.
90 Hekman, 1996, p 9.
91 Alcoff, 1997, pp 8–9.
92 Alcoff, 1997, pp 23–4.
93 Merry, 1994, p 993.

physical injury, and so in this sense beyond cultural construction, but at the same time the injury can only be understood within a context of cultural interpretation. While the real must, of course, be expressed in language, some feminists, Alcoff included, become concerned when analysis 'moves all events to the level of discourse, stories and social categories, turning away completely from questions of truth and justice'.[94]

While this is not the place to attempt to resolve these complex epistemological and ontological issues, I will say this: many poststructuralist feminists, me included, have no intention of turning away from questions of truth and justice. On the contrary, we continue to work with an understanding that violence is both outside representation and always represented in our various stands against violence in itself *and* the many discourses of justification that help to perpetuate it. We also continue to strive to get justice *for* victims – never forgetting, of course, that what counts as justice is as discursively mediated as truth. In this connection, it is instructive to observe that Alcoff continues to engage with postmodern theorists and Foucault in particular in order to develop new articulations of the problem of sexual violence. After equivocating over whether to call her approach 'post-Foucauldian or Foucauldian-informed', she still names her position as that of a 'feminist Foucauldian', one who applies his approach to questions related to sexuality and the body, but disagrees with his substantive view on sexual violence against women and children. Moreover, she insists that a feminist Foucauldian does not draw back, as Foucault did, from 'striking a judgmental pose' with respect to violence in any form.[95] Such a feminist is very judgmental indeed, as readers of this book have discovered.

Conclusion – *for* poststructuralist feminism

In the course of defending women's studies from being subsumed under gender studies, Robyn Weigman comments that one 'does not need poststructuralism to detect the various ways feminism's production of a counter-cultural imaginary has sought both to diagnose and to heal the profound and unsettling social and psychic cost of living under the organisational sign *woman*'.[96] One may not need it, but as I have tried to show here, poststructuralist feminist attentiveness to questions of language and representation has undoubtedly facilitated Western feminism's confrontation with the problem of sexed violence. And that is not all it has done. Its wide-ranging

---

94 Frohmann and Mertz, 1994, pp 840–7.

95 Alcoff, 1996, pp 101 and 111.

96 Wiegman, 2001, p 379, original emphasis. Compare Alison Young's demonstration of the usefulness of a poststructuralist feminist critique of how 'woman' functions as a sign in rape trials: Young, 1998.

dissections of cultural scripts that legitimate specific forms of men's violence and its exposures of the 'discursive tricks' that rename victims of sexual abuse as unharmed or as hysterics or liars have reconfigured feminist approaches to the sex-violence problematic. Moreover, it has reconfigured feminism. Problematisations of a whole host of practices – speaking for others; assuming survivor discourse is in itself liberating; invoking a universalising notion of 'male domination'; relying on law reform to deliver justice for women – have transformed feminism. Power relations between dominant and marginalised women have been queried and global grammars that do not allow for multiple mediations of women's experience of violence challenged. And finally, thanks to those who have endeavoured to build counter-discourses that convey the different experiences of diversely situated women – whether they framed their interventions in explicitly Foucauldian terms or not – language has become a place of struggle *within* the feminist movement, a place in which to articulate multiple voices and form more effective counter-hegemonic cultural practices. As for the violence insistently named in feminist campaigns as 'domestic violence', that analytical field has been troubled from so many different political and theoretical directions as it forced its way into Western government policy that I have delayed its consideration until the next chapter.

Chapter 6

Policy conundrums – reframing 'domestic violence' in the new millennium

At different points in time over the last century, and most intensively over the last four decades, Western feminists have fought with various degrees of success to have men's violence in the private or 'domestic' sphere recognised as a pressing public issue. Not all of this anti-violence work is well known. Some had to be reclaimed by feminist scholarship. An exemplary instance, referred to in Chapter 5, is that of Carol Smart's rediscovery of feminist campaigns in early twentieth-century England to get adult-child sexual contact reinterpreted as harmful. Smart had two aims in charting the early discursive battles between, on the one hand, feminist pressure groups attempting to extend the criminal law to cover various forms of adult-child sex and, on the other, a largely impervious legal profession and judiciary which stood firm in defence of men's sexual rights. Her first aim was to join the 'older voices' of the early 'feminist/purity' and child-saving campaigners to 'the voices of those who are still pushing for reform in this area'. For although it was 'shocking and depressing to find that feminist campaigners in the 1910s and 1920s knew what we think we discovered in the 1970s', she felt it might help buttress arguments that still needed to be made at the turn of the new millennium. Her second, related aim was to help explain why child sexual abuse is still widespread by showing how the discursive struggle to name victims and perpetrators has a long and unfinished history.[1]

Certainly, it is shocking to learn that in the 1920s, English medical reports explained outbreaks of venereal diseases in children as the result of 'accidental' or 'innocent' transmission, say from a towel or bath. It is even more shocking to learn that feminists had to forge a counter-discourse to challenge 'the apparently tenacious belief among men' that intercourse with a virgin, including virgin children, produced a cure for the disease.[2] It is shocking also to learn – from another feminist study – that as recently as the 1970s, English courts of appeal reduced sentences in father-daughter incest

1 Smart, 1999, p 407.
2 Smart, 1999, pp 395–7.

cases if girls had retained their virginity and so had not suffered 'serious harm'; or if a man had turned to his daughter because he had been 'starved of affection by his wife'.[3] Feminist campaigners have continued to battle against what Sally Merry calls the 'discourse of justification' for violence against women.[4] Towards the end of the twentieth century, they succeeded in getting child sexual abuse and, more broadly, other forms of so-called 'family' or 'domestic' violence named as harms, criminal harms no less, in many Western jurisdictions. But as we shall see, no sooner were these harms recognised as criminal harms than some feminists began to question whether criminalisation was the best way to deal with violence perpetrated in the 'private' sphere. One thing was clear: naming and framing men's violence at home was no easy matter.

This chapter looks at what happened when Western states finally began to respond to feminist demands that 'domestic' violence be taken seriously. What happened was that feminists have had to confront the ever-present danger faced by all social justice movements – that of having their demands co-opted by the state. Campaigning to get violence against women and children recognised as a significant social problem has been and continues to be a compromising and tricky business. As Anne Genovese argues in her genealogy of domestic violence policy in late twentieth-century Australia, feminist policy advisors strategically adopted the term 'domestic violence' in the 1970s because they realised that if they were to have any success at getting violence against women on the agenda they needed policymakers on side. They did so *'knowingly'*, aware that the relatively benign term 'domestic violence' was far more acceptable to a 'masculinist state' prepared to 'extend *noblesse oblige*' to battered women supplicants than that much more confrontationist descriptor: 'criminal assault in the home'. Such a compromise was necessary to ensure that 'domestic violence' succeeded as a discourse. As Genovese argues, it also illustrates clearly that 'feminisms have always been problematised by their relationship to the state and the law'.[5] But getting the discourse accepted at the policy level was just the first difficulty. The next was naming violence against women as a serious crime without getting caught up in agendas not of their own making – law and order agendas especially. That was a particularly difficult matter to negotiate.

If Western feminism's relationship with nation states proved to be so difficult in the twentieth century, what has occurred in the field now known as 'domestic violence' in the twenty-first century? What discourses and policies have feminists been prepared to accept under the very changed and

---

3 Mitra, 1987, pp 138–9.
4 Merry, 1994, p 972.
5 Genovese, 2000, pp 123–5, original emphasis, citing Thornton, 1995, p 7.

worsening conditions of the global era? The broader context in which feminists campaign today against violence against women has been described as
one in which a process of 'world-wide *restratification*' is redistributing
privileges and deprivations, wealth and poverty, power and powerlessness,
freedom and constraints in both the developed and developing worlds.[6]
Today, globally inflected neoliberal economic processes, notably the dismantling of the welfare state, a growing polarisation of wealth and poverty
and new immigration patterns are altering the conditions and forms of political participation in Western democracies. On the one hand, new global
inequalities are pushing migrants and asylum seekers into increasingly desperate employments and illegalities, notably forced prostitution; trafficking
in women and children into the sex trade has created a new frontier for anti-
violence campaigners and, at the same time, a sharp global acceleration of
'punishment-by-incarceration' has led to rapidly increasing prison populations in several Western countries.[7] On the other hand, a preoccupation with
'welfare dependency', a product of the economic dogma of the inevitability
of globalisation and the concomitant need to reduce the size of the public
sector, has led Western states to embrace the North American welfare-to-
work model. The resulting welfare cutbacks not only affect women as the
primary recipients of state services, they also retract the space in which
feminists can make claims on the states, especially when national governments accompany the introduction of austerity measures with claims that
globalisation has decreased their ability to provide social services.[8]

How are feminists responding to these challenges? Have they been
spurred on to take new directions in their thinking about violence against
women? And how is feminist anti-violence work being played at the policy
level today? Following some introductory comments about the naming
conundrums besetting anyone trying to put 'men's violence' into policy discourse, Chapter 6 examines an exemplary instance of the practice of naming
and un-naming men's violence in the policy arena: the new millennium
flurry of feminist-influenced policy and consultation activity in the UK
around the new discursive field of 'Violence Against Women'. The launch of
the Blair government's domestic violence awareness campaign in January
1999 gave a new urgency to the politics of naming men's violence in Britain.
It led six years later to the introduction of ground-breaking domestic violence legislation and government boasts that 'tackling domestic violence on
every front' was a policy priority. With the Home Office assuming the policy
lead on the new strategy on violence against women, the question of men's
violence, while not named as such in the flurry of policy documents, or in the

6 Bauman, 1998, p 304, original emphasis.
7 Bauman, 1998, p 114.
8 Bergeron, 2001, p 992.

descriptions of local projects funded under the Violence Against Women Initiative, has been placed firmly on the public agenda. So too has the vexed question of 'prevalence', one that is inextricably associated with the equally vexed question of who is doing what to whom. The stage has thus been set for more discursive battles between, on the one hand, British and British-based feminist activists and scholars who have endeavoured, apparently successfully, to make men's violence against women and children a public issue and, on the other, all those non-feminists who have fought so hard to recuperate for violent men their hegemonic social position. The chapter concludes by pointing to some future directions for anti-violence work.

Naming and framing conundrums

'What's in a name?' – a great deal. As feminists have found, naming unnamed forms of violence in the private sphere is a 'tricky business'. Each act of naming needs to be critically analysed, each has a contentious history as genealogies of 'definitional grappling' with the issues show.[9] One of the first and still definitive accounts is Linda Gordon's history of the politics of family violence in Boston in the period 1880–1960. Her book, *Heroes of Their Own Lives*, is a carefully nuanced study of the 'discovery' of family violence and child abuse by feminist and social purity movements in the late nineteenth century and the 'rediscovery' of child abuse by radiologists peering at x-rays of unexplained broken bones in children in the 1960s. In the intervening period, concern about family violence ebbed and flowed, all too visible one moment, invisible the next. Gordon tracks the history of the political construction of family violence as a social problem back to the late 1870s when Societies for the Prevention of Cruelty to Children became the first social agencies devoted to family-violence problems. Originally focused on child abuse, they were soon drawn into other forms of family violence which Gordon divides into four major types – 'cruelty to children', child neglect, sexual abuse of children and finally, 'wife-beating', brought to the attention of child-welfare agencies by women making complaints about battery and about what is today called marital rape.[10] Gordon traces 'cover-ups' and denials of wife-beating and sexual assaults of children within families at various periods of the twentieth century, notably during 'the long period of the quiescence of feminism between 1920 and 1960', and the importance of women's rights movements in bringing them to light again, reconstituting assailants and aggressors as family men rather than strangers and defining wife-beating as a social problem – 'one of the great achievements of feminism'. Not that Gordon believed that the definition of family

9 MacDonald, 1998, pp 2 and 15.
10 Gordon, 1988, pp 1–7.

violence had been secured. She felt that women would still need to make their own judgments about 'the border between acceptable and unacceptable attempts to coerce' in their own lives.[11]

Similar genealogies can be traced in other Western countries. In Australia, 'wife beating' had been a key concern of late nineteenth-century feminist campaigners, but by the 1960s that phenomenon had once again become 'a problem that had no specific name' and 'no position on public feminist or state agendas'. As in the United States, violence in the home underwent a depoliticisation process through much of the twentieth century. This was all to change in the 1970s with the opening of the first women's refuges and feminist demands for state funding for protecting women and children fleeing violent men.[12] Since then, violence in the home has been named and renamed as a social problem creating a complex web of competing discourses. We now have 'domestic violence', 'family violence', 'intimate partner violence', 'gendered' or gender-based violence, 'sexed violence' and even, astonishingly and against all the odds, including strenuous anti-feminist protests, 'men's violence' or 'violence by men'.[13] Identifying, naming and defining the problem – that was the first crucial step in any campaign and a 'precursor to policy action' as feminists realised while working on the 'impossibly ambitious plan' to eliminate domestic violence in late twentieth-century Australia. Their efforts received a boost from the growing body of research in the field. A case in point is the publication in 1994 of Australia's first published study of domestic violence during pregnancy, which found that violent men see pregnancy 'as a threat to their dominance and the foetus as a rival'.[14] Media coverage of this kind of research helped bring a once privatised problem into the public arena. Today the most commonly used terms in Australia are 'domestic violence', 'violence against women' and the more inclusive term of 'family violence', introduced 'initially to capture the experience of indigenous women and children against whom violence may have been perpetrated by a range of family or community members, not just male partners'. However, this term is resisted by many working in the domestic violence sector because 'family violence' de-genders the violence, implying that any family member could be a perpetrator, just as the term 'domestic violence' has a domesticating and trivialising effect, concealing the profoundly sexed asymmetry of interpersonal violence. It is noticeable too that while 'family violence' may include child abuse, 'typically, in Australia, it does not'.[15]

Australian state and federal governments now locate domestic violence

11 Gordon, 1988, pp 251 and 290–1.
12 Genovese, 2000, pp 118–23.
13 Bacchi, 1999; James, 2006.
14 Dow, 'Pregnancy may Provoke Violence, Say Researchers', *The Age*, 17 October 1994.
15 Murray, 2005, p 29.

within a broader public policy approach to violence against women and name it, along with sexual assault and sexual harassment, as a form of gender-based violence – that is, as violence experienced by women and almost exclusively perpetrated by men. For example, 'Partnerships Against Domestic Violence', a policy initiative of the former conservative federal government, defines domestic violence as 'an abuse of power perpetrated mainly (but not only) by men against women both in relationship and after separation', while the 'Women Safety Strategy' implemented by the Victorian state government aims to 'improve women's safety, well-being and capacity to fully participate in Victorian life by reducing the level, and fear, of violence against women'. Furthermore, these gender-based frameworks of violence against women recognise that domestic violence occurs within the wider context of economic and social disadvantage and of inequality of women relative to men, thereby heightening women's vulnerability. Several studies document that vulnerability. A 1996 Australian Bureau of Statistics women's safety survey found that 23 per cent of women had experienced violence from their male partners and that up to 80 per cent of battered women did not seek assistance from services; an Institute of Criminology study undertaken in 2004 found that one-third of women who had a current or former intimate partner reported experiencing at least one form of violence during their lifetime and a state government report on 'intimate partner violence' in Victoria in 2004 found not only that the vast majority of victims were women, but that intimate partner violence is responsible for more ill-health and premature death in Victorian women under the age of 45 than any other well-known preventable risk factors such as obesity and smoking.[16]

Naming is one thing, but feminist analysts insist that we go 'beyond the rhetoric of naming domestic violence as gendered violence' and examine 'the discourses through which policies are operationalised'. Keeping the focus on recent Australian policy initiatives, it has been observed that strategies to prevent or reduce violence sit within a range of competing discourses. Feminist or 'gendered' discourses mix uncomfortably with 'ungendered' and palpably non-feminist discourses such as those promoting 'family harmony' and law and order agendas.[17] Thus, for example, while the Partnerships Against Domestic Violence initiative names its target as 'gendered violence', the programme is also 'a major part of the Government's strategy for strengthening families, preventing family breakdown and creating healthy and safe communities' – creating an 'Australian culture which is free from violence': that is the main aim.[18] By contrast, in a feminist framework,

16 Murray, 2005, pp 28–9.
17 Murray, 2005, p 30.
18 Partnerships Against Domestic Violence, 1999, p 1.

violence against women is conceptualised as an inextricable part of a gendered social order, not as a breakdown of that order. But the ever present danger with law and order discourses is that violence against women gets subsumed into concerns about 'violence in society', with the result that men and gendered power relationships are lost from view. And that is not all that happens. Law and order approaches tend to translate the problem of men's violence as a safety and protection issue, diverting the policy focus and funds from prevention to criminalisation of dangerous individuals, from community education campaigns targeting men and aggressive forms of masculinity such as those condoned in sport and the media to the criminal justice system.[19] But feminists have long been alert to the dangers of naming domestic violence as a crime.

In 1994, Sally Merry concluded her study of domestic violence cases in nineteenth- and twentieth-century Hawaiian courts, which revealed just how entrenched discourses justifying battery are, on a cautiously optimistic note. Notwithstanding the recurrent theme in the court hearings that battery of women is justifiable, Merry felt that the criminal law offers 'a lively terrain' for contesting the legitimacy of domestic violence and also an opportunity for 'creative cultural work in transforming the boundaries of legitimate violence'.[20] Others have been far less sanguine about law's capacity to deliver justice to women victims of male violence. In her now classic account of feminist-inspired reforms to the law on rape in Canada in the early 1980s, Canadian criminologist Laureen Snider shows how an apparent feminist legal victory – the abolition of rape and its replacement with an offence of sexual assault with three levels of gravity – brought significant disadvantages for women. One notable disadvantage was the increased penalties for sexual assault which flew in the face of feminist demands for a more effective criminal justice system, not a more punitive system. Furthermore, the feminist rape reform proposals were co-opted into a reactionary pro-family law and order agenda with a strong anti-feminist rhetoric, becoming part of a set of new regulations over sexual behaviour, including homosexuality and under-age sex. The feminist-instigated reforms had indeed been a Pyrrhic victory.[21]

A decade later, Snider turned her attention to the larger question of the viability of criminalisation as a feminist strategy for dealing with violent men. Concerned by the tendency of Western feminism to embrace 'agendas of punishment' that legitimised policies of coercive control, she argues that there was 'no persuasive evidence that reliance on criminal justice' had made women complainants safer or male offenders less violent. On the contrary,

---

19 Murray, 2005, pp 30–1.
20 Merry, 1994, p 993.
21 Snider, 1985. See also Smart, 1989, pp 45–6 and Pitch, 1985.

decades of social science research had documented 'the failure of criminal justice systems to improve the safety, life-conditions or life-chances of victims, or to transform offenders'. Furthermore, focusing on wife assault and battery, she points out that 'strategies of criminalisation' had 'benefited privileged white women at the expense of women of colour, aboriginal and immigrant women'.[22] She provides by way of example the adoption in the 1980s in North America of zero tolerance laws increasing sanctions for sexual and domestic assault and introducing mandatory arrest policies. These laws have been counter-productive, leading on the one hand to greater surveillance of those who 'fit hegemonic definitions of "the criminal" ' and, on the other, to increased misery of lower-class women and visible minorities who are more vulnerable to contempt of court charges for refusing to testify against violent male partners. Immigrants to Western countries are especially vulnerable – if their papers are irregular, the whole family can be deported, and for women of colour in Britain, Canada and the United States, increased surveillance means 'increased vulnerability to the actions of racist police'. The lessons for Snider are clear: recognising the 'horrific human cost of violence against women' and seeking to focus public attention on it in the face of 'massive resistance' is one thing; seeking the 'material and ideological resources' that criminalisation provides is quite another. The symbolic denunciation of the criminal does not provide solutions, nor does simply naming problems and 'heaping moral opprobrium' on offenders.[23]

Snider is by no means the only analyst to warn of the dangers of the state co-opting feminist demands for the protection of women and of the problems with zero tolerance laws in particular. M Jacqui Alexander, for example, has explored how Caribbean feminists have resisted state attempts to privatise or domesticate violence, insisting that violence within the domestic sphere did not originate there, but was legitimated by state economic violence which was 'itself responsible for the increase of sexual violence in the home'. According to Alexander, this 'larger feminist vision of the historicised violences of heteropatriarchy' was co-opted by the Bahaman state and brought within its juridical confines as sexual offence and domestic violence legislation in 1991. While this was a symbolic victory for women and feminists inasmuch as incest, sexual harassment and sexual assault of a spouse were introduced as new crimes, there were 'significant disjunctures' between what feminists demanded and the law conceded. Sexual offences were 'spatially separated in the legal text from domestic violence', thereby contradicting feminist research indicating that violent sex is almost always accompanied by violent physical coercion. Furthermore, the new provisions

22 Snider, 1998, pp 2–3.
23 Snider, 1998, pp 9–12.

did not define 'domestic violence', but concentrated instead on the question of the disposition of property within the matrimonial home in the event of a marital breakup. And most worryingly, by providing penalties for women who failed to report the sexual abuse of themselves and their daughters by violent male partners, the new Bahaman law encoded 'a disciplinary narrative' that represented the state's interests, not women's interests.[24]

As these examples illustrate, appeals for strengthening the criminal law to deal with violent men has proved to be a highly problematic feminist strategy, just as Carol Smart had predicted when she reflected on the power of law to disqualify women's experiences of violence.[25] Taking this analysis forward, Snider warns against feminists becoming 'complicit' in the 'surge of punitiveness' that characterises the globalising neoliberal Western state. Feminists, she argues, need to examine whether 'policy initiatives apparently produced at "our" insistence turn out to have repressive consequences', and whether our demands are being heard in ways that authorise expanded surveillance, repression and control, especially at a time when 'punishment has replaced amelioration as the key legitimating function of government'.[26] Once again, she points to the paradox of zero tolerance laws on spousal assault actually producing more female offenders when women refuse to testify against their partners. As Snider notes, such developments 'underline the perils of good intentions – in a culture of punitiveness reforms will be heard in ways that reinforce rather than challenge dominant cultural practices'.[27] They also highlight the importance of taking account of rapidly changing conditions in globalising neoliberal Western societies today. With this in mind, let us turn now to our case study, the introduction of a wide-ranging domestic violence policy in Britain.

The politics of naming and un-naming – a case study

By 2000, violence against women became a policy priority in the UK. Responding to three decades of feminist campaigning, the Blair government pushed through a raft of new policies in the field that it had begun to call 'Violence Against Women' (VAW). A wide-ranging consultation led by the Home Office led to the publication of *Safety and Justice: the Government's Proposals on Domestic Violence* in 2003. This provided the legislative framework for the Domestic Violence, Crime and Victims Act passed the following year. In 2005, the Home Office published a national report setting out the government's progress and detailed a National Action Plan that

24 Alexander, 1997, pp 72–4.
25 Smart, 1989.
26 Snider, 2003, pp 355–6.
27 Snider, 2003, p 369.

promised to further improve support for victims, for example, by intervening earlier with offenders and by expanding a network of specialist domestic
violence courts. By recording the road travelled so far and signalling future
directions, the Home Office Minister hoped that the report would convince
those working in the domestic violence field that their work has been recognised and that the government was fully committed to confronting VAW
in Britain.[28]

The new policies were announced with much fanfare. Addressing a feminist conference in London in July 2003, the then Solicitor-General Harriet
Harman announced that the *Safety and Justice* proposals were an important
step in ending the 'culture of excuses' for men's violence against women.
Setting up a new legal framework for, as Harman put it, 'making her safe
and bringing him to justice', the consultation paper proposed a three-
element strategy of prevention, 'protection and justice' and support for
domestic violence victims.[29] The centerpiece of this policy initiative was
clearly the second strand, focusing on improving legal protection for victims. A broad range of 'protection and justice' proposals addressed the problem of providing an effective police response to domestic violence cases and
improving the prosecution of these cases to ensure that sentences reflected
the seriousness of the crime. Specific proposals included making common
assault and breaches of civil order arrestable offences and improving the
relationship between civil and criminal courts. The hope was that this the
biggest overhaul of domestic violence legislation for over 30 years would
ensure effective responses from criminal justice agencies and maximum protection for victims.

The new policy initiative got off to a good start, with the Home Office
naming the problem to be addressed under the rubric of 'VAW' and recommending that domestic violence forums become VAW forums. Moreover, in
its 1999 policy document, *Living without Fear*, it promised an 'integrated
approach to tackling VAW' that committed the government to reducing
crimes of domestic violence, rape and sexual assault.[30] Starting with the
widely-publicised British Crime Survey finding that one in four women
experience domestic violence at some stage in their lives, *Living without
Fear* stated categorically that violence against women is a crime. It also
noted that 70 per cent of women fear rape, that domestic violence often
starts off and escalates during pregnancy and that reports of rape increased
by 165 per cent since 1989. Concededly, there were some worrying signs in
the document. VAW was labelled a 'serious crime' that the government was

---

28 Home Office, 2005. This section develops the analysis of these policy initiatives in
    Howe, 2006.
29 Harman, 2003; Home Office, 2003, pp 6–8.
30 Home Office, 1999, p 6.

committed to tackling 'with vigour' and women may have had the right to 'live their lives without the fear of violence'. Yet already by the second sentence in the foreword women are transmogrified into mothers having a right to raise their children in safety, and in next to no time, protecting women's rights takes a second place to 'building a better society for our children to grow up in'.[31] Worryingly too, when the government's primary concern is framed as that of making Britain 'a place where *we* can live our lives without fear', a gendered understanding of the people most likely to live in fear of domestic violence disappears.[32] It is also noticeable that men are not named as the perpetrators of the vast majority of violent acts against women. Then again, men's invisibility in government policy is hardly surprising, given that stating that domestic violence is overwhelmingly perpetrated by men led to 'near apoplexy' in non-feminists, including some domestic violence sector representatives at domestic violence forums held at that time.[33] Still, for all that, it was quite an achievement that the Home Office did recognise VAW in its myriad forms as the social problem to be addressed in *Living without Fear*.

It did not do so for long. In 2003, the Home Office reverted to naming the problem in its *Safety and Justice* proposals as 'domestic violence', thereby foregoing its promised 'integrated' strategy and omitting rape and sexual assault in the process. While repeating the one-in-four women statistic, the consultation paper adds that one in six men will be a victim of domestic violence in their lifetime, a classic gender-neutralising discursive manoeuvre which flattens out the starkly gendered asymmetry of interpersonal violence revealed in every national survey. The source for the one-in-six men statistic, a domestic violence self-completion questionnaire distributed as part of the 1996 British Crime Survey, is described as 'the most robust data for domestic violence'.[34] Yet a powerful critique of conventional survey methodologies published in 2001, in time to have been included in the consultation paper, listed several limitations of national surveys, including the British Crime Survey, which have led to a serious underestimation of the extent of VAW. Most notably, when the partner of a woman was involved in the completion of the questionnaire, the rate of reporting of lifetime domestic violence dropped to less than half the rate when no one else was present and the lack of data on sexual assault and rape was noted as a serious omission. Coming under fire too was the use in crime surveys of the so-called 'Conflict Tactile Scale', which names as violence any method of dealing with conflict, be it verbal reasoning or serious violence. Crime

---

31 Home Office, 1999, p 1.
32 Home Office, 1999, p 5, emphasis added.
33 Itzin, 2000, p 378.
34 Home Office, 2003, pp 9 and 58.

surveys using this scale tend to find that men are as likely to be the victim of domestic violence as women, but they overlook the much more serious nature of the injuries sustained by women, the fear factor and the likelihood that women who hit men are responding in self-defence.[35] Indeed, the researcher responsible for producing the one-in-six men statistic acknowledged that women were twice as likely to have been injured by a partner in the previous year and three times more likely to have suffered 'frightening threats'. They were also 'far more likely to be "chronic" victims than men'.[36] Including these statistics in *Safety and Justice* would have provided a more accurate picture of domestic violence, and given less ammunition to the professional apologists for men's violence seeking to prove that women are as violent as men, discussed in Chapter 2. So too would a reference to research indicating that, as one English newspaper headline put it in 2001, 'Murder is biggest cause of death in pregnancy'.[37]

Certainly, VAW seems to be taken seriously when it is asserted that one (ungendered) 'incident' of domestic violence is reported to police 'every minute' and that it has the highest rate of (again ungendered) repeat victimisation of any crime. But the gendered asymmetry of that violence would have been revealed to be so much starker if, for example, it had been noted that on average two women per week are killed by a male partner and that nearly one-half of all women murder victims are killed by a male partner or ex-partner. The consultation paper notes that only 8 per cent of men who are murdered are killed in a domestic context and, in parentheses, that of the 30 men killed by women partners each year, 'some' had been killed in self-defence by their battered women partners.[38] Not only does this significantly understate the evidence from all Western jurisdictions that most women who kill men do so after a long history of violence; the Home Office has nothing to say directly about the very different circumstances in which men kill women. It briefly mentions the fact that the Law Commission was about to undertake a review of partial defences to homicide because of 'concern' about the way in which the law on murder operates in relation to domestic violence cases, and particularly about the operation of the provocation defence. One area of concern, it is noted, was domestic homicide where the provocation relied on is sexual jealousy or infidelity. Another was that sentencing in cases of manslaughter by reason of provocation does not adequately reflect the seriousness of the cases and the loss of life.[39] But no mention is made of the fact that it was men who were getting away with

35 Walby and Myhill, 2001, pp 509–19.
36 Of those suffering repeat victimisation, 73 per cent were women: Mirrlees-Black, 1999, p 26.
37 *The Independent*, 21 March 2001.
38 Home Office, 2003, p 9.
39 Home Office, 2003, p 37.

murdering women on the basis of feeble excuses, nor that Solicitor-General Harman was at that very moment spearheading a campaign to abolish the provocation defence, law's premier excuse for men who kill women, as part of the government's drive to tackle domestic violence.[40] An important opportunity to state clearly and categorically who was doing what to whom and also to reinforce the links between domestic violence and domestic homicide, so essential to a broad-gauged approach to VAW, thus went begging.

Already by 2003, the integrated approach promised in 1999 had well and truly disintegrated. Clearly, the government had failed to grasp the significance of key innovations in conceptualising violence against women within the British feminist movement. New millennium feminist anti-violence campaigners no longer spoke of 'domestic' violence, but rather of the 'co-occurrence' of physical and sexual violence and abuse against women and children in the home *and* 'extrafamilial' child sexual abuse and exploitation and rape of women.[41] The emphasis now was on linking different forms of violence against diversely situated women. Speaking at a conference in 2000, prominent feminist academic consultant in the VAW field, Liz Kelly, acknowledged that globalisation and migration were 'breaking down boundaries' and bringing forced marriage, honour crimes and trafficking in women into the heart of feminist analysis. As for *Living Without Fear*, the government's 1999 policy statement, she noted that while it had prioritised an integrated approach to tackling VAW, the document itself and 'everything that happened since betrays how poorly this is understood by policy makers in this country'. The key problem as she saw it was that policymakers were slipping and sliding from one term, 'VAW', to another, 'domestic violence', instead of thinking in terms of connections and making other forms of VAW a core part of its response.[42]

Safety and Justice fell precisely into this trap. Focusing narrowly on a generically framed 'domestic violence', the Home Office's efforts to incorporate diversely situated women into its proposals were tokenistic at best. Its brief reference in *Safety and Justice* to the problems faced by domestic violence victims who are subject to immigration control is a case in point. Boasting that the government's reform measures had provided 'a significant improvement' for victims of domestic violence who were still subject to immigration control, the Home Office referred to the introduction in 1999 of the domestic violence 'concession' for immigrant women victims who left their spouse during the probationary period of one year that was then in force for foreign nationals wanting to settle in the UK on the basis of

40 See Howe, 2004b and 2008.
41 Itzin, 2000, pp 359–60.
42 Kelly, 2000, pp 3–6.

marriage.[43] The 'concession' to the one-year rule allowed women who left their spouse or partner during the probation year, and who could prove by a court conviction or order that the relationship had ended because of domestic violence, to apply for residency and access to state support. But the reforms fell far short of feminist demands for the abolition of both the one-year rule and the prohibition on recourse to public funds on the grounds that these policies were racist and discriminatory. As for the impact of domestic violence on black and minority ethnic (BME) communities, all that the Home Office had to say in *Safety and Justice* was that minority ethnic women 'may be discouraged from speaking out about violence for fear of bringing dishonour upon their family or community'.[44] Forced marriages and honour killings – issues which Asian feminists had insisted must be incorporated into domestic violence policies and legislation[45] – were not even mentioned. Recognised and named as forms of men's violence in the wider feminist movement, they remained un-named in the government's anti-violence strategy.

In fact, the Home Office had trouble naming men's violence at all. A case in point is the statement in *Safety and Justice* that 'people' in the LGBT (lesbian, gay, bisexual and transgender) community 'experience domestic violence in a similar proportion to the rest of the population (about one in four)'. The basis for this claim is a single report of a survey of non-heterosexually identified victims who supposedly represent a cross-section of this 'community'. Whatever the validity of this survey, it helps to pave the way for the bland claim that domestic violence occurs 'across society, regardless of age, gender, race, sexuality, wealth and geography' that once again mutes a VAW focus. Only fleetingly does *Safety and Justice* acknowledge that the statistics show that domestic violence is 'predominantly violence by men against women'.[46]

Interestingly, the Home Office indicated that a more in-depth study of sexual and domestic violence conducted in conjunction with the 2001 British Crime Survey would provide a 'more detailed picture of the prevalence and incidence of domestic violence'.[47] And so it has. Described as the most reliable findings to date on the extent and nature of interpersonal violence in England and Wales, this study spotlights the 'Man' question by underlining the asymmetrical nature of men's and women's violence, something that *Safety and Justice* singularly failed to do. Defining interpersonal

---

43 Home Office, 2003, p 45. The one-year rule requires that people coming to the UK to join their spouse must remain in the marriage for at least one year before they can apply to stay permanently.
44 Home Office, 2003, p 10.
45 Siddiqui, 2003a, p 6.
46 Home Office, 2003, p 9.
47 Home Office, 2003, p 10.

violence as including 'non-sexual domestic violence', sexual assault and stalking, the researchers found that 45 per cent of women compared with 26 per cent of men aged 16–59 had experienced at least one incident of inter-personal violence; that 24 per cent of women and only 5 per cent of men had been subject to some form of sexual assault at least once in their lifetime; that 7 per cent of women had suffered a serious sexual assault in their lives compared with 1.5 per cent of men, and that half of the women who had been subjected to 'domestic force' had also been subject to frightening threats and nearly half to emotional and financial abuse, whereas only 9 per cent of the men subject to domestic force had also experienced these forms of abuse. They found too that in the 12-month period prior to interview, 2.8 per cent of women were subjected to sexual assault, including an esti-mated 190,000 incidents of serious sexual assault, compared with only 0.2 per cent of men. Indeed, the numbers of reported incidents of serious sexual assault of men were 'too few for reliable further analysis'.[48] Furthermore, the data on the worst incidents revealed 'a significant gender asymmetry in the impact of domestic violence'. Women made up 89 per cent of the 'most heavily abused group', defined as those who report being subject to domestic violence four or more times. They were more likely to have sustained some form of injury, and much more likely than men to have suffered mental or emotional problems or severe physical injuries, including broken bones and teeth and severe bruising.[49] At a time when policymakers were 'increasingly addressing domestic violence and other forms of interpersonal violence as crimes', the researchers felt that it was important to reinforce the fact that domestic violence is indeed predominantly violence by men against women.[50]

Finally, it is worth noting that *Safety and Justice* deployed a cost-benefit analysis to measure the financial cost of implementing the proposed policies against the annual cost of domestic violence of approximately £5.25 billion, a figure based, as it conceded, on recorded crime figures that did not reflect the 'chronic under-reporting of domestic violence'. It was estimated that the legislative measures, which included criminalising breaches of civil non-molestation orders, making common assault an arrestable offence and establishing a multi-agency review of domestic murders, would cost approximately £102 million. By contrast, only £18 million was to be allo-cated for developing new refuges in partnership with local authorities. While there were to be some other allocations for 'similar projects', it was clear that the 'justice' component of the government's 'three element strategy' that received most of the government's attention was to get the bulk of the resources, while the support element favoured by feminist campaigners was

48 Walby and Allen, 2004, pp 11 and 18–19.
49 Walby and Allen, 2004, pp 33–4.
50 Walby and Allen, 2004, p 42.

to be left seriously under-funded.[51] Furthermore, research funded by the Women and Equality Unit and published in 2004 found that the Home Office had seriously underestimated the cost of domestic violence. The study calculated that the total cost, taking into account the cost to the criminal justice system, health and social services, housing and the economy (measured in terms of the cost of time of work due to injuries), was approximately £23 billion.[52] With such a huge discrepancy between this calculation and that of the Home Office the previous year, major adjustments would need to be made by the government if a cost-benefit analysis was to provide a better understanding of the full cost of domestic violence and a sound basis for effective policy.

Co-option conundrums – challenging the recourse to law

What are we to make of policy initiatives that had promised so much but delivered so little, converting a broad-gauged feminist anti-violence campaign into a narrowly circumscribed crime-focused 'domestic violence' policy within such a short space of time? Is this yet another instance of a social justice campaign being subsumed by a law and order agenda? Tackling this difficult issue first, let us revisit Laureen Snider's query about whether the policy initiatives produced in response to feminist campaigners have repressive consequences and whether their demands are heard in ways that authorise expanded surveillance and control. Have British feminists become complicit in the surge of punitiveness that characterises the contemporary British state? Was it unwise, at a time when a law and order agenda was leading inexorably to a drastically increased prison population in England and Wales, to highlight 'the consistent lack of sanctions' against violent men through low levels of prosecutions and high attrition rates across all forms of VAW?[53] Given the enhanced status of imprisonment in the Blair government's criminal policy, should feminists have reconsidered their demand that the state tighten its criminal laws? And why bother anyway, when there is little to inspire confidence that reform of more criminal laws will guarantee safety and justice for women? On the contrary, a great deal of evidence exists that it does no such thing, and some that it can, in fact, worsen the situation for women at risk of further violence from male partners if they report them to the police.

This is the view taken by a leading feminist criminologist in a recent assessment of the 'recourse to law' as a strategy for responding to violence

---

51 Home Office, 2003, pp 59–69. The prevention element was not costed.
52 Walby and Allen, 2004.
53 Womankind Worldwide, 2004, p 3. See Howe, 2006, p 410.

against women in the UK. Reflecting on the new legislation which extends the reach of the legal system in tackling domestic violence cases, Sandra Walklate observes that 'the drive to apply existing legal options in the private sphere along with making previously legal behaviour illegal, taken together, constitute an important change in the criminalisation of violence against women'. While it was too soon to say to what extent this was likely to result in 'long-term effects' of the negative kind that had been monitored in North American states with pro-arrest policies, she has no hesitation in declaring this kind of 'crime-centered approach' to be harmful to 'those already harmed by state intervention', notably, when interventions go against the wishes of women afraid of the consequences for themselves if their male partners are subjected to an intervention. The main difficulty, as she sees it, is 'a belief in the symbolic power of the law and an acceptance of a process that criminalises behaviour that a short time ago was (and still is, by many) seen to be acceptable'. Walklate is prepared to concede that these developments 'vindicate those feminists who campaigned for the private experiences of women to be taken seriously' and that 'all may not be lost by this investment in the symbolic power of the legal system'. Some studies do show that the criminal justice system can provide some protection for women in violent relationships. But beyond the symbolism, alliances with criminal justice professionals can have unintended consequences – the voices of the women themselves are lost and the campaigns are '(potentially) co-opted in the interests of the state'. So why hold on to 'the power of arrest response'? Besides, reforms to the criminal law had done nothing to assist the problem of attrition in rape cases – a record-high attrition rate that sees only 5.6 per cent of rape allegations ending in a conviction in England and Wales is still attracting adverse publicity today.[54]

The thrust of Walklate's complaint is that the feminist movement 'remains focused on the law and the criminal justice system and, in policy terms, almost to the exclusion of exploring other options' in the VAW field.[55] But that is not my reading of new millennium feminist anti-violence work in Britain. On the contrary, campaigners have canvassed many options to assist victims of violence. Nor does it tally with what I witnessed in vibrant consultation meetings around *Safety and Justice* that were held in London by Women for Justice and other feminist groups. These meetings provided a platform for a range of different and conflicting viewpoints, including those of participants who asked hard questions about the government's proposals to extend the criminal law. Feminist lawyers, in particular, were troubled by the suggestion in the consultation paper that courts could make restraining orders against men who are violent towards women when there

54 Walklate, 2008, pp 42–5.
55 Walklate, 2008, p 44.

is insufficient evidence to convict. Why, one asked, would there be insufficient evidence to convict? Was it because a woman might be unwilling to give evidence? If so, should a man be 'subject to a quasi-criminal penality' if the main witness did not give evidence against him? And if judges took decisive steps on every breach of a civil order, would not prisons be 'full to overflowing'? In her view, this was 'a dilemma'.[56] Indeed it is, and these questions serve to highlight the broader conundrums facing feminists calling for an end to the 'global culture of impunity where there are minimal sanctions' against violent men.[57] The fact that prisons in England and Wales were already full to overflowing by the time *Safety and Justice* was published underlies this dilemma. As Bauman amongst others has noted, a sharp global acceleration of incarceration policies at the turn of the twentieth century saw the targeting in Western countries of new and large sections of the population 'for one reason or another as a threat to social order', and Britain was no exception.[58] By 2003, the North American supermax prison which functions as a warehouse to contain globalisation's losers – the casualties of new informal economies pushing new migrants and asylum seekers into increasingly desperate employments and illegalities – was threatening to become a reality in England and Wales, where prison populations hit record levels.[59] In such an illiberal political climate, it is surely incumbent on feminists – perhaps especially on one who has written at length about the power to punish[60] – to consider closely possible untoward effects of criminal justice reform proposals and the worsening penal context in which we make them.

One might start by noting that British prisons were not then and are still not today overflowing with men convicted of violent offences against women. Nor do criminal law reforms automatically lead to an increase in the prison population, as indeed the failure of legislative reforms to assist rape victims or increase the conviction rate attests. Moreover, in 2006, in moves designed to relieve pressure on overcrowded prisons, the Sentencing Guidelines Council recommended that jail terms for convicted rapists be slashed and that men convicted of domestic violence crimes escape prison terms if they convince the courts they were 'capable of changing'.[61] In these

---

56 Woodcraft, 2003; See also Kennedy, 2003, p x.
57 Kelly, 2000, p 5.
58 Bauman, 1998, p 114.
59 By the end of 2002, the prison population reached an all-time high of over 74,000, or a rate of 141 per 100,000, the highest rate in the European Union: Walmsley, 2003. It remained a highly racialised dispossessed – 11 per cent were foreign nationals and African Caribbeans accounted for one in six of all inmates. See Howe, 2006, p 410.
60 Howe, 1994.
61 J Doward and G Hinsliff, 'Judges Told: Slash Jail Terms for Rapists', *The Observer*, 12 March 2006. By 2007, there had been another shift with the inter-departmental Ministerial Group on Sexual Offending declaring that the then current rate of serious sexual offences convicted was unacceptable: HM Government, 2007, p 29.

circumstances, it appears that concerns about feminist proposals to extend law's reach to men whose violence against women is, *contra* Bauman, inextricably part of the contemporary gendered social order, rather than a threat to it, are somewhat premature. The worry expressed in 2003 by leading barrister Helena Kennedy QC about justice for women being 'secured by reducing justice for men' is a case in point. While she felt it was all very well to campaign for victims' rights in rape and domestic violence cases where their experiences had been so readily dismissed, Kennedy was adamant that the campaigning had been 'highjacked by the law and order lobby to make inroads into the rights of the accused – male or female'. In her view, this was yet another 'lesson in unforeseen consequences' and she felt strongly that feminism had to 'take a good hard look at itself and not only look where it is heading but also who its bedfellows are'.[62]

It is surely ironic that Baroness Kennedy expresses this view in a preface to a book documenting the work of Southall Black Sisters (SBS), a group – as we are about to see – that has done so much to put the under-policing of crimes of violence against BME women on the agenda of the wider feminist movement. It is perhaps even more ironic that Kennedy acknowledges that SBS has 'played a significant role, enriching feminist activity and providing truly important insights into an experience outside the reach of white women' – a role that has included assisting BME women wanting to proceed with prosecutions of men who abuse them – before going on to castigate the VAW sector for wanting to criminalise violent men.[63] That aside, it seems to me that feminism, and the British anti-violence movement in particular, has been taking a good hard look at itself for some time. Not only that, bringing violent men to justice was only ever part of its agenda and since 2003, campaigners have worked hard to retrieve the rest of their anti-violence strategy from the wreck of the government's gender-neutralising and narrow crime-focused approach in *Safety and Justice*.

Consider, for example, the position taken by Kelly and Lovett in the course of making, or rather re-making, the case for an 'integrated VAW strategy' in *What a Waste*, published in 2005. In their assessment, the Blair government might have shown a 'greater recognition of the range of forms of VAW at policy and practice levels' than most other European countries, but its 'silo thinking' separating domestic violence from sexual assault, forced marriage, female genital mutilation, trafficking and other forms of VAW seriously undermined the new policies. So had its failure to make the connection between VAW and child abuse – 'a connection highlighted for more than a decade, including in virtually every child death enquiry'. Notwithstanding the 'improved policy context' under the new Labour

---

62 Kennedy, 2003, p x.
63 Kennedy, 2003, p ix.

government, there was still 'no overall strategic direction for the UK'. In fact, the government's approach to dealing with the range of different forms of VAW was 'entirely disconnected'.[64] Their own approach, by contrast, evinced a desire to move forward with a multi-pronged, integrated strategy that not only addressed all forms of VAW simultaneously, but also mainstreamed it into all relevant areas of government policy in order to encourage and enable integration in policy areas like prevention and public awareness.[65] Furthermore, here as in other recent campaign statements, it is clear that the movement's focus had shifted decisively from the suffering of a generically defined 'woman' to the multiple difficulties faced by diversely situated women, a shift underlined by a recognition that under rapidly changing global conditions – conditions that impact more harshly on racial-ised migrants and on minority ethnic women – it was no longer appropriate, if it ever was, to call VAW a 'domestic' problem.

One of the biggest impetuses for rethinking domestic violence policy and, importantly, for holding onto the power of arrest response that so troubles some of the movement's feminist critics, has been the very effective interven-tion of black and Asian feminist groups in new millennium feminist anti-violence work. In the 1980s, as we saw in Chapter 5, black and Asian women had resisted the claims of white feminism to speak for all women and specifically criticised feminist campaigns around sexual violence that failed to address the question of race and the lived realities of poor racialised women. Their challenges have now come to be recognised as pivotal turning points in the movement against violence against women in Britain.[66] For by the turn of the twentieth century, black and Asian feminist groups had not only succeeded in bringing the plight of BME women wanting to flee from violent men to the heart of feminist VAW campaigns; they had placed immi-gration law on the feminist agenda.

The longest-surviving and most influential agenda-setting minority group is SBS, a London-based group set up in 1979 to meet the needs of Asian and African-Caribbean women and to 'tackle sexual oppression'.[67] As promin-ent spokeswoman Hannana Siddiqui puts it, 'SBS started off as one of a number of radical black women's organisations, but in the 1990s the mantle of leadership of British Asian feminists, especially concerning the issue of domestic violence against Asian women, fell to SBS "by default" '.[68] Domestic violence became the mainstay of SBS's work in the 1990s because that was the 'recurrent issue' which women brought to them. Since then, SBS

64 Kelly and Lovett, 2005, pp 5 and 15–21.
65 Kelly and Lovett, 2005, p 27.
66 Feminist Review, 2005, pp 201–7.
67 Gupta, 2003, p 2.
68 Siddiqui, 2003b, p 279.

has become involved in a number of campaigns, including some with white feminist groups such as Women for Justice, to raise the profiles of women jailed for killing violent men and to reform homicide laws. But what quickly became clear to SBS was that domestic violence 'manifests itself differently in different communities'.[69] Forced marriage, for example, was a form of domestic abuse in South Asian communities and SBS fought hard that it be recognised as such. Not that they wanted a new offence created. Instead, they demanded that it be 'mainstreamed' in feminist domestic violence campaigns and incorporated in the government's national strategy on violence against women and children.[70]

By 2000, SBS had become an experienced casework and advocacy agency that found itself 'driven to the law for redress' because community leaders, mostly men, failed to address the problem of domestic violence.[71] Many of the women who came to their centre were migrants, predominantly from South Asia, whose right to stay in the UK depended on them remaining in violent relationships. To assist them, SBS campaigned long and hard to reform discriminatory immigration rules that trapped women in violent marriages.[72] These campaigns on behalf of women who are subject to immigration control – non-citizens or 'partial' citizens living for the most part outside the public sphere and support networks, without recourse to public funds yet subjected to intolerable levels of male violence – have ensured that reforms to immigration laws became integral to feminist policy. But crucially, they also found themselves driven to the criminal law for redress. Not that they were impressed with the 'newish strategy' that focused on the criminal law in cases of domestic violence. They felt it still had a 'long way to go'.[73] In particular, as advocates for women trying to flee violent men, they had considerable experience with a police force reluctant to arrest violent men or to help minority women who wanted to obtain injunctions. They had also observed the magistracy handing out light sentences for breaches of injunctions. It was these experiences that led them to explore civil law options and human rights law to '*compel* the criminal justice system to protect women from violence in the home'.[74]

It is at this point that I would like to return to Walklate's criticism of the VAW movement's continued commitment to a pro-arrest stand 'in total disregard of the evidence' of how police have used their power of arrest under

69 Gupta, 2003, pp 8–9.
70 Siddiqui, 2003c, pp 88 and 91.
71 Patel 2003a, pp 235–6.
72 For an account of their campaign against the one-year rule and their other efforts to address the problem of accommodating women with insecure immigration status and no recourse to public funds see Joshi, 2003, pp 135–7.
73 Johal, 2003, pp 44–5.
74 Patel, 2003a, p 235, emphasis added.

the North American model of mandatory arrest. Interestingly, she claims that researchers who had taken a pro-arrest stance later pointed out that the violence worsened 'especially for ethnic minority women'.[75] By contrast, SBS has been very critical of chronic under-policing of domestic violence in BME communities, insisting that the introduction in the 1990s of a 'partnership' approach to policing domestic violence through multi-agency forums had seriously undermined the criminal justice system as 'a legitimate option of redress for women'. The problem as they see it is that directives to police to liaise with local agencies via multi-agency forums subsumed the need for effective criminal justice responses, displacing police responsibility for dealing with domestic violence.[76] Moreover, theirs was a long-standing and bitterly felt objection – the limitations of multi-agency initiatives which encouraged mediation and the use of civil remedies had been exposed when an Asian woman was murdered by her husband in 'the supposed safety' of a Domestic Violence Unit at a London police station in 1991. Demanding more effective police responses to complaints by BME women about men's violence, SBS also expressed concern about the growing acceptance of the multi-agency approach by many women's aid groups which muted feminist criticism of the police. As for the debate about what type of police intervention feminists should be demanding in domestic violence cases – a pro-arrest or a 'softer' approach – SBS case work showed that the police 'fail at both approaches' in minority communities. Worse, by actively preventing BME women from gaining access to the criminal justice system, the police fed 'the myth' that women are reluctant to press charges when in fact many of the women seeking SBS's intervention had wanted to proceed with prosecutions of their assailants.[77] SBS also opposed the 'excuse of multiculturalism' – the police invoking of language, cultural or religious differences as reasons for non-intervention in response to Asian women's demands for protection from violent men. They had always been at pains to point out that 'all women experience violence in a cultural context and that differences of culture should not lead to a denial of civil rights for minority women'.[78]

While SBS remains wary of the wider women's movement, believing it to be less openly critical of the state's response to domestic violence, they have acknowledged that white feminists are becoming more vocal about other areas of VAW. Prostitution and trafficking in women have become 'the new battle-grounds', and yet, SBS stalwart Hannana Siddiqui claims there is still

---

75 Walklate 2008, p 41.
76 Other problems included a shift to a new corporatism within local authority and police governance, a widening of the social control net, the co-option of state and voluntary agencies and, 'most importantly, the breakdown of political resistance': Patel, 2003b, pp 162–8.
77 Patel, 2003b, pp 170–4.
78 Patel, 2003b, pp 176–80.

no adequate analysis of 'the intersection of race and gender shaping the experiences of trafficked women'. She does not exempt black women from her critique – 'we too', she insists, need to become more active in relation to the international trafficking in women into prostitution.[79] Nevertheless, SBS's achievements in the broad field of VAW should not be underestimated. Thanks largely to their efforts, forced marriage and honour crimes now sit next to rape, forced prostitution and trafficking in women at the centre of British feminist anti-violence campaigns.

Changing feminist agendas in the global era

For their part, white feminists have acknowledged the significant contribution made by SBS to the remapping of the feminist VAW agenda. Thus, for example, when making their case for an integrated violence against women strategy in 2005, Kelly and Lovett noted that SBS has played 'an inspirational role in the UK voluntary sector for two decades', assisting BME women suffering from all forms of VAW in both the public and private sphere, including domestic violence, sexual assault, harassment, forced marriage, dowry-related abuse and honour crimes. They also ran a project on gender violence which aims to 'mainstream' recognition and representation of BME women's experiences of domestic and sexual violence, including trafficking and prostitution, into practice and intervention strategies.[80] Speaking at a conference five years earlier, Kelly had acknowledged SBS's part in giving the wider feminist movement the impetus to question what she called 'our orthodoxies' and to think 'beyond the confines of current practices and organisational structures'. Deploying the term 'gender violence' as utilised in UN and international policy documents, she urged feminists to think in terms of connections at local, national and international levels.[81] Feminist stakeholders in VAW policy appear to be taking this path. Simultaneously with participating in consultation processes, feminist groups are formulating a VAW strategic framework that looks to international conventions, especially those concerned to protect women's rights to life, equality, health, personal freedom and security. Within this framework, VAW is increasingly being named as a human rights issue in order to hold the government accountable for failing to protect women, thereby denying them full enjoyment of their human rights. One tactic has involved exploring the potential of the UK Human Rights Act 1998. As SBS spokeswoman Meena Patel puts it, the passing of this Act opens up the possibility of using the 'very

79 Siddiqui, 2003c, pp 285–6.
80 Kelly and Lovett, 2005, p 25.
81 Kelly, 2000, pp 3–7.

language of human rights to hold the state accountable for the policing and prosecution of crimes against women'.[82]

Another tactic is to use global instruments such as the UN Declaration on the Elimination of VAW.[83] The pivotal international instrument, however, is the Convention for the Elimination of Discrimination Against Women (CEDAW), one of the UN's six core human rights treaties and the major treaty governing women's status. CEDAW is noteworthy for addressing discrimination in private spheres, including family and cultural practices that may constitute discrimination against women. Importantly, the CEDAW Committee has interpreted the convention to include VAW as a form of discrimination that inhibits women's ability to enjoy their human rights on an equal basis with men. While the UK government is required to report on its implementation of CEDAW and the progress it has made on women's human rights, non-governmental organisations (NGOs) can also report on whether the government is fulfilling its international obligations. British feminist groups have exploited this window of opportunity to hold it to account. To take one example, in 2003 Womankind Worldwide, a feminist charity, utilised CEDAW to produce a report on VAW for submission to the UN committee monitoring whether the UK government is honouring its commitments to human rights. The report, which insisted that violence impacts on all areas of women's lives and should not be seen only as a domestic or private issue, assessed the government's efforts to introduce new legislation and its commitments to tackling VAW and found them wanting. The government still lacked a national strategy with clear goals, resulting in an 'over focus on domestic violence in policy, research and provision' and a failure to make links between forms of gender-based violence and between VAW and economic, social and cultural rights.[84] Consequently, despite encouraging local initiatives to develop awareness, especially about domestic violence, there has been virtually no government investment with respect to rape, sexual assault, forced marriages, honour crimes, female genital mutilation, trafficking, the sex industry or the situation of refugee and asylum-seeking women, all of which now concerned the feminist movement against violence against women and children.

In proclaiming that VAW 'undermines the ability of women to participate as full and equal citizens in UK society', Womankind Worldwide's report acknowledges the work of groups like SBS who have highlighted how immigration policy discriminates against women with uncertain immigration

---

82 Patel, 2003a, p 236.
83 This Declaration, signed by the UK in 1993, defines VAW as 'any act of gender-based violence that results in physical, sexual or psychological harm or suffering to women, including threats of such acts, coercion or arbitrary deprivation of liberty, whether occurring in public or private life'.
84 Womankind Worldwide, 2004, pp iii and 2–3.

status who experience gender-based violence. It also notes how restrictive immigration policies created 'gendered access' to legal migration favouring men and male-dominated industries, while forcing women to take illegal and dangerous routes to the UK, notably the sex industry. Adopting an analytical framework that negotiates between the local and global dimensions of VAW, the report urges the government to make a 'strategic response' that understands and challenges the links between national and international trafficking, the growth of the local sex industry and VAW.[85] This initiative exemplifies the broad approach taken today by the British feminist movement against VAW, one that is based on a recognition that membership in a territorially exclusive nation-state has ceased to be the only ground for the realisation of women's rights. More crucially, it signals a willingness to listen to minority groups like SBS in order to open up spaces for the development of a vigorous and – *contra* Walklate – multi-option strategic plan. It is thanks to the advocacy work of these groups that the wider feminist movement has been forced to rethink 'domestic' violence as violence with a global inflection.

Strategies for the global era – towards transnational feminist anti-violence work

Where to next in the politics of naming and framing in the fraught field that is increasingly being framed as VAW? Hannana Siddiqui believes that the new economic world order has 'thrown up opportunities as never before for us as women living in the West to show solidarity with women's struggles worldwide'. She points to the successes of the anti-capitalist protestors and the opportunities afforded by the globalisation of women's struggles to make connections with other social movements.[86] Western feminists wishing to continue to think strategically about the impact of globalisation on their anti-violence agendas would also do well to consider the rich body of feminist theoretical work that has been 'un-domesticating' domestic violence by laying the foundations for a multicultural, globally-aware, anti-violence feminist campaign for over two decades.

As we saw in Chapter 5, Third World feminist scholar Chandra Mohanty was one of the first to offer advice to Western feminists on how to develop a strategy that articulated the local with the global. We saw too that she also provided a checklist of how *not* to articulate VAW – do not constitute yourselves as political subjects while representing migrant and Third World women as a racialised, powerless and undifferentiated group of

---

85 Womankind Worldwide, 2004, pp 4 and 20–1.
86 Siddiqui, 2003c, p 287.

down-trodden women; do not invoke an 'ethnocentric universalism' that assumes women are globally oppressed by men, regardless of their location, or a global sisterhood of first and Third World women. And finally, if you decide to take men's violence as a campaign focus, theorise it 'within specific societies'.[87] Revisiting 'Under Western Eyes' over a decade later, Mohanty still held to an analytic framework that attends to 'the micropolitics of everyday life as well as to the macropolitics of global economic and political processes', but she now takes account of the fact that globalisation has become more brutal, exacerbating economic, racial and gender inequalities. What was now required, she suggested, was transnational feminist organisation against capitalism informed by an analysis of the effects of corporate globalisation restructuring on the 'raced, classed, national and sexual bodies of women'. Whereas 'Under Western Eyes' had challenged the false universality of Eurocentric feminist discourse, Mohanty now felt the need to re-emphasise the necessity of cross-national feminist solidarity that makes connections between local and universal. More specifically, she advocated an analysis that centralises 'racialised gender' and begins from the place of the most marginalised and disenfranchised communities of women – poor women of all colours in affluent and neocolonial nations and women of the Third World. This, she believes, provides 'the most inclusive paradigm for thinking about social justice'.[88] As we have seen, this is precisely the kind of thinking and strategising – from spaces occupied by some of most marginalised women in Britain – that is informing feminist anti-violence work in Britain today.

Mohanty is not the only analyst to argue for a new form of transnational feminist organisation against global capital. A self-defining 'transnational' or 'critical multicultural feminism' emerged in North America in the 1990s, where salutary lessons have been learnt about the limitations of domestic violence legislation *and* of inadequately theorised feminist policies in late modernity. Transnational feminists seek to form transnational alliances while addressing asymmetrical global power relations. For them, taking account of the global context of VAW work today is axiomatic. As Ella Shohat puts it, multicultural feminism must take as its starting point the consequences of the worldwide movements and dislocations of people associated with the development of global or transnational capitalism.[89] For her, 'the global nature of the colonising process, the global flow of transnational capital and the global reach of contemporary communication technologies *virtually oblige* the multicultural feminist critic to move beyond the

87 Mohanty, 1988, pp 64–5 and 67.
88 Mohanty, 2002, pp 509–10.
89 Shohat, 1998, p 1.

restrictive framework of the nation-state as a unit of analysis'.[90] These processes also require her to reconceptualise power relations between cultural communities within and beyond the nation-state.

The implications of this kind of analysis for domestic violence work are spelled out clearly in Anannya Bhattacharjee's case study of the different meanings of 'home' for poor immigrant women in South Asian communities in the United States. Her analysis derives from a double dissatisfaction – first, with the fact that most domestic violence work, at least in the 1990s, focused exclusively on the family home. Working with immigrants in those communities, she found that 'home' had multiple significations for them – first, 'home' in the 'conventional domestic sphere of the heterosexual and patriarchal family'; second, that of an extended ethnic community, and a third 'home' for many immigrant communities is their nations of origin. Bhattacharjee's second source of dissatisfaction is the 'conventional' feminist mapping of the distinction between the private and public spheres and its understanding of the state as 'definitionally public' – 'organised around male power and expressed in law', it remains 'conveniently outside of private homes'. It follows that the feminist goal is to ensure that the state pays attention to violence in the privacy of the home so that battered women have public recourse.[91] Taking issue with these assumptions, Bhattacharjee argues that because feminist jurisprudence has omitted an analysis of nationhood, the nation-state and immigration, taking for granted women's status as legally recognised members of the public, its construction of the private and the public is largely imaginary. Most crucially, it ignores how immigration laws have *privatised* the nation', turning it into 'a bounded space into which only some of the people can walk some of the time'.[92] Here, an employer's control over a domestic worker in the home who is more often than not a poor immigrant woman, or a man's control over his migrant wife 'extends to controlling her recognition as a member of what constitutes the public – in this case being a legal resident of a national community (in itself a private concept)'. In South Asian immigrant communities, the figure of the undocumented woman who is an 'illegal alien' is 'a reminder of the not-public – that is, private – basis of the nation-state'. For this woman, 'home' is not a clearly demarcated space; what is presumed to be 'public' and 'private' shifts and changes. If she is battered and wants to leave her abuser, she not only risks alienating her family and community, but also her standing as 'an appropriate member' of her ethnic community, partly because this community 'occupies a public space policed by U.S. federal laws'. And crucially, her situation points to the limitations of a Western feminist analysis that

---

90 Shohat, 1998, p 47, emphasis added.
91 Bhattacharjee, 1997, pp 308–17.
92 Bhattacharjee, 1997, p 317, original emphasis.

assumes that public space is a space of recourse from injuries endured in 'private' – a zone 'automatically lying outside an easily and singularly recognised "home" '.[93]

For transnational feminists, it follows that any strategy against domestic violence that takes the lives of immigrant women seriously 'has to be seen as global'. This is so not only because domestic violence 'affects women everywhere', but because the immigrant woman's experiences of violence 'spans the patriarchal home, the community, the host nation and the nation of origin'. Attending to the global parameters of 'domestic' violence not only challenges, once again, conventionally accepted spaces of private and public; it demonstrates that 'an un-nuanced belief in social change through intervention in public spaces is an illusion'. It is not enough, then, to fight violence in the home. Globalising and 'undomesticating' domestic violence work, Bhattacharjee predicted in the late 1990s, was the road ahead for campaigners whose work has too often been 'domesticated as social service', thereby losing its critical edge.[94]

It should be emphasised that globalisation, from this perspective, is not a new development; it must be seen as part of the much longer history of colonialism. As critical multicultural feminist Ella Shohat points out, the migration of poverty-stricken women attempting to survive in 'the age of the IMF-generated debt crisis' is 'only the most recent episode of imperialism'. Feminists today must navigate between the local and the global 'without romanticising either transnational globalism as a form of universalism or localism as salvation'. Thus, for example, immigration – as we have seen, currently a focal concern of the British feminist VAW movement – cannot be discussed 'only from the receiving end'. It must be traced back to its origins in transnational economies that generate the displacement. A critical multicultural or transnational feminism that privileges a 'multiply situated analysis' must see the necessity of strategising both locally and globally.[95]

Negotiating the local and the global

Clearly, there are huge challenges ahead for Western feminist movements against VAW. On the one hand, white feminists have to avoid the danger of reinscription into a discourse of 'global feminism' that lumps women into one unified voice against a supposedly unified capitalist world market, distracting feminists from recognising continuing inequalities of power. For example, while human rights discourse has helped to raise the issue of

93 Bhattacharjee, 1997, pp 317–20.
94 Bhattacharjee, 1997, pp 322–4, original emphasis.
95 Shohat, 1998, pp 50–2.

violence against women onto 'the world stage',[96] entering into the fray of human rights advocacy for women subject to immigration control can be fraught. At face value, the climate of international women's human rights appears to have been important for advocates of women's rights to asylum. For example, Canada and the United States have granted refugee status to women fleeing persecutions such as forced marriage. But in an incisive analysis, Sherene Razack underlines the problematic ways in which gender-based harms become visible within the racial context of the refugee hearing in Canada. In her view, the concept of gender persecution might be 'the most significant legal gain for women in this century, opening the door to the recognition that women can be persecuted as women, and that this is a violation of their human rights'. However, gender persecution, as it is deployed in refugee discourse, can 'function as a deeply racialised concept' requiring 'Third World women to speak of their experience of sexual violence at the expense of their realities as colonised peoples'.[97]

On the other hand, Western feminists need to unlearn Eurocentric narrative strategies and representational politics that run the risk of privileging violence against Third World or BME women as the worst forms of VAW.[98] In the British context, where BME groups are well-represented in feminism forums, it needs to be remembered that even if the inequalities produced by economic globalisation were not forcing vulnerable people to move across state borders, there would still be violence against women already living there. The issues that transnational feminists seize upon – refugees, illegal migration, trafficking – can only be part of the local story in any given place. British anti-violence campaigns will need to continue to be relevant to the large population of British-born majority ethnic women subjected to fear and violence 'at home'.[99] Campaigners also need to be alert to the possibility that poor white women who experience violence are less likely than BME women to seek refuge in a shelter, secure protection orders or call the police.[100] Relatedly, feminists have yet to fully explore how VAW is connected to what has been called in the North American context 'State-sponsored violence', involving a 'coupling of domestic violence and the state' that occurs when the 'state-sponsored safety net' is dismantled. This has resulted in severe curtailments in women's access to welfare, shelter and

96 Mohanty, 2002, p 529.
97 Razack, 1995, p 48.
98 Bergeron, 2001, p 1000. For further elaboration of these points, see Kaplan et al, 1999.
99 I am grateful to Katie Curchin for bringing my attention to this issue and formulating it so lucidly.
100 An American study found that African-American women who reported experiences of domestic violence were more likely to report the abuse than battered white women: Fine and Weis, 2000, pp 1139–40.

higher education – the routes through which poor and working-class women escaped violence in the past.[101]

The question of how 'the local' and 'the global' should figure in the formation of transnational identities has been the subject of debate in Britain. Advocating a feminist 'politics of location' that is 'simultaneously local and global', Ugandan academic and founding SBS member Avtar Brah argues that one of the most important developments in the feminism movement has been the emergence of a politics that is simultaneously local and global. It is based on an understanding of a 'diasporic space' that is inhabited not only by migrants and their descendants, but equally by those 'represented as indigenous' – in the UK, white populations. It includes the entanglement of the genealogies of dispersion with those of 'staying put'. A case in point is 'the diasporic space called "England"', where African-Caribbean, Irish, Asian, Jewish and other diasporas 'intersect among themselves as well as with the entity constructed as "Englishness", thoroughly re-inscribing it in the process'. Such decentring processes challenge 'the minoritising and peripheralising impulses' of dominant cultures – including that of the wider feminist movement.[102]

Western feminist anti-violence work has done a great deal to conceive of VAW in multi-axial terms, thereby helping to keep in check peripheralising impulses within the contemporary feminist anti-violence movements. In Britain, for example, it has highlighted the needs of impoverished migrant and refugee women as well as first- and second-generation black and Asian women trying to escape violent men 'at home'. Feminist campaigns now situated violence against women in a global context. But while the scope of political activity has expanded, it needs to be remembered that globalisation is 'just another way of saying (and doing) imperialism'.[103] Of course, for Foucauldians, saying *is* doing, so a constant interrogation of feminist discursive practices – checking them for orientalist, neoimperialist and racist narrations of VAW – is in order. As Inderpal Grewal counsels, in cases of global activism or activism in multicultural contexts, representational practices matter profoundly. She singles out 'the objects of rescue created by human rights discourse' and also the 'subject formation' of those who deploy this discourse. It is imperative, she reminds us, to examine practices that depict 'the objects of violations as well as the subject-constitution of those doing the depicting and representing'. Are Western feminists representing themselves as saviours and rescuers of oppressed Third World and minority ethnic victims? – 'Who speaks for whom? What relations of power enable some to speak for others? What forms of violence do these

101 Fine and Weis, 2000, pp 1140–1.
102 Brah, 1996, pp 209–10, original emphasis.
103 Katz, 2001, p 1214.

representations perform?'[104] Importantly, the practices and claims of NGOs and other 'grass roots' groups, including black and minority groups, cannot be exempt from this scrutiny.

Nor can the claims of transnational feminists themselves. Sceptical critics claim that for all the hype around the 'new buzz word' of transnational feminism, it is no fitter to negotiate the different positions and interests of women in the era of globalisation than the much-maligned universalising and essentialising notion of 'global sisterhood' paraded by radical feminists in the 1970s and 1980s. In fact, is has been suggested that little differentiates these feminisms. According to marxist critic Breny Mendoza, the new transnationalist postcolonial feminists have made some advances. By focusing on issues related to immigration, forced removals, diasporas and asylum, they have produced 'an intersectional analysis and a transversal politics' not possible within a global sisterhood framework that universalises the oppression of women. They have made possible the analysis of gender, race and sexuality beyond national borders and some – Mendoza singles out Chandra Mohanty – have pointed out the centrality of Third World women's work to global capitalism. However, in Mendoza's view, their analysis is flawed inasmuch as transnationality and class alliances appear to be limited to Third World women workers across the first/Third World divide, while class alliances formed by non-Third World women workers in other sectors of the global economy are ignored.[105] Blinded by a romanticism of Third World activism in the global arena, transnational feminists have 'arrogated the global terrain to themselves without a clear basis of legitimation from local constituencies', thereby failing to provide 'a political form of consciousness and organisation that is any more fit to negotiate the different positions and interests of women' in the global era than the old idea of 'global sisterhood'.[106]

For analysts like Mendoza, new feminist theories with their fancy global inflections will not usher in a golden age that will end the violation of women's rights. But I am hardly going to end the story there, with a marxist who bemoans the advent of poststructuralism and does not address any of the focal concerns of this book! Let us conclude rather with the positives and with the feminists who have done so much to reconceptualise the problem of violence against women as a question of negotiation between the national and the global and as one involving advocacy on behalf of poor and marginalised women from older indigenous and contemporary diasporic communities in order to grasp critical possibilities of feminist alliances across discrepant material conditions. Let us respect their understanding that if

104 Grewal, 1998, pp 502–4.
105 Mendoza, 2002, pp 300–4.
106 Mendoza, 2002, pp 309–10.

men's violence is taken as a campaign focus, it has to be theorised at both the local and global levels, and accept their endorsement of 'the piecemeal approach of postmodern feminism' that enables 'co-operation around specific issues without making generalised claims for women's rights'.[107] And let us side, too, with those who recognise that if current feminist theory or practice is inadequate to the task of 'local-global analysis' and action, it should be 'called to account, or indeed abandoned', as the journal *Feminist Review* recently editorialised.[108]

Lest today's challenges appear too daunting, let us take heart from what our case study of the British VAW sector shows has been achieved so far. Feminist academics and activists are participating in feminist-initiated consultations about domestic violence policy directives to ensure that states incorporate differently situated women such as refugee and migrant women. Simultaneously, they are exploring international mechanisms for holding the government to account for infringements of women's human rights. Moreover, if in the early 1990s it could be said that 'white feminist movements in the West have rarely engaged questions of immigration and nationality',[109] influential agenda-setting groups such as SBS, Rights of Women and Womankind Worldwide are ensuring that the wider feminist movement in the UK is engaging those trans-boundary questions now in the ongoing fight against violence against women and children. In doing so, it is contributing to a new type of globally-inflected politics that continues the long, hard fight to find new ways of naming and combating that violence.

At the same time, the movement has kept a watchful eye on local needs and has been richly rewarded for its hard-fought efforts with widespread media coverage of its campaigns and finally, government action. In particular, its work towards the establishment of an integrated VAW strategy appears to have been a resounding success. The Home Office Domestic Violence mini-site informs us that domestic violence has not only been steadily ascending the political agenda, but is also recognised as a cross-government priority. Moreover, the government is promising a more co-ordinated approach for action on domestic violence at the local level and greater collaboration between its domestic violence and sexual assault service delivery plans in the future. Signs of the new collaborative approach can be seen in the establishment of a joint Foreign Office/Home Office Forced Marriage Unit. It is epitomised too in the launching in 2007 of the UK Action Plan on Tackling Human Trafficking to tackle trafficking across government departments, and the Cross Government Action Plan on Sexual Violence and Abuse, the latter without doubt being one of the pinnacles of

107 Gutpa, 2003, pp 264–5 quoting Nira Yuval-Davis.
108 Hemmings, Gedalof and Bland, 2006, p 3.
109 Mohanty, 1991, p 23.

feminist achievement. Here at last we find government recognition that sexual violence and abuse should be catapulted into the 'the most serious crimes' category; that sexual violence and child sexual abuse are a 'dangerous element of domestic violence' and, more broadly, that sexual violence is linked to a whole range of other forms of gender-based violence – domestic violence, forced marriage, honour crimes, female genital mutilation, prostitution and trafficking.[110] The integrated VAW strategy promised by the Blair government at the close of the twentieth century is finally well and truly back on track.

A final word from Foucault – *for* co-option

One final point: commenting on 'the centrality that sexual violence has achieved for policy action within the criminal justice process in England and Wales', Sandra Walklate observes that violence against women is now 'squarely on the policy agenda'. But in her view, this feminist success story 'also hints at the problems of co-option'. Not only has the problem of attrition in cases of rape and domestic violence remained the same or, indeed, 'worsened', but because feminists have continued to focus on the criminal justice system as an appropriate arena for action, demanding 'as robust policing response as possible in risk-assessing repeat domestic violence', it is possible to 'trace all the elements' of a 'culture of control' in responses to violence against women developed over the last 25 years. Most notably, the recourse to law and criminalisation has led feminist campaigners down the unholy path of enhancing and fuelling the activities of police and prosecutors in the face of accumulating evidence that organisations charged with the implementation of an expanded criminal law will not deliver safety and justice to victims. To support her argument, Walklate makes the obligatory reference to Carol Smart's warning, all those years ago, about the power of law to disqualify women's experiences of violence and highjack feminist law reform efforts.[111] It therefore pays to return to Smart to see how, having canvassed all the problems and paradoxes attending involvement in rape law reform, she concluded her ground-breaking Foucauldian critique of the feminist recourse to law. She did so by saying that to follow the argument about unintended consequences and co-option to its logical conclusion

110 HM Government, 2007, p iii.
111 Walklate, 2008, pp 46–50. For a brilliant, nuanced consideration of critiques of social control in the context of family and child welfare agencies' handling of family violence cases, see Gordon, 2007. First published in 1986, it has stood the test of time. My misgivings about Walklate's analysis notwithstanding, trenchant and convincing critiques of the feminist recourse to law do exist. See, e.g. the argument that a feminist emphasis on legislative intervention against sexual trafficking can be counter-productive, reinforcing punitive migration policies in O'Connell Davidson, 2006.

would 'lead to total inactivity and political paralysis'. She continued: 'I am not recommending that feminist policy should stop campaigning around rape and the law. Rape is already in the legal domain, therefore it *must* be addressed on that terrain'.[112] It is worth recalling too that while Smart concluded her study of twentieth-century feminist efforts to get child sexual abuse recognised as a social problem by remarking that the criminal justice system and legal practice are 'the most problematic sites for radical redefinitions' of harm to take root, she began her analysis declaring that she remained convinced that 'law, understood in its widest meaning, is still one of the most important sites of engagement and counter-discourse'.[113]

It is in that spirit that I have continued to work on the project of framing violence against women as a harm – a social harm no less and one requiring legal redress.[114] I have also continued to work for the reform of the criminal law, specifically the law of homicide. Rape law reform, on the other hand, is something I have assiduously eschewed. Placing it in the too-hard basket, admiring from afar feminist lawyers, activists and campaigners who persist in pointing out that there is still today something spectacularly wrong and unjust about the way in which criminal justice systems handle rape cases, has always seemed to me the better part of valour. For some time now though, I have been involved in feminist campaigns to reform partial defences to murder, focusing my attention on the provocation defence, law's premier excuse for men's lethal violence against their current and departed women partners. My view that the provocation defence should be abolished is grounded in a reading of a great deal of case law that demonstrates how frequently men get away with murdering women on the most feeble of excuses – she made derogatory comments about his manhood, she had an affair, she wanted to leave him. There is no space here to rehearse my abolitionist position, let alone to expand on how my argument has been shaped by a reading of homosexual advance cases and of alternative and sometimes conflicting feminist approaches to the problem of partial defences to murder.[115] Suffice it to say that I have paid the usual price for taking such a presumptuous stand against a man's right to avoid a murder conviction after killing his wife by pleading guilty to manslaughter by reason of provocation and receiving a lesser sentence. On one occasion, while working in the community legal sector, I was castigated as a law and order ideologue and a racist bent on imprisoning more Aboriginal men charged with killing their wives by depriving them of their best chance of avoiding a lengthy prison sentence.[116] Paralysis-inducing though such slanders can be, I have

---

112 Smart, 1989, p 49, emphasis added.
113 Smart, 1999, pp 407 and 392.
114 E.g. Howe, 1987, 1990, 1997b and see the Introduction to Cain and Howe, 2008.
115 See Howe, 2000c, 2002 and 2004b.
116 See Howe, 2002.

continued to advocate that the provocation defence be abolished. And now that it has been in my home state of Victoria, I wait to see how defence lawyers frame the provocation narrative as a plea of mitigation at sentencing after their client has been found guilty of murdering his wayward wife. But I remain confident that in the courts as in the world at large, that age-old 'nagging and shagging' provocation script will continue to provide a site for engagement, counter-discourse and that modest Foucauldian project of shifting thresholds of tolerance – in this case, thresholds of tolerance for men's lethal anger at annoying or departing women partners.[117]

Speaking of Foucauldian projects, Foucault himself did not shy away from the problems and dangers attending engagement with law and the state. He believed strongly that the 'necessity of reform mustn't be allowed to become a form of blackmail, serving to limit, reduce or halt the exercise of criticism'. After all, critique is 'an instrument for those who fight, those who resist and refuse what is'.[118] But this, as Keith Gandal points out, is 'not to say that refusal or criticism was the be-all and end-all of Foucault's efforts or that he was not interested in seeing reforms carried out'. Nor, crucially, did he reject reform because it meant co-option. In Foucault's view, to practise a 'progressive politics', one had to 'overcome the fear of reformism and stop using it as a bogey to insure adherence' to a supposedly more radical stance. Seeing that co-option was inevitable, he set about developing 'new possibilities of reformism'. Referring to one of the prison reforms enacted by the French government in the 1970s in response to demands of a prisoners' rights group in which he was actively involved, Foucault said that it would not alter the essential situation of the prison:

> It would be silly for us to see in that fact a victory for the movement, but it would be just as silly to see in it the proof that our movement has been co-opted . . . to be sure, some political groups have long felt this fear of being co-opted. Won't everything that is said be inscribed in the very mechanisms that we are trying to denounce? Well, I think it is absolutely necessary that it should happen this way: if the discourse can be co-opted, it is not because it is vitiated by nature, but because it is inscribed in a process of struggle.

Co-option, he suggests, is the 'best valorisation of the stakes', and 'as in judo, the best answer to the opponent's manœuver is never to step back, but

---

117 Foucault, 1981, pp 11–12.
118 Foucault, 1981, p 13. I am aware of the irony of citing Foucault's comments about reformism in a context where he would have agreed with Walklate's social control perspective. Let him groan and protest.

to re-use it to your own advantage as a base for the next phase . . . Now it is our return to reply'.[119]

When it comes to taking on masculinist institutions and entrenched cultures of excuse and justification in the matter of men's violence against women and children, feminists have been doing just that for over a hundred years. It is going to take something more than fear of co-option to stop us now, secure as we are in the conviction that it is absolutely necessary that it should happen this way – that the co-option of our discourse will inscribe it in an ongoing process of resistance. I can live with that sort of valorisation of our work. Can you?

---

119 Quoted in Gandal, 1986, p 131. After all this time, I still rate Gandal's defence of Foucault's work as unsurpassable, and I still describe it to students as a gift.

Epilogue

It is now 30 years since Baudrillard famously told us to forget Foucault. The only reason, he said, that Foucault had been able to talk with 'such definitive "understanding" ' about such things as 'power, sexuality, the body and discipline, even down to their most delicate metamorphoses' was because 'at some point *all this is here and now over with*'.[1] It had been 'the most dazzling display of analysis', but its time had passed. Adding to this negative appraisal some 10 years later, Lacanian theorist Slavoj Žižek declared that the time had come to move 'beyond' discourse analysis. Dissolve 'reality' into its discursive constitution? So passé.[2] Why bring this up now, and why mention this psychoanalytical theorist at all? Certainly not to engage with his anti-poststructuralism and 'disturbing anti-feminism'.[3] My much more self-limiting purpose here is to say that early dismissals of Foucault and his analytical framework have proven to be premature. At least, they have been from the perspective of anyone casting a critical eye over non-feminist representations of sexed violence. Take, for example, our Lacanian's contribution to the so-called 'false memory debate'. He dismisses – in a footnote, perhaps to better register his contempt – survivors' memories of child sexual abuse unearthed through 'the suggestive help of the all-too-willing therapist'. Such 'memories' – he problematises them with inverted commas – are, he says, 'often revealed to be fake and fantasised'. But '*even if they are factually true*, (that is, even if the child was actually molested by a parent or a close relative)', which he doubts very much, they are still '*false*'. Why? Because they permit the subject to assume 'the neutral position of a passive victim of external injurious circumstances, obliterating the

---

1 Baudrillard, 1987, p 11, original emphasis. *Forget Foucault* was originally published as *Oublier Foucault* in 1977.
2 Žižek, 1990, p 249.
3 Alcoff, 2000, p 859 referring to Judith Butler's 1993 critique of Žižek's position in the course of their debate about the 'real'.

crucial question of his or her *own libidinal investment* in what happened to him or her'.[4]

Now there's a claim worthy of Foucault, an excellent match indeed for *his* cavalier dismissal of the sexual assault of a young girl as a harmless bucolic pleasure. A passive victim of external injurious circumstances – what a splendid discursive manoeuvre it is, utterly erasing the abuser while loading up the child with responsibility for his or her victimisation and targeting therapists for facilitating preposterous fantasies. Both of these eminent theorists, it seems, are past masters in the art of denial and erasure when it comes to registering the suffering inflicted by rapists and paedophiles. But what is of more interest is how they both gloss over the insight, taken as read in most fields of critical inquiry, that such representations of violence are themselves violent since they confirm stereotypes of willing victims while implicitly endorsing the entitlement of abusers to abuse. This oversight is perhaps more remarkable in Foucault's case inasmuch as the underlying premise of his work was that representational practices matter profoundly. Žižek, on the other hand, feels that too much has been made of the dis-cursive. Now it is true that I have succumbed here to what Žižek derides as 'the usual critical-feminist temptation' of fussing over masculinist discursive constructions of the real.[5] But far be it for me to venture beyond that. Specu-lating about why he says what he says, wondering about the blinding effects of his own and Foucault's libidinal investments in narrations of abuse, that is not my brief. I leave it to those more qualified to throw light on the enduring mystery of that stubborn drive to excuse abuses of power by deny-ing harms to victims.[6]

My far more modest goal in this book has been that of contributing to the Foucauldian project of breaching the self-evidence of the way things are – of trying to change the way people perceive and talk about sexed violence. I have tried, more particularly, to help displace forms of sensibility and thresholds of tolerance in the fraught field that has been increasingly named as men's violence against women. There is a great deal of work still to be done. Here it is well to recall that for Foucault, critical work consists in 'analysing and reflecting on limits' and recognising the contingency of such limits for the purpose of 'possible transgression'. Critique, he said in 'What is Enlightenment?' is 'an experiment with the possibility' of going beyond limits. One embarks on this work by developing a certain 'attitude'. He calls

---

4 Žižek, 2000, p 135, n 55, original emphasis. For an insightful study of the role played by fantasy in survivors' memories of child sexual abuse, see Haakan, 1994.

5 Žižek, 1990, p 257.

6 I also leave it them – to you? – to query why power has to be 'not only violent but also cruel or savage or sadistic' and why it has to generate a measure of 'enjoyment' for those who exercise it, whether via state power, or colonial rule or 'male domination': Balibar, 1998, p 12. See further Howe, 2004b.

it the 'attitude of modernity' – 'a philosophical ethos that could be described as a permanent critique of our historical era'. It is also a 'permanent critique of ourselves', of 'what we are saying, thinking and doing'.[7] Such 'thinking with attitude', as Foucauldian Moya Lloyd translates this advice, is a 'process of denaturalisation or problematisation that grounds the politics of refusal'. Practising criticism, as Foucault puts it, involves ensuring that 'what is accepted as self-evident will no longer be accepted as such'; it is 'a matter of making facile gestures difficult' or as Lloyd puts it, of rendering 'alien' modes of thought that 'we accept as normal and everyday'.[8] And that as it happens is the sort of criticism I have tried to practise in this book. By offering a myriad of examples of the perceptual limits imposed by hegemonic representations of men's violence, I have invited readers to refuse their self-evidence, and to think hard about what we and others are saying and doing when we put that violence into discourse. It is my hope that this book encourages readers to continue to engage with the politics of refusal around masculinist modes of thought accepted as normal and everyday. I hope too, that they learn to perceive critical work, again adapting Foucault, as 'the art of not being governed quite so much' by the facile gestures of masculinity hegemony and that they are won over to the idea of practising critique as he envisaged it – as 'the art of voluntary insubordination'.[9] Take from him, I entreat you, the analytical tools that enable a re-imagining of dominant regimes of truth as events – 'nothing more, nothing less than events' – that are fixed according to their own conditions of acceptability, but are also fields of 'openings, indecisions, reversals and possible dislocations' which make them fragile and temporary.[10]

Finally, it needs to be said that asking the 'Man' question in any field, but perhaps especially in the fields explored in this book, is a very risky business. So many dangers lie in wait – being mistaken for a radical feminist or some other unspecified kind of 'extremist'; being traduced on the one hand as a nihilist and on the other as a law-and-order ideologue; spending inordinate amounts of time unpacking discourses of justification for men's violence only to be told that the time of discourse analysis is past; recalling – too late, alas – a warning posted three decades ago that a Foucauldian concern with the discursive production of sex, violence and power was already well and truly over with way back then. As if that were not enough to give pause, one also needs to confront that fact that 'any move that is made *against* violence will have to come to terms with a backlash'. It has to be recognised, too, that it is simply not possible to offer 'a programme for the complete elimination

---

7 Foucault, 1984c, pp 39–50.
8 Lloyd, 1996, p 244 quoting Foucault, 1988e, p 155.
9 Foucault, 1997, pp 29 and 32.
10 Foucault, 1997, p 60.

of violence'. Face it: 'there is no non-violence'.[11] But do not despair. Join Foucault, the master theorist of the discursive production of truth, in delighting that 'everything is dangerous'. For if everything is dangerous, 'we always have something to do'.[12] So readers take heart, your work is cut out. I leave it to you to continue the job of making facile gestures difficult when anyone starts talking about that massively resistant analytical object, 'men's violence against women'. Good luck.

11 Balibar, 1998, p 6, original emphasis and p 18.
12 Foucault, 1983, pp 231–2.

References

Adelson, J 1986 'Back to Criminal Psychology' 8 *Commentary* 44

Alarcón, N 1990 'The Theoretical Subject(s) of *This Bridge Called My Back* and Anglo-American Feminism' in G Anzaldúa (ed) *Making Face, Making Soul, Hacinedo Caras: Creative and Critical Perspectives by Women of Colour* San Francisco: Aunt Lute Foundation Books

Alcoff, L 1990–1 'The Problem of Speaking for Others' Winter *Cultural Critique* 5

Alcoff, L 1996 'Dangerous Pleasures: Foucault and the Politics of Paedophilia' in S Hekman (ed) *Feminist Interpretations of Michel Foucault* University Park: Pennsylvania State University Press

Alcoff, L 1997 'The Politics of Postmodern Feminism, Revisited' Spring *Cultural Critique* 5

Alcoff, L 2000 'Philosophical Matters: A Review of Recent Work in Feminist Philosophy' 25(3) *Signs: Journal of Women in Culture and Society* 841

Alcoff, L and Gray, L 1993 'Survivor Discourse: Transgression or Recuperation?' 18(2) *Signs: Journal of Women in Culture and Society* 260

Alexander, MJ 1997 'Erotic Autonomy as a Politics of Decolonisation: An Anatomy of Feminist and State Practice in the Bahamas Tourist Economy' in MJ Alexander and CT Mohanty (eds) *Feminist Genealogies, Colonial Legacies, Democratic Futures* New York: Routledge

Alexander, MJ and Mohanty, CT 1997 (eds) *Feminist Genealogies, Colonial Legacies, Democratic Futures* New York: Routledge

Allen, H 1987 'Rendering Them Harmless: The Professional Portrayal of Women Charged with Serious Violent Crimes' in P Carlen and A Worrall (eds) *Gender, Crime and Justice* Milton Keynes: Open University Press

Allen, H 1988 'One Law for all Reasonable Persons?' 16 *International Journal of the Sociology of Law* 419

Allen, A 1996 'Foucault on Power: A Theory for Feminists' in S Hekman (ed) *Feminist Interpretations of Michel Foucault* University Park: Pennsylvania State University Press

Amos, V and Parmar, P 1984 'Challenging Imperial Feminism' 17 *Feminist Review* 3

Archer, J 2000a 'Sex Differences in Aggression Between Heterosexual Partners: A Meta-analytic Review' 126(5) *Psychological Bulletin* 651

Archer, J 2000b 'Sex Differences in Physical Aggression to Partners: A Reply to Frieze, O'Leary and White, Smith, Koss and Figueredo' 126(5) *Psychological Bulletin* 697

Ashe, M 1995 'Mind's Opportunity: Birthing a Poststructuralist Feminist Jurisprudence' in J Leonard (ed) *Legal Studies as Critical Studies: A Reader in (Post)modern Critical Theory* Albany: State University of New York Press

Bacchi, C 1999 *Women, Policy and Politics: The Construction of Policy Problems* London: Sage

Balibar, E 1998 'Violence, Ideality and Cruelty' 35 *New Formations* 7

Bandalli, S 1995 'Provocation: a Cautionary Tale' 22 *Journal of Law and Society* 398

Bar On, B 1993 'Marginality and Epistemic Privilege' in L Alcoff and E Potter (eds) *Feminist Epistemologies* New York: Routledge

Barbaree, HE *et al* 1989 'Brief Research Report: The Reliability of the Rape Index in a Sample of Rapists and Nonrapists' 4(4) *Violence and Victims* 299

Baudrillard, J 1987 *Forget Foucault* New York: Semiotext(e)

Bauman, Z 1998 *Globalisation: the Human Consequences* Oxford: Polity

Bell, V 1991 'Beyond the "Thorny Question": Feminism, Foucault and the Desexualisation of Rape' 19 *International Journal of the Sociology of Law* 1

Bell, V 1993 *Interrogating Incest: Feminism, Foucault and the Law* London: Routledge

Bergeron, S 2001 'Political Economy Discourses of Globalisation and Feminist Politics' 26(4) *Signs* 983

Berlant, L and Warner, M 1998 'Sex in Public' 24 *Critical Inquiry* 547

Bhattacharjee, A 1997 'Mapping Homes and Undomesticating Violence Work in the South Asian Immigrant Community' in MJ Alexander and CT Mohanty (eds) *Feminist Genealogies, Colonial Legacies Democratic Futures* New York: Routledge

Bittner, E 1976 'Review: I, Pierre Rivière' 82 *American Journal of Sociology* 256

Bottomley, A 2004 'Shock to Thought: An Encounter (of a Third Kind) with Legal Feminism' 12 *Feminist Legal Studies* 29

Brah, A 1996 *Cartographies of Diaspora: Contesting Identities* Routledge: London

Braithwaite, J 1987 'Review Essay: the Mesomorphs Strike Back' 20 *Australian and New Zealand Journal of Criminology* 45

Bronfen, E 1992 *Over Her Dead Body* Manchester: Manchester University Press

Brown, B 1981 'A Feminist Interest in Pornography – Some Modest Proposals' 5/6 *m/f* 5

Brown, B 1985 'Women and Crime: The Dark Figures of Criminology' 15(3) *Economy and Society* 355

Brown, B 1990 'Debating Pornography: The Symbolic Dimensions' 1(2) *Law and Critique* 131

Brown, W 1995 *States of Injury: Power and Freedom in Late Modernity* Princeton: Princeton University Press

Butler, J 1990 *Gender Trouble: Feminism and the Subversion of Identity* New York: Routledge

Butler, J 1992 'Contingent Foundations: Feminism and the Question of "Post-modernism"' in J Butler and JW Scott (eds) *Feminists Theorise the Political* London: Routledge

Butler, J 1993 *Bodies That Matter: On the Discursive Limits of 'Sex'* New York: Routledge

Cain, M 1990 'Towards Transgression: New Directions in Feminist Criminology' 18 *International Journal of the Sociology of Law* 1

Cain, M and Howe, A 2008 'Women, Crime and Social Harm: Towards a Criminology for the Global Era Oxford: Hart Publishing

Cameron, D 1994 'St-i-i-ll Going ... The Quest for Jack the Ripper' 40 Social Text 147

Cameron, D and Frazer, E 1987 The Lust to Kill: A Feminist Investigation of Sexual Murder Cambridge: Polity Press

Caputi, J 1987 The Age of Sex Crime London: The Women's Press

Carlen, P 1985 (ed) Criminal Women Cambridge: Polity Press

Carlen, P 1990 'Women, Crime, Feminism and Realism' 17(4) Social Justice 106

Carlen, P 2002 'Critical Criminology? In Praise of an Oxymoron and its Enemies' in K Carrington and R Hogg (eds) Critical Criminologies: An Introduction Cullompton: Willan Publishers

Carrington, K 2002 'Feminism and Critical Criminology: Confronting Genealogies' in K Carrington and R Hogg (eds) Critical Criminologies: An Introduction Cullompton: Willan Publishers

Carrington, K and Hogg, R 2002 (eds) Critical Criminologies: An Introduction Cullompton: Willan Publishers

Castel, R 1982 'The Doctors and Judges' in M Foucault (ed) I, Pierre Rivière Having Slaughtered My Mother, My Sister and My Brother Lincoln: Bison Books

Chan, W and Rigakos, GS 2002 'Risk, Crime and Gender' 42 British Journal of Criminology 743

Cobb, R 1978 'A Triple Life' New Society June 8

Cohen, S 1994 'Social Control and the Politics of Reconstuction' in D Nelken (ed) The Futures of Criminology London: Sage

Cohen, S 2001 States of Denial: Knowing about Atrocities and Suffering Cambridge: Polity

Collier, R 1997 'After Dunbane: Crime, Corporality and the (Hetero)sexing of the Bodies of Men' 24(2) Journal of Law and Society 177

Collier, R 2004 'Masculinities and Crime: Rethinking the "Man" Question?' in C Sumner (ed) The Blackwell Companion to Criminology Oxford: Blackwell Publishing

Combahee River Collective, 1983 'A Black Feminist Statement' in C Moraga and G Anzaldúa G (eds) This Bridge Called My Back: Writings by Radical Women of Colour Boston: South End Press

Connell, RW 1987 Gender and Power: Society, the Person and Sexual Politics Cambridge: Polity Press

Connell, RW 2002 'On Hegemonic Masculinity and Violence: Response to Jefferson and Hall' 6(1) Theoretical Criminology 89

Couzens Hoy, D 'Foucault: Modern or Postmodern?' in J Arac (ed) After Foucault: Humanistic Knowledge, Postmodern Challenges New Brunswick: Rutgers University Press

Coward, R 1987 Female Desire: Women's Sexuality Today London: Paladin

Davies, S and Rhodes-Little, A 1993 'History, Sexuality and Power: Deconstructing the "Lesbian Vampire Case" ' 12 Australian Cultural History 14

de Haan, W and Loader, I 2002 'On the Emotions of Crime, Punishment and Social Control' 6(3) Theoretical Criminology 243

de Lauretis, T 1984 Alice Doesn't: Feminism, Semiotics, Cinema Bloomington: Indiana University Press

de Lauretis, T 1987 *The Technology of Gender* Bloomington: Indiana University Press

de Lauretis, T 1990 'Eccentric Subjects: Feminist Theory and Historical Consciousness' 16 *Feminist Studies* 115

Deveaux, M 1996 'Feminism and Empowerment: A Critical Reading of Foucault' in S Hekman (ed) *Feminist Interpretations of Michel Foucault* University Park: Pennsylvania State University Press

Dobash, P *et al* 1992 'The Myth of Sexual Symmetry in Marital Violence' 39(1) *Social Problems* 71

Duncan, S 1995 'Law's Sexual Discipline: Visibility, Violence and Consent' 22(3) *Journal of Law and Society* 326

Duncker, P 1997 *Hallucinating Foucault* London: Picador

Editorial 1991 'Letters to the Editors' 14(5) *Women's Studies International Forum* 505

Edwards, A 1989 'The Sex/Gender Distinction: Has it Outlived its Usefulness?' 10 *Australian Feminist Studies* 1

Feminist Review 2005 'Roundtable on the Un/certainties of the Routes of the Collective and the Journal' 80 *Feminist Review* 198

Ferguson, K 1993 *The Man Question: Visions of Subjectivity in Feminist Theory* Berkeley: University of California Press

Ferrell, J 1997 'Criminological *Verstehen*: Inside the Immediacy of Crime' 14(1) *Justice Quarterly* 3

Fine, M and Weis, L (2000) 'Disappearing Acts: The State and Violence Against Women' 25(4) *Signs* 1139

Foucault, M 1973 *The Order of Things: An Archaeology of the Human Sciences* New York: Vintage

Foucault, M 1979 *The History of Sexuality: An Introduction* London: Allen Lane

Foucault, M 1980a 'Prison Talk' in C Gordon (ed) *Power/Knowledge: Michel Foucault* Brighton: Harvester Press

Foucault, M 1980b 'The History of Sexuality' in C Gordon (ed) *Power/Knowledge: Michel Foucault* Brighton: Harvester Press

Foucault, M 1980c 'Two Lectures' in C Gordon (ed) *Power/Knowledge: Michel Foucault* Brighton: Harvester Press

Foucault, M 1980d 'Truth and Power' in C Gordon (ed) *Power/Knowledge: Michel Foucault* Brighton: Harvester Press

Foucault, M 1981 'Questions of Method: An Interview with Michel Foucault' 8 *Ideology and Consciousness* 3

Foucault, 1982a (ed) *I, Pierre Rivière Having Slaughtered My Mother, My Sister and My Brother* Lincoln: Bison Books

Foucault, M 1982b 'The Subject and Power' in HL Dreyfus and P Rabinow (eds) *Michel Foucault: Beyond Structuralism and Hermeneutics* Brighton: Harvester Press

Foucault, M 1983 'On the Genealogy of Ethics: An Overview of Work in Progress' in HL Dreyfus and P Rabinow (eds) *Michel Foucault: Beyond Structuralism and Hermeneutics* 2nd edition; Chicago: University of Chicago Press

Foucault, M 1984a 'Polemics, Politics and Problematisations: An Interview with Michel Foucault' in P Rabinow (ed) *The Foucault Reader* New York: Pantheon Books

Foucault, M 1984b 'The Order of Discourse' in M Shapiro (ed) *Language and Politics* Oxford: Basil Blackwell

Foucault, M 1984c 'What is Enlightenment?' in P Rabinow (ed) *The Foucault Reader* New York: Pantheon Books

Foucault, M 1985 *The Use of Pleasure: The History of Sexuality* vol 2 Harmondsworth: Penguin

Foucault, M 1988a 'Confinement, Psychiatry, Prison' in LD Kritzman (ed) *Michel Foucault: Politics, Philosophy, Culture* New York: Routledge

Foucault, M 1988b 'The Dangerous Individual' in LD Kritzman (ed) *Michel Foucault: Politics, Philosophy, Culture* New York: Routledge

Foucault, M 1988c 'The Concern for Truth' in LD Kritzman (ed) *Michel Foucault: Politics, Philosophy, Culture* New York: Routledge

Foucault, M 1988d 'The Ethic of Care for the Self as a Practice of Freedom' in J Bernauer and D Rasmussen (eds) *The Final Foucault* Cambridge: MIT Press

Foucault, M 1988e 'Practising Criticism' in LD Kritzman (ed) *Michel Foucault: Politics, Philosophy, Culture* New York: Routledge

Foucault, M 1989a 'How Much does it Cost for Reason to Tell the Truth?' in J Johnston and S Lotringer (eds) *Foucault Live: (Interviews, 1966–84)* New York: Semiotext(e)

Foucault, M 1989b 'I, Pierre Rivière' in J Johnston and S Lotringer (eds) *Foucault Live: (Interviews, 1966–84)* New York: Semiotext(e)

Foucault, M 1997 'What is Critique?' in S Lotringer and L Hochroth (eds) *The Politics of Truth: Michel Foucault* New York: Semiotext(e)

Foucault, M 2000 'Structuralism and Post-Structuralism' in JD Faubion (ed) *Michel Foucault: Aesthetics, Method and Epistemology* vol 2 London: Penguin

Foucault, M 2002 'Truth and Juridical Form' in JD Faubion (ed) *Michel Foucault: Power* vol 3 London: Pengiun

Foucault, M 2003 *Society Must be Defended: Lectures at the Collège de France, 1975–76* London: Penguin

Frazer, E 1989 'Review: *The Age of Sex Crime*' 17 *International Journal of the Sociology of Law* 231

Frohmann, L and Mertz, E 1994 'Legal Reform and Social Construction: Violence, Gender and the Law' 19(4) *Law & Social Inquiry* 829

Gandal, K 1986 'Michel Foucault: Intellectual Work and Politics' 67 *Telos* 121

Gatens, M 1996 *Imaginary Bodies: Ethics, Power and Corporeality* London: Routledge

Gavey, N 1989 'Feminist Poststructuralism and Discourse Analysis' 13 *Psychology of Women Quarterly* 459

Gelsthorpe, L and Morris, A 1990 (eds) *Gender, Crime and Justice* Milton Keynes: Open University Press

Genovese, A 2000 'The Politics of Naming: 70s Feminisms, Genealogy and "Domestic Violence" ' in R Walker *et al* (eds) *Anatomies of Violence: An Interdisciplinary Investigation* Sydney: Research Institute of Humanities and Social Sciences

Goode, E 1990 'Symposium' 19 *Contemporary Sociology* 5

Gordon, L 1988 *Heroes of Their Own Lives: The Politics and History of Family Violence* New York: Penguin

Gordon, L 2007 'Family Violence, Feminism and Social Control' in L O'Toole *et al* (eds) *Gender Violence: Interdisciplinary Perspectives* New York: New York University Press

Grewal, I 1998 'On the New Global Feminism and the Family of Nations: Dilemmas of Transnational Feminist Practice' in E Shohat (ed) *Talking Visions: Multicultural Feminism in a Transnational Age* Cambridge: MIT Press

Gunew, S 1990 'Questions of Multi-culturalism' in S Harasym (ed) *The Post-Colonial Critic* New York: Routledge

Gunew, S 1991 'Margins: Acting Like a (Foreign) Woman' 17(1) *Hecate* 31

Gupta, R 2003 'Walls into Bridges: The Losses and Gains of Making Alliances' in R Gupta (ed) *From Homebreakers to Jailbreakers: Southall Black Sisters* London: Zed Books

Haakan, J 1994 'Sexual Abuse, Recovered Memory and Therapeutic Practice' 40 *Social Text* 115

Hall, C 1991 'Politics, Post-structuralism and Feminist History' 3(2) *Gender & History* 204

Hall, S 2002 'Daubing the Drudges of Fury: Men, Violence and the Piety of the "Hegemonic Masculinity" Thesis' 6(1) *Theoretical Criminology* 35

Halperin, D 1995 *Saint Foucault: Towards a Gay Hagiography* New York: Oxford University Press

Haraway, D 1997 *Modest_Witness@Second_Millenium.FemaleMan©_Meets_ OncoMouse™* New York: Routledge

Harman, H 2003 Keynote Address, 'Rights of Women: Challenges within the Law' Conference 3 July London

Haug, F *et al* 1987 *Female Sexualisation: A Collective Work of Memory* London: Verso

Hearn, J 1996 'Is Masculinity Dead? A Critique of the Concept of Masculinity?' in M Mac an Ghaill (ed) *Understanding Masculinities* Buckingham: Open University Press

Hearn, J 2003 ' "Just Men Doing Crime" (and Criminology)' 53 *Criminal Justice Matters* 12

Hekman, S 1996 (ed) *Feminist Interpretations of Michel Foucault* University Park: Pennsylvania State University Press

Helliwell, C 2000 ' "It's Only a Penis": Rape, Feminism and Difference' 25(3) *Signs: Journal of Women in Culture and Society* 789

Hemmings, C, Gedalof, I and Bland, L 2006 'Editorial: Sexual Moralities' 83 *Feminist Review* 1

Hengehold, L 2000 'Remapping the Event: Institutional Discourses and the Trauma of Rape' 26(1) *Signs: Journal of Women in Culture and Society* 189

Henry, S and Milovanovic, D 1994 'The Constitution of Constitutive Criminology: A Postmodern Approach to Criminological Theory' in D Nelken (ed) *The Futures of Criminology* London: Sage

Henry, S and Milovanovic, D 1996 *Constitutive Criminology: Beyond Postmodernism* London: Sage

Hickey, E 1991 *Serial Murderers and their Victims* Pacific Grove: Brooks/Cole Publishing

Hirsch, SF 1994 'Interpreting Media Representations of a "Night of Madness": Law and Culture in the Construction of Rape Identities' 19(4) *Law & Social Inquiry* 1023

Hirst, P and Thompson, G 1996 *Globalisation in Question* Cambridge: Polity Press

HM Government 2007 *Cross Government Action Plan on Sexual Violence and Abuse* London: Home Office www.homeoffice.gov.uk/documents/Sexual-violence-action-plan

Hollway, W 1981 ' "I Just Wanted to Kill a Woman" Why? The Ripper and Male Sexuality' 9 *Feminist Review* 33

Holmes, RM and De Burger, J 1988 *Serial Murder* Newbury Park: Sage

Holub, R 1992 *Antonio Gramsci: Beyond Marxism and Postmodernism* London: Routledge

Home Office 1999 *Living Without Fear: An Integrated Approach to Tackling Violence Against Women* London: Home Office

Home Office 2003 *Safety and Justice: The Government's Proposals on Domestic Violence* London: Home Office

Home Office 2005 *Domestic Violence: A National Report* London: Home Office

hooks, b 1990 *Yearning: Race, Gender and Cultural Politics* Boston: South End Press

Howe, A 1987 'Social Injury Revisited: Towards a Feminist Theory of Social Justice' 15 *International Journal of the Sociology of Law* 428

Howe, A 1990 'The Problem of Privatised Injuries: Feminist Strategies for Litigation' 10 *Studies in Law, Politics and Society* 119

Howe, A 1994 *Punish and Critique: Towards a Feminist Theory of Penality* London: Routledge

Howe, A 1995 'White Western Feminism Meets International Law – Challenges/ Complicity, Erasures/Encounters' 4 *Australian Feminist Law Journal* 63

Howe, A 1997a 'Postmodern Feminism Meets Criminology (and Has a Nice Day)' in B Maclean and D Milovanovic (eds) *New Directions in Critical Criminology* Vancouver: Collective Press

Howe, A 1997b 'Family Relationships, Fiduciary Law and Civil Incest Suits: Re-framing the Injury of Incestuous Assault' 8 *Australian Feminist Law Journal* 59

Howe, A 1998 (ed) *Sexed Crime in the News* Sydney: Federation Press

Howe, A 2000a 'Law out of Context (Or: Who's Afraid of Sex and Violence in Legal Education' 25(6) *Alternative Law Journal* 274

Howe, A 2000b 'Postmodern Criminology and its Feminist Discontents' 33(2) *Australian and New Zealand Journal of Criminology* 221

Howe, A 2000c 'Homosexual Advances in Law: Murderous Excuse, Pluralised Ignorance and the Privilege of Unknowing' in D Herman and C Stychin (eds) *Sexuality in the Legal Arena* London: Athlone

Howe, A 2002 'Provoking Polemic: Provoked Killings and the Ethical Paradoxes of the Postmodern Feminist Condition' 10 *Feminist Legal Studies* 39

Howe, A 2004a 'Managing "Men's Violence" in the Criminological Arena' in C Sumner (ed) *Blackwell's Companion to Criminology* Oxford: Blackwell Publishing

Howe, A 2004b 'Provocation in Crisis – Law's Passion at the Crossroads? New Directions for Feminist Strategists' 21 *Australian Feminist Law Journal* 55

Howe, A 2005 *Lindy Chamberlain Revisited: A Twenty-fifth Anniversary Retrospective* Sydney: Lhr Press

Howe, A 2006 'New Policies for Battered Women: Negotiating the Local and the Global in Blair's Britain' 34(3) *Policy and Politics* 407

Howe, A 2008 ' "Sex Violence Policy" Conundrums – in Search of "Really Active Crime Prevention" ' in G Letherby *et al* (eds) *Sex as Crime* Collumpton: Willan Publishers

Hoy, DC 1988 'Foucault: Modern or Postmodern?' in J Arac (ed) *After Foucault: Humanist Knowledge, Postmodern Challenges* New Brunswick: Rutgers University Press

Hubbard, R 1996 'Gender and Genitals: Constructs of Sex and Gender' 46/47 *Social Text* 157

Huet, M 1993 *Monstrous Imagination* Cambridge: Harvard University Press

Huggins, J *et al* 1991 'Letters to the Editors' 14(5) *Women's Studies International Forum* 506

Itzin, C 2000 'Gendering Domestic Violence: The Influence of Feminism on Policy and Practice' in J Hanmer and C Itzin (eds) *Home Truths about Domestic Violence: Feminist Influences on Policy and Practice – A Reader* London: Routledge

James, C 2006 'Media, Men and Violence in Australian Divorce' 31 *Alternative Law Journal* 6

Jefferson, T 1994 'Theorising Masculine Subjectivity' in T Newburn and E Stanko (eds) *Just Boys Doing Business? Men, Masculinities and Crime* London: Routledge

Jefferson, T 1996a 'Introduction: Special Issue' 36(3) *British Journal of Criminology* 337

Jefferson, T 1996b 'From "Little Fairy Boy" to "the Complete Destroyer": Subjectivity and Transformation in the Biography of Mike Tyson' in M Mac an Ghaill (ed) *Understanding Masculinities* Buckingham: Open University Press

Jefferson, T 1997a 'Masculinities and Crimes' in M Maguire *et al* (eds) *The Oxford Handbook of Criminology* 2nd edn Oxford: Clarendon

Jefferson, T 1997b 'The Tyson Rape Trial: The Law, Feminism and Emotional "Truth" ' 6(2) *Social & Legal Studies* 281

Jefferson, T 2002a 'For a Psychosocial Criminology' in K Carrington and R Hogg (eds) *Critical Criminologies: An Introduction* Cullompton, Devon: Willan Publishers

Jefferson, T 2002b 'Subordinating Hegemonic Masculinity' 6(1) *Theoretical Criminology* 63

Jenkins, P 1987 'Review Essay: *Crime and Human Nature?*' 10(3) *Crime, Law and Social Change* 329

Jenkins, P 1994 *Using Murder: The Social Construction of Serial Homicide* New York: A de Gruyter

Jenkins, P 1998 'African-Americans and Serial Homicide' in RM Holmes and ST Holmes (eds) *Contemporary Serial Murder* London: Sage

Johal, A 2003 'Struggle not Submission: Domestic Violence in the 1990s' in R Gupta (ed) *From Homebreakers to Jailbreakers: Southall Black Sisters* London: Zed Books

Jones, S 1998 *Criminology* London, Butterworths

Joshi, P 2003 'Jumping Through Hoops' in R Gupta (ed) *From Homebreakers to Jailbreakers: Southall Black Sisters* London: Zed Books

Kaplan, C et al 1999 (eds) Between Women: Nationalisms, Transnational Feminisms and the State Durham: Duke University Press

Katz, J 1988 Seductions of Crime: Moral and Sensual Attractions in Doing Evil New York: Basic Books

Katz, C 2001 'On the Grounds of Globalisation: A Topography for Feminist Political Engagement' 26(4) Signs 1213

Katz, J 2002 'Symposium on How Emotions Work' 6(3) Theoretical Criminology 375

Katz, SB 1989 'Review: Seductions of Crime' 80 Journal of Criminal Law and Criminology 352

Kelly, L 1987 'The Continuum of Sexual Violence' in J Hanmer and M Maynard (eds) Women, Violence and Social Control London: MacMillan

Kelly, L 2000 Speech at 'Domestic Violence: Enough is Enough' Conference, London

Kelly, L and Lovett, J 2005 'What a Waste: The Case for an Integrated Violence Against Women Strategy' London: Home Office

Kennedy, H 2003 'Foreword' in R Gupta (ed) From Homebreakers to Jailbreakers: Southall Black Sisters London: Zed Books

Klee, E 1976 'Review: I, Pierre Rivière' 12 Journal of the History of the Behavioural Sciences 192

Kundera, M 1992 The Book of Laughter and Forgetting London: Faber & Faber

Kurzweil, E 1977 'Michel Foucault: Ending the Era of Man' 4 Theory and Society 395

Lees, S 1986 Losing Out: Sexuality and Adolescent Girls London: Hutchinson

Letellier, P 1994 'Gay and Bisexual Male Domestic Violence Victimisation: Challenges to Feminist Theory and Responses to Violence' 9(2) Violence and Victims 95

Levi, M 1997 'Violent Crime' in M Maguire, R Morgan and R Reiner (eds) The Oxford Handbook of Criminology Oxford: Clarendon

Leyton, E 2003 Hunting Humans London: John Blake

Lippens, R 1998 'Alternatives to What Kind of Suffering? Towards a Border-crossing Criminology' 2 Theoretical Criminology 311

Lloyd, G 1984 The Man of Reason: 'Male and Female' in Western Philosophy London: Methuen

Lloyd, G 1989 'Woman as Other: Sex, Gender and Subjectivity' 10 Australian Feminist Studies 13

Lloyd, M 1993 'The (F)utility of a Feminist Turn to Foucault' 22 Economy and Society 437

Lloyd, M 1996 'A Feminist Mapping of Foucauldian Politics' in S Hekman (ed) Feminist Interpretations of Michel Foucault University Park: Pennsylvania State University Press

Lorde, A 1983 'The Master's Tools will Never Dismantle the Master's House' in C Moraga and G Anzaldúa (eds) This Bridge Called My Back: Writings by Radical Women of Colour Boston: South End Press

Lumby, C 1999 Gotcha: Life in a Tabloid World St Leonards: Allen & Unwin

Lutz, CA 1988 Unnatural Emotions: Everyday Sentiments on a Micronesian Atoll and their Challenge to Western Theory Chicago: University of Chicago Press

Lyng, S 1990 'Edgework: A Social Psychological Analysis of Voluntary Risk Taking' 95 American Journal of Sociology 851

Lyng, S 1991 'Edgework Revisited: Reply to Miller' 96 American Journal of Sociology 1534

MacDonald, H, 1998 *What's in a Name? Definitions and Domestic Violence* Melbourne: Domestic Violence and Incest Centre

MacKinnon, CA 1982a 'Towards Feminist Jurisprudence' 34 *Stanford Law Review* 703

MacKinnon, CA 1982b 'Feminism, Marxism, Method and the State: An Agenda for Theory' 7 *Signs: Journal of Women in Culture and Society* 515

MacKinnon, CA 1983 'Feminism, Marxism, Method and the State: Toward Feminist Jurisprudence' 8 *Signs: Journal of Women in Culture and Society* 635

MacKinnon, CA 1987 *Feminism Unmodified: Discourses on Life and Law* Cambridge: Harvard University Press

MacKinnon, CA 1989 'Sexuality, Pornography and Method: "Pleasure under Patriarchy" ' 99 *Ethics* 314

MacLean, BD and Milovanovic, D 1997 (eds) *Thinking Critically about Crime* Vancouver: Collective Press

MacLeod, M and Saraga, E 1988 'Against Orthodoxy' July *New Statesman and Society* 15

Marcus, J 1989 'The Death of the Family: Pierre Rivière, Foucault and Gender' 2 *Criticism, Heresy and Interpretation* 67

Marcus, S 1992 'Fighting Bodies, Fighting Words' in J Butler and J Scott (eds) *Feminists Theorise the Political* New York: Routledge

Markowitz, S 2001 'Pelvic Politics: Sexual Dimorphism and Racial Difference' 26(2) *Signs: Journal of Women in Culture and Society* 389

Matza, D 1964 *Delinquency and Drift* New York: Wiley

Matza, D 1969 *Becoming Deviant* Englewood Cliffs: Prentice-Hall

McCallum, EL 1996 'Technologies of Truth and the Function of Gender in Foucault' in S Hekman (ed) *Feminist Interpretations of Michel Foucault* University Park: Pennsylvania State University Press

McIntosh, M 1988 'Family Secrets as Public Drama' 28 *Feminist Review* 6

McNay, L 1992 *Foucault and Feminism* Boston: Northeastern University Press

Mendoza, B 2002 'Transnational Feminism in Question' 3(3) *Feminist Theory* 295

Merry, S 1994 'Narrating Domestic Violence: Producing the "Truth" of Violence in 19th and 20th Century Hawaiian Courts' 19(4) *Law & Social Inquiry* 967

Miller, E 1991 'Assessing the Risk of Inattention to Class, Race/Ethnicity and Gender: Comment on Lyng' 96 *American Journal of Sociology* 1530

Milovanovic, D 1996 'Postmodern Criminology: Mapping the Terrain' 13 *Justice Quarterly* 567

Milovanovic, D 2000 'Transgressions: Towards an Affirmative Postmodern Analysis' 33 *Australian and New Zealand Journal of Criminology* 202

Mirrlees-Black, C 1999 *Domestic Violence: Finding from a New British Crime Survey Self-Completion Questionnaire* Home Office Research Study, no 191 London: Home Office

Mitra, C 1987 'Judicial Discourse on Father-Daughter Incest Appeal Cases' 15 *International Journal of the Sociology of Law* 121

Mohanty, CT 1988 'Under Western Eyes: Feminist Scholarship and Colonial Discourses' 30 *Feminist Review* 61

Mohanty, CT 1989–90 'On Race and Voice: Challenges for Liberal Education' Winter *Cultural Critique* 179

Mohanty, CT 1991 'Cartographies of Struggle: Third World Women and the Politics of Feminism' in CT Mohanty *et al* (eds) *Third World Women and the Politics of Feminism* Bloomington: Indiana University Press

Mohanty, CT 1992 'Feminist Encounters: Locating the Politics of Difference' in M Barrett and A Phillips (eds) *Destablising Theory: Contemporary Feminist Debates* Stanford: Standford University Press

Mohanty, CT 2002 ' "Under Western Eyes" Revisited: Feminist Solidarity Through Anti-Capitalist Struggles' 28(2) *Signs: Journal of Women in Culture and Society* 499

Moir, A and Jessel, D 1995 *A Mind to Crime* London: Michael Joseph

Moore, H 1994a 'The Problem of Explaining Violence in the Social Sciences' in P Harvey and P Gow (eds) *Sex and Violence* New York: Routledge

Moore, H 1994b ' "Divided we Stand": Sex, Gender and Sexual Difference' 47 *Feminist Review* 78

Moraga, C 1983 'La Guera' in C Moraga and G Anzaldúa (eds) *This Bridge Called My Back: Writings by Radical Women of Colour* Boston: South End Press

Moraga, C and Anzaldúa, G 1983 (eds) *This Bridge Called My Back: Writings by Radical Women of Colour* Boston: South End Press

Moreton-Robinson, A 2003 *Blacklines: Contemporary Critical Writing by Indigenous Australians* Melbourne: Melbourne University Press

Morris, M 1988 *The Pirate's Fiancée: Feminism, Reading, Postmodernism* London: Verso

Morrison, W 1995 *Theoretical Criminology: From Modernity to Post-Modernism* London: Cavendish

Moulin, P 1982 'Extenuating Circumstances' in M Foucault (ed) *I, Pierre Rivière Having Slaughtered My Mother, My Sister and My Brother* Lincoln: Bison Books

Muncie, J *et al* 1996 *Criminological Perspectives: A Reader* London: Sage

Murphy, T 1997 'Feminism on Flesh' VIII *Law and Critique* 37

Murray, S 2005 'An Impossibly Ambitious Plan? Australian Policy and the Elimination of Domestic Violence' 38 *Just Policy* 28

Naffine, N 1995 'Criminal Conversation' V1 *Law and Critique* 193

Naffine, N 1997 *Feminism and Criminology* Cambridge: Polity Press

Naffine, N, 2003 'The "Man Question" of Crime, Criminology and Law' Autumn *Criminal Justice Matters* 53

National Committee on Violence 1990 *Violence: Directions for Australia* Canberra: Australian Institute of Criminology

Nelken, D 1994 (ed) *The Futures of Criminology* London: Sage

Newburn, T and Stanko, B 1994 (eds) *Just Boys Doing Business? Men, Masculinities and Crime* London: Routledge

Newman, G 1990 'Review Essay: Jack Katz, *Seductions of Crime*' 14 *Contemporary Crises* 179

Norris, J 1988 *Serial Killers: The Growing Menace* New York: Doubleday

O'Brien, P 1978 'Crime and Punishment as Historical Problem' 11 *Journal of Social History* 508

O'Brien, RM 1988 'Exploring the Intersexual Nature of Violent Crime' 26(1) *Criminology* 151

O'Connell Davidson, J 2006 'Will the Real Sex Slave Please Stand up?' 83 *Feminist Review* 4

O'Malley, P and Mugford, J 1994 'Crime, Excitement and Modernity' in G Barak (ed) *Varieties of Criminology* Westport: Praeger

Partnerships Against Domestic Violence 1999 *First Report of the Taskforce 1999–2000* Canberra: Commonwealth of Australia

Patel 2003a 'Shifting Terrains: Old Struggles for New?' in R Gupta (ed) *From Homebreakers to Jailbreakers: Southall Black Sisters* London: Zed Books

Patel 2003b in 'The Tricky Blue Line: Black Women and Policing' in R Gupta (ed) *From Homebreakers to Jailbreakers: Southall Black Sisters* London: Zed Books

Perera, S 1985 'How Long Does it Take to get it Right? Migrant Women and the Women's Movement' May *Refractory Girl* 13

Peter JP and Favret J 1982 'The Animal, the Madman and Death' in M Foucault (ed) *I, Pierre Rivière* Lincoln: Bison Books

Philadelphoff-Puren, N 2004 'Derelection: Women, Rape and Football' 21 *Australian Feminist Law Review* 35

Pitch, T 1985 'Critical Criminology, the Construction of Social Problems and the Question of Rape' 13(1) *International Journal of the Sociology of Law* 35

Probyn, E 1993 *Sexing the Self: Gendered Positions in Cultural Studies* London: Routledge

Puren, N 1995 'Hymeneal Acts: Interrogating the Hegemony of Rape and Romance' 5 *Australian Feminist Law Review* 15

Rajchman, J 1985 *Michel Foucault: The Freedom of Philosophy* New York: Columbia University Press

Ramazanoglu, C 1993 (ed) *Up Against Foucault: Explorations of Some Tensions between Foucault and Feminism* London: Routledge

Razack, S 1994 'What is to be Gained by Looking White People in the Eye? Culture, Race and Gender in Cases of Sexual Violence' 19 *Signs: Journal of Women in Culture and Society* 894

Razack, S 1995 'Domestic Violence as Gender Persecution: Policing the Borders of Nation, Race and Gender' 8 *Canadian Journal of Women and the Law* 45

Reekie, G 1988 'Feminism and Men's Bodies: More Thoughts on Male Sexuality' 6 *Australian Feminist Studies* 31

Ressler, RK *et al* 1988 *Sexual Homicide: Patterns and Motives* New York: Lexington Books

Sandland, R 1998 'Seeing Double? Or, Why "To Be Or Not To Be Is" (Not) the Question for Feminist Legal Studies' 7(3) *Social & Legal Studies* 307

Schwartz, J 2005–6 'How Much can Genetics Tell us about the Causes of Crime and Violence' 62 *Criminal Justice Matters* 20

Seltzer, M 1995 'Serial Killers (11): The Pathological Public Sphere' 22 *Critical Inquiry* 122

Seltzer, M 1998 *Serial Killers: Death and Life in America's Wound Culture* New York: Routledge

Shohat, E 1998 *Talking Visions: Multicultural Feminism in a Transnational Age* Cambridge: MIT Press

Siddiqui, H 2003a 'Empowering Women to Escape Violence: Interview with Hannana Siddiqui' 23 *Refugee Women's News* 6

Siddiqui, H 2003b 'Black Feminism in the Twenty-first Century: The Age of Women?' in R Gupta (ed) *From Homebreakers to Jailbreakers: Southall Black Sisters* London: Zed Books

Siddiqui, H 2003c ' "It was Written in her Kismet": Forced Marriage' in R Gupta (ed) *From Homebreakers to Jailbreakers: Southall Black Sisters* London: Zed Books

Simon, J 1998 'Ghosts of the Disciplinary Machine: Lee Harvey Oswald, Life-History and the Truth of Crime' 10 *Yale Journal of Law and the Humanities* 75

Simon, W 1996 *Postmodern Sexualities* London: Routledge

Smart, B 1986 'The Politics of Truth' in DC Hoy (ed) *Foucault: A Critical Reader* Oxford: Basil Blackwell

Smart, C 1989 *Feminism and the Power of Law* London: Routledge

Smart, C 1990a 'Feminist Approaches to Criminology: Or Postmodern Woman Meets Atavistic Man' in L Gelsthorpe and A Morris (eds) *Feminist Perspectives in Criminology* Milton Keynes: Open University Press

Smart, C 1990b 'Law's Power, the Sexed Body and Feminist Discourse' 17(2) *Journal of Law and Society* 194

Smart, C 1994 'Law, Feminism and Sexuality: From Essence to Ethics?' 9(1) *Canadian Journal of Law and Society* 15

Smart, C 1995 *Law, Crime and Sexuality: Essays in Feminism* London: Sage

Smart, C 1999 'A History of Ambivalence and Conflict in the Discursive Construction of the "Child Victim" of Sexual Abuse' 8(3) *Social & Legal Studies* 391

Smith, B and Smith, B 1983 'Across the Kitchen Table: A Sister-to-Sister Dialogue' in C Moraga and G Anzaldúa (eds) *This Bridge Called My Back: Writings by Radical Women of Colour* Boston: South End Press

Snider, L 1985 'Legal Reform and Social Control: The Dangers of Abolishing Rape' 13 *International Journal of the Sociology of Law* 337

Snider, L 1998 'Towards Safer Societies: Punishment, Maculinities and Violence Against Women' 38(1) *British Journal of Criminology* 1

Snider, L 2003 'Constituting the Punishable Woman: Atavistic Man Incarcerates Postmodern Woman' 43(2) *British Journal of Criminology* 354

Soothill, K and Walby, S 1991 *Sex Crime in the News* London: Routledge

Spelman, E 1989 'Anger and Insubordination' in A Garry and M Pearsall (eds) *Women, Knowledge and Reality: Explorations in Feminist Philosophy* Boston: Unwin Hyman

Spivak, G 1990 'Questions of Multi-culturalism' in S Harasym (ed) *The Post-Colonial Critic* New York: Routledge

Stanko, B 1997 'Conceptualising Women's Risk Assessment as a "Technology of the Soul" ' 1(4) *Theoretical Criminology Quarterly* 479

Stanko, B 2002 'Symposium on *How Emotions Work*' 6(3) *Theoretical Criminology* 368

Stoler, AL 1995 *Race and the Education of Desire: Foucault's History of Sexuality and the Colonial Order of Things* Durham: Duke University Press

Straus, M and Gelles, RJ 1986 'Societal Change and Change in Family Violence from 1975 to 1985 as Revealed by Two National Surveys' 48(3) *Journal of Marriage and the Family* 465

Tatar, M 1995 *Lustmord: Sexual Murder in Weimar Germany* Princeton, New Jersey: Princeton University Press

Taylor, I, Walton, P and Young, P 1973 *The New Criminology* London: Routledge & Kegan Paul

Thompson, D 1989 'The Sex/Gender Distinction: A Reconsideration' 10 *Australian Feminist Studies* 23

Thornton, M 1995 *Public and Private: Feminist Legal Debates* Melbourne: Oxford University Press

Thornton, M 1996 *Dissonance and Distrust: Women in the Legal Profession* Melbourne: Oxford University Press

Thornton, M 2006 'The Dissolution of the Social in the Legal Academy' 25 *Australian Feminist Law Journal* 3

Trinh, TM 1989 *Woman, Native, Other; Writing Postcoloniality and Feminism* Bloomington: Indiana University Press

Vega, J 1988 'Coercion and Consent: Classic Liberal Concepts in Texts on Sexual Violence' 16 *International Journal of the Sociology of Law* 75

Volpp, L 1996 'Talking "Culture": Gender, Race, Nation and the Politics of Multiculturalism' 20 *Criminal Law Journal* 1573

Walby, S and Allen, J 2004 *Domestic Violence, Sexual Assault and Stalking: Findings from the British Crime Survey* Home Office Research Study 276 London: Home Office Research, Development and Statistics Directorate

Walby, S and Myhill, A 2001 'New Survey Methodologies in Researching Violence Against Women' 41(3) *British Journal of Criminology* 502

Walklate, S 1995 *Gender and Crime: An Introduction* London: Prentice Hall/ Harvester Wheatsheaf

Walklate, S 1997 'Risk and Criminal Victimisation' 37(1) *British Criminology Journal* 35

Walklate, S 2008, 'What is to be done about Violence Against Women?' 48 *British Journal of Criminology* 39

Walmsley, R 2003 'World Prison Population List' 5th edn Home Office Research, Development and Statistics Directorate www.homeoffice.gov.uk/rds/

Ware, V 1992 *Beyond the Pale: White Women, Racism and History* London: Verso.

Weedon, C 1987 *Feminist Practice and Poststructuralist Theory* Oxford: Basil Blackwell

West, DJ 1987 *Sexual Crimes and Confrontations* Aldershot: Gower Publishing

Wiegman, R 2001 'Object Lessons: Men, Masculinity and the Sign *Woman*' 26(2) *Signs: Journal of Women in Culture and Society* 355

Williamson, S et al 1987 'Violence: Criminal Psychopaths and Their Victims' 19(4) *Canadian Journal of Behavioral Science* 454

Wilson, JQ and Herrnstein, RJ 1985 *Crime and Human Nature* New York: Simon and Schuster

Womankind Worldwide 2004 *CEDAW Thematic Shadow Report 2003: Violence Against Women in the UK* London: Womankind Worldwide

Wong, N 1983 'In Search of the Self as Hero: Confetti of Voices on New Year's Night' in C Moraga and G Anzaldúa (eds) *This Bridge Called My Back: Writings by Radical Women of Colour* Boston: South End Press

Woodcraft, E 2003 Untitled Paper 'Rights of Women: Challenges within the Law' Conference 3 July London

Wykes, M 2001 *News, Crime and Culture* London: Pluto Press

Yeatman, A 1993 'Voice and Representation in the Politics of Difference' in S Gunew and A Yeatman (eds) *Feminism and the Politics of Difference* St Leonards: Allen & Unwin

Young, A 1996 *Imagining Crime* London: Sage

Young, A 1998 'The Wasteland of the Law, the Worldless Song of the Rape Victim' 22(2) *Melbourne University Law Review* 442

Young, J 1981 'Thinking Seriously about Crime: Some Models of Criminology' in M Fitzgerald *et al* (eds) *Crime and Society: Readings in History and Theory* London: Routledge & Kegan Paul

Young, J 2003 'Merton with Energy, Katz with Structure' 7(3) *Theoretical Criminology* 389

Žižek, S 1990 'Beyond Discourse-Analysis' in E Laclau *New Reflections on the Revolution of our Times* London: Verso

Žižek, S 2000 'Class Struggle or Postmodernism. Yes, Please!' in J Butler *et al* (eds) *Contingency, Hegemony, Universality: Contemporary Dialogues on the Left* London: Verso

Magazine articles

Bakos, SC 1991a 'Why He Wants You to do That' *Cosmopolitan* February

Bakos, SC 1991b 'The Two Sex Acts Men Want More Of' *Cosmopolitan* February

Bakos, SC 1993 'Everything There is to Know about Orgasm' *Cosmopolitan* April

Borno, H 2003 'Say No to Soul-less Sex' *Cosmopolitan* October

Campbell, C 1994 'Why Men go to Prostitutes' *Cosmopolitan* February

Editorial 2003 *Cosmopolitan* October

Elder, J 1999 'I was Raped by Another Woman' *Cleo* August

Feltz, V 1992a 'The Great Swallowing Controversy and Other Dilemmas of Modern Sex' *Cosmopolitan* March

Feltz, V 1992b 'If You Can't Make It – Fake It!' *Cosmopolitan* July

Fennell, T 1999a '20 Really Dirty Things All Men Want You to do in Bed' *Cleo* May

Fennell, T 1999b 'Things That Go Through a Man's Mind . . .' *Cleo* August

Kelly, E 2002 'Male Order Orgasms' *Cosmopolitan* October

Krizanovich, K 1996 '6 Steps to Joygasmic Sex' *Cosmopolitan* April

Swift, R 1993 'How to Have an Orgasm as Often as You Want' *Cleo* April

Williams, Z 2003 'A Bit Behind' *Guardian Magazine* 10 May

Zorn, R 1991 'Sex is Back' *Cosmopolitan* February

Subject index

Author index